LOG HOUSE PLANS
B. ALLAN MACKIE

LOG HOUSE PLANS

B. ALLAN MACKIE

Charles Scribner's Sons
New York, New York

Log House Plans
©Canada 1979 First Edition
Log House Publishing Company Ltd.

1st published 1979 in Canada by
Log House Publishing Co.
of Prince George, British Columbia

U.S. edition published by
Charles Scribner's Sons 1981

1 3 5 7 9 11 13 15 17 19   I/C   20 18 16 14 12 10 8 6 4 2

Printed in Canada

Library of Congress Catalogue
Card Number 80-53967
ISBN 0-684-16960-6

LOG HOUSE PLANS

Table of Contents

Note: The 37 House Plans contained in this book are subject to review at all times. The publisher reserves the right to update and alter plans from time to time.

Acknowledgments

I would like to express my thanks to those who contributed ideas and materials to this book and to all the people who have welcomed me and my sketch pad into their homes.

Allan Mackie

Introduction

The evolution of log house design has become so rapid and so exciting, in the last few years, that I have been slow to put this book into print. Everywhere I looked, there were new ideas, new methods, and new concepts being demonstrated. I wanted to wait until the final direction had been established.

In addition, the belated respectability being accorded to the environmentalists is exerting a new influence, too, insisting that we examine our basic housing morality. A few of the exponents of better design are now being heard, and I wanted to consider their views carefully.

But, at last, it occurred to me that the final direction for log house design may never be wholly established in my lifetime. Certainly, there is no limit to the distance any realistic direction may be pursued. Therefore, I began to look differently at my own book of log house design and to accept the fact that it is composed of actual houses. It is, then, more in the nature of an archives of today's reality that it is an instrument of prophecy.

In any event, this book could have been delayed no longer. People keep asking for it. And so, in spite of the feelings I have that log house design — perhaps all house design — will be changing radically in the next few years, I know that such changes will be brought about by the people who are doing things. This book is a direct response to them, the people who are building and exploring the possibilities, for these are the ones who will initiate changes for the better, and not the people who limit their activities to conjecture. I therefore dedicate this book to the people who build. I offer these designs and houseplans as a source of ideas and help for those who anticipate being a part of the improved architecture of the coming years.

I have developed these plans through a number of years of being crouched intermittently over a draughting board. Except for the several houses designed for some personal needs, they are mostly developed in response to requests from other individuals. Often they represent an idealized home.

The full sets of plans (¼ inch to 1 foot scale) are available from Log House Publishing Company Ltd., and will normally be supplied in three copies to a set. If additional copies are required, these may be supplied by special arrangement.

It should be understood that the builder or homeowner may also take some liberties in making alterations directly onto the blueprints. Major structural changes should be avoided. But a reasonable amount of minor alteration can be accomplished right on the blueprints without losing legibility. This can sometimes take care of a special personal need at a great saving of time and money required to obtain custom-drawn plans.

The complete plans for each design are printed in this book. In this way, the builder may require no further assistance with his blueprint. He may draw his own, using the book as a guide.

Plans are of the utmost importance in the total success of a building and should always be fully completed before any construction gets under way.

Houseplans cost only a small fraction of the total cost of a building project, and good plans can save their initial price many, many times over.

Log house plans are unique in several important ways. With the aid of this book, then, I sincerely hope that any person seriously determined to build a good solid log home will be able, at very little cost, to either copy his own blueprints directly from the book, or develop his own original design with the guidance of this book, or purchase a ready-made blueprint selected from one of the designs shown here.

It would please me greatly to hear from any reader when you've achieved your goal. I certainly wish you good luck, clear weather, and a sharp axe. And now, let us get on with our studies of log house plans.

"Log building", as it has become known, has been around for a few years now. Never mind that people have been building with logs for centuries, it's today in which we are now interested. It has become a welcome alternative to the high cost and bad performance of what is commonly called regular or standard housing. Many hundreds of log builders are now engaged in either private or commercial construction. They are approaching this opportunity with a fresh and hopeful attitude. For them, log construction is a totally new ball game. The old historic buildings and ancient methods serve as an exciting guide and inspiration ... but today's rules are all changed. The purpose, scope, and expectations of a habitation are different today.

This is perhaps an awkward time to present a book of log house plans because it can only be a segment of the development to date. So much more is yet to come. We tremble on the threshold of an entirely different approach both to living and to building. That new approach will soon manifest itself in fresh design. There will be new concepts in total environment living and in the utlization of space, of energy, of waste, and of building materials. Certainly, this means that houses will become far more sensitive to the needs of the inhabitants as well as to the reality of the world in which we live. As such, houses will in future probably be smaller. They will be made much more energy-efficient. And above all, I hope they will be much more self-contained, self-sufficient, and independent. If, they are that, they'll also be more delightful, and more comforting places in which to live.

Up to this point in architectural development, the so-called alternative methods and materials have simply tried to make it possible for people to continue living in the same wasteful manner as the consumer industries have taught them to become accustomed to. But flushing feces into the nearest supply of public drinking water, no matter how pretty the pastel colour of the toilet itself, is an abomination that surely will pass from civic practice, just as one example. This whole destructive cycle can be totally turned around by the concept of the home becoming self-sufficient. But we're only starting, hesitatingly, on this new road to survival. In the meantime, it is wise to brace oneself with Romer's Rule: "The initial survival value of a favourable innovation is . . . that it renders possible the maintenance of a traditional way of life in the face of changed circumstances."

Consequently, the log house designs which people have selected in these early recent years of its new popularity have been the romanticised versions of regular suburban houses, or, simply log-walled ticky-tacky. There was indeed justification for this approach. Many of those first modern log home owners feared they were being marked as dissidents when they built with logs and so the apology they made was to appear as nearly "conventional" as possible. There was reason for their feeling. Brain washing is not restricted to any one nation and the western world simply calls it advertising. By means of advertising, we're given clear signals as to how we must live, look, walk, talk, eat, sleep, smell, and more. But I am convinced in my heart that people eventually see through all that and are entirely capable of recognizing and supporting a worthy new trend or product even if it has never once been advertised. And so the general public has swung around to an almost overwhelming endorsement of log homes.

The exception to this is government. Because it has become necessary to seek the approval of one bureaucrat after another, for almost every simple human undertaking, one is inclined to confuse the support and endorsement of one's neighbours with that of one's government . . . nothing could be farther from the truth. Government appears to fear any new trend, any show of independence. This is a great and continuing puzzlement to me.

So, while many of the homes shown in this book do represent that early development, a translation into logs of a commonplace style of modern housing, there is certainly nothing to say that they cannot be enjoyed in a more imaginative way of life. After all, it is the style of living or restrictions upon the style of living which are largely responsible for some of the healthy criticisms being directed at housing. Solar heat or wood heating can be used in any house. Houses of any shape or location can always be made more efficient in energy consumption. New

Cottage of the early 1900's.

homes can be better located and oriented to fit in with the environment both in respect to efficiency, appearance, and human needs. Quality construction can reduce heat loss. Waste can be reduced by reclaiming and recycling. Many, many natural things can be re-introduced into a home to make the life-support system more harmonious with physical and emotional needs. In short, any house can be a real home. And any building can be improved.

This book addresses primarily those people who are going to build their own once-in-a-lifetime home. It may, I hope, make that experience pleasant and successful enough that a good portion of those builders may go on to build other log homes in future. So I would like to pass on to them the ideas and experience gained over many years of building. In the hope that it will assist in making their projects as satisfactory and as satisfying as possible, I make a number of recommendations now. These are based on conclusions I have reached the hard way and the most enjoyable way: by doing it.

1. To me, it is not so important what materials you build your house of; the important thing is that you build it yourself. There are many reasons for this. Skilled labour is expensive, a service which in reality is affordable only by people with money. Despite fat, available mortgage funds, the truth is that for people of modest means who hope to live in their home without anxiety, the hiring of skilled labour and the fat mortgage is out of the question. But you can indeed acquire the necessary skills and understanding to do the job yourself. In the end, it will mean more to you.

By doing the work yourself, every dollar you avoid borrowing is more like $4.00 saved because of the cost of the interest on the loan.

Also, by doing the work yourself, you acquire a set of skills which, from then on, are a real asset in your life.

The owner-builder develops a commitment to a house in which he has directly invested himself, his time, a part of his life. The rest of the family will feel this way, too, most likely. It does something to people. I've seen a person change, develop, and flourish in a dramatic way, with the confidence and commitment that comes through building. I've seen it happen to men, to women, and to children. And I've been proud, every time I've seen it happen. It's such a basic thing, a home. It's such a splendid new feeling of power that a person has (so rare in an urban, industrialized society) when he confronts the timber and builds a thing of beauty and it not only meets that human need but it also sets him free. That alone is worth going after: that tremendous sense of personal value, competence, and independence.

Another satisfying spin-off is the help that comes from friends, neighbours, and often passersby or strangers wanting to learn and who are willing to supply free labour, fun and continuing friendship for the privilege of learning.

There are profound satisfactions from all this. And to know that you have, even to some small extent, avoided the mortgage trap, too, helps keep you going when things get tough. I know of no better way of earning money than to build your own home.

I am talking about log houses here because that is my specialty. But the choice is up to the builder as to what material he uses to build with, as long as the design is good, the material is good, and the workmanship is good . . . then the house will be good. I admire stone houses and brick houses, concrete block buildings and some frame houses. I just prefer log houses.

The log house can be a lot of work — perhaps as much work as building a stone house. So do be sure that it actually is a log house you want. But if you're thinking that because logs are cheaper you can therefore acquire a house of proportions that would otherwise be beyond your means, think about that very carefully. First, there is a tremendous amount of work involved in the completion of any house and, in a log house, probably a lot more. Not only are you going to be considerably depleted over the period of time required to build but the strain will also be carried in part by everyone who is close to you. Determination is a wonderful thing but blind determination is something else. We start with a concept and often extend ourselves beyond reasonable limits in order to see the concept take on a three-dimensional form. This form of enthusiasm is thoroughly acceptable in a society which offers only a limited number of approved ways of committing suicide. Working to death is one of the approved ways. So consider very carefully whether or not you do wish to undertake this workload and, if you do, resolve to take time once in a while to renew yourself and those around you. The spiritual revitalization will probably put the project ahead in the long run but even if it doesn't the project will be more successful if there's still a family around to live in it.

If, however, your basic wish is to build a large inefficient log house just because you could never afford to build a large inefficient house of any other material, then you are plunging into two basic errors. First, it's going to cost as much as a frame house. And second, it's going to be an inefficient house all the same and so costly to maintain.

2) My second recommendation, then, is that the person looking for a low-cost home should build a small house.

There is much to recommend smallness. It is obviously less expensive to build. It is less expensive to heat.

A large house was the vogue in the late 1920s and was wiped out by the stock market decline, the subsequent depression, and then world war two. Then the small house became not only a thing of necessity but a refuge from poverty and scarcity. As affluence became a way of post-war life, it was a remarkable phenomenon to know that families were living in a new kind of poverty: trapped in large, costly, inefficient houses which bled them financially, tied them to jobs which tortured their peace

Open planning helps to keep a house smaller. If a dining area and living room overlap, each may be considered larger and why not. They're not usually in use at the same time. Make use of all the space. Large spaces under the eaves and roof may be redesigned to be accessible either as storage or as living space ... and, if not, then it should be eliminated. Well designed roof insulation will permit this (Fig. I).

Recommendation #3 is to maximize thermal efficiency. The great costs in upkeep, other than mortgage costs and taxes, are in energy-consumption. Two of these expenses can be eliminated from your home or, with determined planning, greatly reduced.

of mind, and often drove them into a totally new kind of endeavour, "moonlighting", in order to make ends meet. For them, the large, inefficient house was an artificial illusion of grandeur and social importance. Now, at last, we seem to be breaking through this toward a firmer sense of reality.

For my part, I admire with near reverence a small, exquisitely designed and executed house. Yet time after time people will come to me, saying, "Did you see that new log house on such-and-such road, wow! It must be at least 4,000 square feet ..." and they wonder why I am not impressed by its mere vastness. On examination, the house may be well built or well designed or have some other things to recommend it, but, to me, the important question is: why was it built. What were its purposes and is it fulfilling those real needs. I have seen far too many people enslaved, in one way or another, by the "bigger is better" motivation.

So I urge any prospective home-owner, because of the labour to be undertaken and the costs involved, to examine his resources and his lifestyle, and to make realistic decisions early, during the initial planning stage.

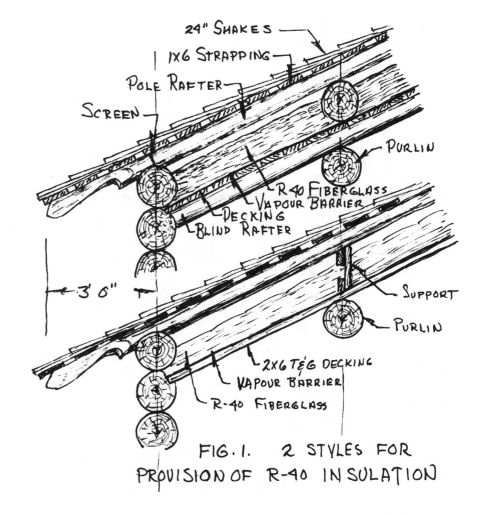

FIG. 1.   2 STYLES FOR PROVISION OF R-40 INSULATION

Heat efficiency can be improved in many ways. The first, of course, is by the choice of a small, space-conscious house and by building it well. Then, by locating or siting it wisely. These are long steps in the right direction.

The use of skylights instead of some wall windows may vastly increase the interior light, thus shortening the hours when artificial lighting is required. Skylights are delightful additions in many ways, providing so much more light per square foot and putting it down directly upon one's

work areas or on the plants, and generally creating a new, pleasurable kind of indoor sunlight. It's a joy to look up at night and see the stars twinkling, too.

Well-fitted logs provide a near-perfect insulation which is safeguarded by the careful application of air-sealing strips such as moss, fibreglass, or oakum down the lateral grooves during construction.

But the floor and roof areas can be the most vulnerable unless they are well-sealed and heavily insulated against air leakage. Many people believe that almost any investment in floor- and roof-insulation is worthwhile as it is repaid in fuel savings within a remarkably short period of time.

Masonry can provide heat sumps (Fig. 2) and with the large selection of wood-burning stoves and heaters on the market today, the fossil fuels and electricity can be reserved for back-up application.

Heat which, otherwise, would be lost should be recovered from a stove or fireplace and used to heat water (Fig. 3). Several such units are on the market or they can be reasonably made on site and either built into fireplaces or added onto existing facilities.

Hot water can be directed into a sump before it is allowed to run into a septic system, in order to extract the heat it contains.

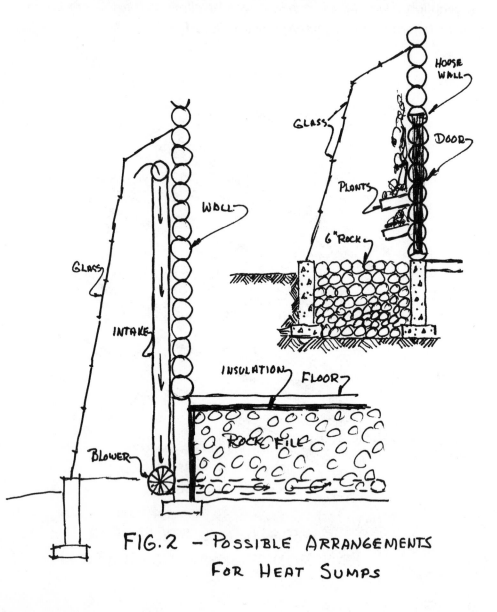

FIG. 2 — POSSIBLE ARRANGEMENTS FOR HEAT SUMPS

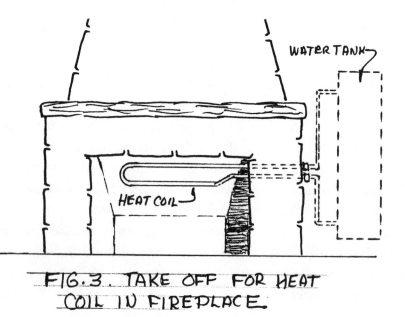

FIG. 3. TAKE OFF FOR HEAT COIL IN FIREPLACE

Insulated shutters are a very desirable feature in a house and solar radiation should be trapped and utilized to whatever extent is practical. Many books on this subject are now available.

Recommendation #4 is that the prospective builder learn to sketch. Because logs are not of uniform size and shape, they do not lend themselves fully to traditional square and ruler types of drawings. And because intersecting logs can be a half-log higher than the one at right angles to it, difficulties can be encountered at floors, doors, and window-height and in roof layout, particularly if roofs intersect at different pitches. By developing working drawings through sketching, improvements may be made to many features and what is perhaps most important, disastrous errors may be avoided. Log walls, like no others, cannot be altered once they're built, without demolishing the work down to the level requiring the alteration. Self-preservation demands the avoidance of this kind of activity.

Sketching comes easily to most people who get interested in home building. And since sketching is largely a function of observation, the activity may well develop into a pleasurable occupation after the building is complete. In any event, preserve your original drawings as part of the family archives. They become all the more intriguing as the years go by.

Sometimes a person ends up with a whole armful of drawings. Details and ideas make a most interesting history of the development of the building. They can provide an educational hour or two (and save you a lot of repetitious conversation) for visitors, along with the slides and photos of construction.

Scale models of the proposed building can also be of assistance although I have seen some of these carried to such a high degree of accuracy that they consumed almost as much time as the actual housebuilding would have. This, I often think, is a displacement activity replacing the responsibilities of undertaking the real thing. I recommend that cardboard bits held in place with masking tape will do this mock-up job as well as little logs; certainly, well enough to give you an idea of proportions and to show up major flaws in your roof design, support for walls and floors, and traffic flow, to name the more obvious.

Recommendation #5: a Survival Check List. Plan books often contain a Habitability Check List and these are well worth reading. However, most of the usual points concern themselves with passive conveniences. I believe that a ceiling outlet in the living room will be of little real help when the power goes off.

So I would like therefore to propose a check-list of survival features that might be considered for incorporation into a building that will serve its occupants come what may. In my opinion, these are the areas in which the individual is left on his own and which are the very ones that ought to be as fully developed as possible. The secret is that they bring profit to nobody but you and it's for this very reason that I recommend this check-list.

Sun Power

* As a heat source. Does your house have provision for solar heat, a solar greenhouse, or solar water heating? Can a heat sump be included in the house or added?

* Food production. Can a solar greenhouse be included in the design for growing plants, for added heat retention for the building, for the humidity it provides in the internal atmosphere, and for the added sunlight?

* Light source. Can skylights be used to advantage? (If even one single 100-watt lightbulb can be eliminated, this, I believe, would be called an advantage worthy of a skylight.) Can electric lights be eliminated, at some times, and in some areas, by the use of light wells? Reflectors? Or better window arrangements?

Wind Power

* Is maximum protection from the wind provided?

* Can the available wind be used to generate electricity and to run integrated equipment such as a heat pump, pumps for solar heated water, or sufficient power to sustain the operation of a composting toilet?

* Are the ventilation possibilities, using the wind, employed to the fullest?

Energy Storage

* Can a heat sump be installed and used?

* Can masonry masses be considered as a means of storing and regulating the household heat?

Site Selection

* Is the building sited to make use of the sun?

* Are the prevailing winds avoided as much as possible?

* Are natural features such as slope used to the fullest extent?

* Can existing trees and shrubs be preserved to provide winter and/or summer protection?

Waste

* Can heat be extracted from waste or grey water?

* Can the grey water be caught and recycled through the toilets as a flushing medium?

* Can the residual wastes be used as compost?

* Can other household waste be used as fuel?

Electricity

* Is the house totally dependent upon outside sources?

Food

* Is there provision for dry storage for several months?

* Is there provision for cool, dark storage for the garden produce and preserves?

* Can a root cellar be added to the house?

* Is there a truly functional area in which butter could be churned, or other large-scale food production activities efficiently undertaken?

Vulnerability and Self-Sufficiency

* Can the operation of this household be fully sustained over a given minimum period — a month, six months, a year — without external support?

Many people ask if, before they order a certain set of blueprints, they can travel to someone's private home to "view" the real thing. I always wish that the question had never been asked; for it is impossible for me to provide access to the private life of anyone, even of my own family members.

My strong belief is that a home is a sacred place. One visits another's home only upon invitation. And one knocks on the door of a stranger's house only if the purpose of the visit brings the real possibility of pleasure or significance to the owner, primarily, and the visitor, secondarily. Anyone who, like my wife, has been virtually pushed to one side while her home was inspected from top to bottom, will readily understand the perils involved. Some log home owners have actually been driven from their homes by the persistent invasions.

I have, in my opinion, been granted a rare privilege in being invited to see some of the log homes in this country. Now and then, the generous-hearted owner has agreed to permit photographs, and to share the approximate design of their home. I consider that a personal trust. I never have sent and never will send strangers to that house.

This, then, is the basis of my consistent refusal to provide the names and addresses of people who have struggled, sweat, and worked to attain the log house of their dreams and who, having won that noble battle, are fully entitled to the peace and enjoyment of that log home.

This I believe is how you, too, will want things when you've achieved the house of your dreams.

Now and then, somebody asks if a certain log house design is "C.M.&H.C. approved" which only tends to tell me that the questioner doesn't understand very much about mortgage approvals. So may I offer these few points, by way of clarification.

First: when a person seeks out mortgage money, it's the person who comes up for approval, primarily. These points must be met:
* adequate income
* secure employment prospects
* good credit rating

In essence, the person must prove that he can sustain the burden of the monthly repayment plan. There is no way that a set of blueprints can do that for him.

Second: the C.M.&H.C. mortgage, or any other type of mortgage, will also depend heavily upon where you intend to build. Site is, in some strange fashion, linked to the government's notion of re-sale values which they feel are centred downtown. This is in case they should be forced to repossess the property by reason of default on mortgage repayment. It is further linked with the government-financed sewage systems operational in most cities. Thus you can readily get approval for a plan if it's to be built within city limits but you might be totally unable to get mortgage funds if it's to be built 10 or 20 miles out into the countryside. No set of blueprints can predict where the house is to be built.

Third: some sections of the land are managed either by city council, regional districts, developers or co-op groups. Part of their overall plan may be that all houses conform to certain square footage. In my opinion, this is an abomination as it tends to impose a cookie-cutter conformity upon large segments of a community which inhibits spontaneity and diversity. One section of my home city is given over to churches, for example. Six days a week this strip of boulevard is a barren wasteland; on Sunday mornings, however, it looks as if it's $1.49 day. Surely the church belongs in the neighbourhood, where it shields and comforts the nearby parishioners and they, in turn, maintain and protect the church *building itself.*

Another section is given over to large houses which, it was hoped, would bring all the millionaires together and exclude the artists and artisans. I enjoy the fact that there are always more "For Sale" signs in this section of town than in any other, and I much prefer the old riverfront area which has a historic (if now and then tumbledown) sequence of buildings of all sizes and shapes. Unfortunately, as the old suburb started to win a new loyalty, the city planners stepped in and decided that its main street should be commercialized and semi-industrial so that the earthy, colourful residential flair is now very quickly being destroyed. Planning departments seem excellent only in theory. In practice, they commit blunders which they themselves would never for a moment permit an ordinary citizen to imitate in any way. And it is part of my belief that an ordinary citizen, as part of his growth and experiential processes, has every right to test out theories knowing that occasionally he may make an error which, of course, he will correct of his own accord (he being a person of intelligence, just as Planning personnel are). As I see it, the great peril of having our lives and homes and communities fully planned by a government department, is that all of this experiential process is eliminated from our daily lives. And with that, goes creativity.

So remember that C.M.&H.C. does approve log construction (if that's your underlying question) and that they even have log home plans of their own design. Use that information if ever you're unfortunate enough to be dealing with an employee who does not understand log construction. Stand your ground because it is he who is uninformed, not you.

Remember, as well, that these same employees who are totally unfamiliar with log construction may, in the final analysis, request that an engineer put his stamp of approval on a set of blueprints. This, he feels, protects him from the decision-making process, of which he is entirely unsure. Sometimes this is a simple matter, however, and the engineer will charge only about $50 or less for the service. But here again, the engineer may also know nothing of log construction so, to protect himself from the unfamiliar, he will begin sketching in metal parts, drift pins, steel spikes, and generally messing up a good design. The danger here is that he will insert "hang-ups" which, over the years, will prevent

the natural settling of the log structure. An experienced log builder comes to terms early in his training with the settling of walls and roof logs. He learns to work with the process, leaving spaces where necessary, so that in the years to come all the logwork settles down tighter, firmer, and more positively. Consider the perils of someone not understanding this, and one who inserts metal hardware to prevent it. It could be the ruination of the home. So first of all ask the engineer if he's familiar with log construction.

A question which mortgage lenders, be they C.M.&H.C. or others, do not ask is one which I feel to be of critical importance, namely, who is the builder. The entire success of the building rests in the builder's hands, and here again, even the best blueprints in the world can in no way guarantee you a fine building if a wood-butcher is executing the plan. The builder is the key element, the artisan who builds safety, durability, beauty, and grace into the walls, the roof, the windows, the doors, and he can do this with a poor plan (with more difficulty) or with a superb plan. The blueprints themselves can't guarantee that the builder can execute the plan to its fullest.

Sometimes, I feel, that the person who asks if the design is "C.M.&H.C. approved" is really asking if log construction is approved. And here I urge the would-be home-owner to smarten up his act. Never approach the mortgage lender, hat in hand, worry written all over you, with the appalling admission that you, yourself, feel uncertain that log construction is "acceptable". The tragedy here is that because of the commercialized brainwashing that passes for advertising in today's consumer society, many of us fear something self-built and handmade as being not quite as good as something plasticized, factory-built, and advertised on the 24" screen. If it has distorted your appreciation of log construction, work that out before you try for a mortgage. Because, consider for half a moment, in a more familiar setting, how you'd feel if you'd never met Joe Blpflks before and somebody approached you (hat in hand, worry written all over his face) asking, "Will you accept Joe Blpflks as a guest for dinner tomorrow . . .?" and, right now, you're wondering just what you're getting into: what's wrong with Joe Blpflks. On the other hand, approached with confidence by somebody who says, amiably, that Joe Blpflks is a great guy and he'll be available tomorrow, you're all ready to meet him. All right, then, present log construction in the same amiable, confident, and positive way and you'll find that the mortgage employee, being only human after all, will respond to your way of seeing things.

The Kerry Street house, Design #764, I built in the city of Prince George precisely to try and knock on the head, once and for all, this nonsense about "approval". There was a C.M.&H.C. mortgage on it. But, as I'm sure you'll understand, now, there's no way that the same house could've won that mortgage if it had not been within city limits. There is another C.M.&H.C. type of mortgage for "Rural and Remote Housing" which should be investigated. But in all cases, approval depends upon many things and the same blueprints which sail past ten building inspectors may be the very blueprints which become the subject of a full scale battle with the eleventh. There is no way of ensuring that a plan will gain you open door access to mortgages, building permits, fire insurance, or a long life. But we believe they're the best log house plans available in the world today and, should any official wish to suggest improvements to any of them, I'll be pleased to consider the suggestion in the light of what I know about building with logs, and to incorporate that information into the blueprints if it would improve them.

I do not believe that there is any houseplan on the market, anywhere, which purports to be anything other than a houseplan. And that is how I see it, too.

Design Considerations For Log Buildings

The suggestions made here concern only those aspects of design which are particular to log construction. All other design recommendations, from the height of counter tops to the distance from shopping "centres", are adequately analyzed elsewhere.

For the builder or homeowner who is choosing a house design or preferably developing his own design, there are a few rules basic to log construction.

1) Foundations

Because log buildings are heavier than frame buildings, a heavier foundation should be employed. Generally, use 10-inch concrete or 12-inch masonry as minimum specifications. The life expectancy of the building is related in a most direct way to the quality of the foundation upon which it rests. (Please refer again to the section on FINISHING AND PRESERVING.)

2) Log Size

Wall logs should have a minimum 10-inch midpoint diameter, although perhaps for very small houses, smaller logs would do. The quality of the fitting is, in fact, more relevant than is the size of the logs.

There have been town planners and building inspectors who, because of their unfamiliarity with logs, have made some remarkable personal calculations and come up with decisions calling, for example, for log walls to have a minimum 24-inch thickness, before they met R-factor requirements. The situation became so preposterous that eventually, Eastern Forest Products Laboratory in Ottawa did an invaluable service to longsuffering citizens by proving what most of us already knew: that log buildings are remarkable for their ability to remain warm in winter, cool in summer. The EFPL report is No. 6-3-307 titled "Thermal Resistivity of White Pine" and is available for use as a blunt instrument whenever the hard head of a civic employee or bank manager blocks the progress of a building permit or a bank loan for log construction. This report went so far as to prove that the log wall actually resists more and more, as the weather outdoors gets colder and colder. Further, the EFPL scientists developed a device for on-the-job measurements of any material for their R-values, be they logs, walls, windows, whatever. So my sincere hope is that we've heard the last of this foolish debate which painted all log home owners as virtually clinging to life, huddled, half-frozen, in their miserable hutches. But I also hope that it is never forgotten that the critical element in the building of a properly warm log home lies in the workmanship, in particular, in the tightly fitting scribed fit of one log to another. A massive log offers little protection if a 2" gap is left between it and the next one.

3) Wall Support for Horizontal Log Buildings

Cross walls or stub walls must be incorporated into the design of a solid log structure every 16 to 24 feet. Have these partitions or stub walls as harmonious as possible with the rest of the design.

For example, a principal floor joist may be directly under a supporting partition which, in turn, is directly under a principal rafter. The support is then continuous from foundation to ridge.

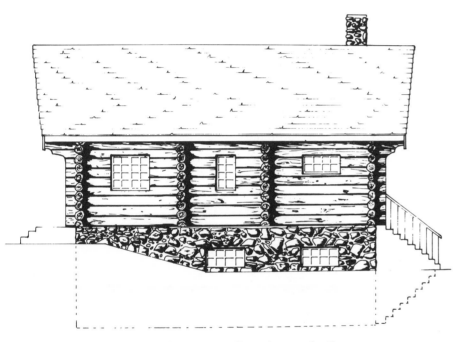

Above — Through partition walls produce good wall support.

4) Provide Support at Doors

I have often seen designs that do not supply adequate support on either side of a door. Good support should be arranged by including stub walls, heavier door framing, or log partition walls as in the previous illustration, as well as the required beams, posts or footings.

5) Avoid Hang-ups

In the literal sense, the hang-up of logs is the most common and devastating error in log construction. Horizontal log walls will settle more than anyone could wish for. Therefore, masonry, built solidly into a new wall, into overhead beams, or into floor joists, will guarantee serious problems of hang-up, later on.

Similarly, upright posts used structurally and mixed with horizontal log work must have adjustment provided, for example, in the case of a central post under the ridgelog, with log gable ends. Other common offenders are partitions that are jammed under logwork without telescopic provision and doors and windows installed without adequate settling space.

6) Rafter Clearance

Log gable ends will settle. This will cause a dimensional change for rafters. Therefore, provision must be made, to allow for this, at the top or at the bottom of the rafters.

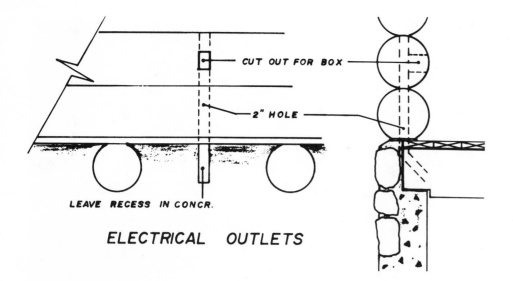

ELECTRICAL OUTLETS

CUT OUT FOR BOX

2" HOLE

LEAVE RECESS IN CONCR.

7) Stairs

Stairs should be constructed so that they will fit when the building has reached a settled condition. The possibility of movement must be incorporated into the design to allow for this.

8) Plumbing and Electrical

Two factors cannot be escaped when designing for plumbing and electricity in a log building.

One is that settling will have its effect upon pipes and conduit unless proper provision is made.

The other is that routing for unsightly vent pipes and for service hardware should be carefully thought out and blueprinted before the building is started. In this way, they can be concealed satisfactorily without mechanical damage to logs or long unlovely lengths of pipe making their pilgrimmage in full view.

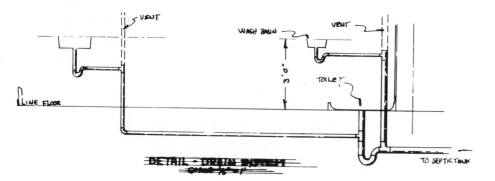

9) Weather Protection

I am always asked what kind of finish or preservative should be applied to logs. Please refer to the section on "Finish and Preservation" but, for here, I'd simply state that in my opinion no artificial finish or protection, applied to the logs, is as good as designed weather-protection.

If shelter from wind and sun are provided in the site selection, and protection from rain is designed into the roof itself, you will have gone most of the way toward insuring the well-being of the log building.

10) Notches

A properly executed round notch, for all its simplicity and ease of achieving, is certainly a good enough notch. For special applications, however, other notches may be more suitable. Designers should inform themselves as to the variety of notches and the particular qualities of each one, specifying the particular ones they consider to be suitable for any application. (See NOTCHES OF ALL KINDS, A Book of Timber Joinery.)

Right — Long roof overhang provides good protection.

Legend

Plans are generally drawn to a scale of ¼ inch = 1 foot.

In this book, the reduction of my original drawings to approximately 8 inches by 12 inches will reduce this scale to about 1/12th of an inch = 1 foot.

I have included all possible details in this book so as to enable persons to prepare their own blueprints if they wish to do so. But I would like to add some cautionary directions here.

Do not take a page from this book, for example, and have it mechanically expanded as distortion is bound to occur.

Never measure (or scale) from a ruler laid upon a print, whether it is from this book or from a blueprint already in your possession, because any printing process may have built in a distortion. Instead, all dimensions required should be shown in figures on the drawing, so calculate them, according to scale, from the dimensions provided.

Here is an example:

Since the full distance of 36'0" is given, the portion of wall containing the window is 36'0" less 18'0" = 18'0".

Be extremely careful that your calculations are double-checked for correctness, too. For this and other reasons, it may be a decided economy to purchase a set of ready-made blueprints. These are available from Log House Publishing Co. Ltd. for all log house designs shown in this book.

Logs are generally drawn as being 12 inch diameter cylinders since the variety of shapes and sizes which may be available is great.

All heights given on log walls are for the wall in a settled state (at 5 years) and additional height must be built, depending on the moisture condition of the logs. Add ¾" per foot of wall for green or near-green wood (e.g., for a 9'0" wall, build 9'6-¾").

All walls built with horizontal logs will settle. But there is not appreciable shrinkage of logs in a longitudinal direction.

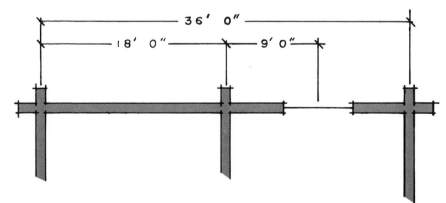

LINES

MAIN OUTLINES

SECONDARY LINES

INVISIBLE FEATURES

DIMENSION LINES

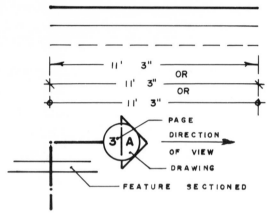

SECTION LINE

PAGE

DIRECTION

OF VIEW

DRAWING

FEATURE SECTIONED

ELECTRICAL

OUTLET BOX LOCATION

LIGHT FIXTURE

RAZOR OUTLET   R

SWITCH $

220 VOLT OUTLET   220

WIRE CONNECTION

FLUORESCENT FIXTURE   FLU

SERVICE PANEL   P

WINDOWS and DOORS

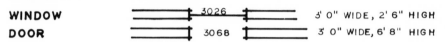

WINDOW   3026   3' 0" WIDE, 2' 6" HIGH

DOOR   3068   3' 0" WIDE, 6' 8" HIGH

OTHER SYMBOLS

MAIN LOG WALLS

STUD WALLS

SECTIONED MATERIAL

CONCRETE IN SECTION

GLASS

STONE

EARTH IN PLACE

LOG HOUSE PLANS

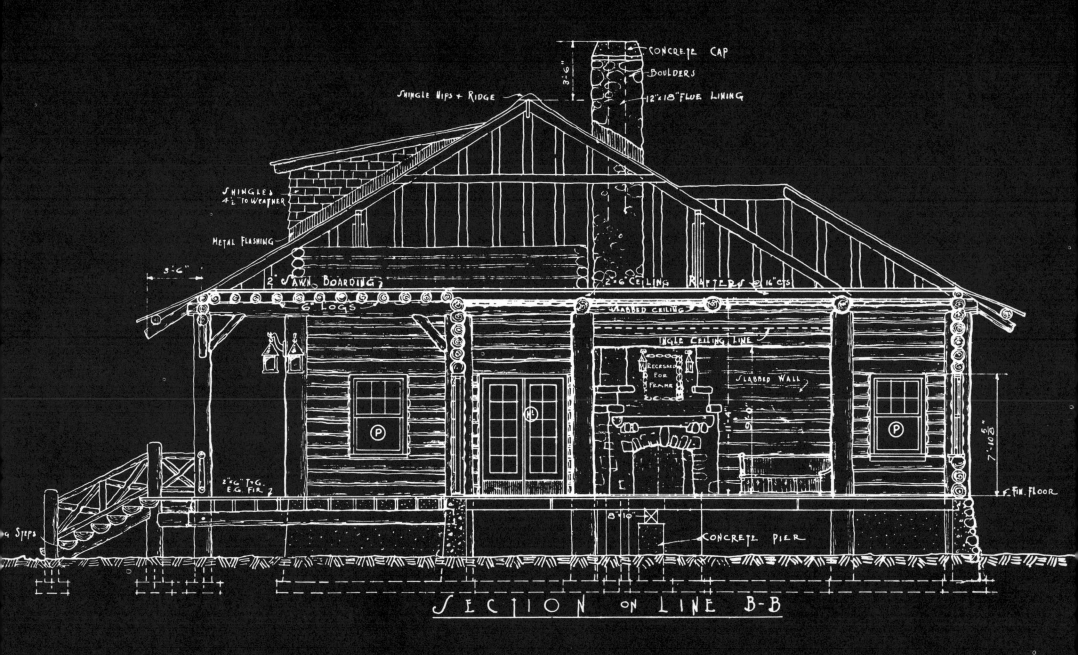

CONCRETE CAP
BOULDERS
12"×18" FLUE LINING

SHINGLE HIPS + RIDGE

SHINGLES 4½" TO WEATHER

METAL FLASHING

2" SAWN BOARDING

6" LOGS

2"×6" CEILING RAFTERS @ 16" CTS

SLABBED CEILING

SINGLE CEILING LINE

RECESSED FOR FRAME

SLABBED WALL

2"×6" T&G. E.G. FIR

F. FIN. FLOOR

CONCRETE PIER

LOG STEPS

SECTION ON LINE B-B

#791   *Square feet: 1,140*

This is our house and a dear little home, we feel. This quality is largely attributable to the many good people who have visited it, the many good times that the little house has seen, and perhaps most especially to the way it was built: by the family.

The house was not planned. It started out to be only a ski lodge. But the quiet isolation of the location, 26 miles from downtown, convinced us to live there full-time. We enjoyed 4 years amongst the bears, the squirrels, the geese and ducks on the lake, before the property became the B. Allan Mackie School of Log Building.

The house has no bathroom. We were reluctant, when faced with the final decision, to partition off or cut into any portion of the pine log walls.

A great deal of the building was constructed by my own children at the ages of 12 and 13, and the upper logs and roof were used to teach my nephew how to build. Consequently some of the workmanship is of a learner's quality but somehow, in our family, more valuable because of that.

The house is heated by a large fieldstone fireplace and is generally a delightful place to live.

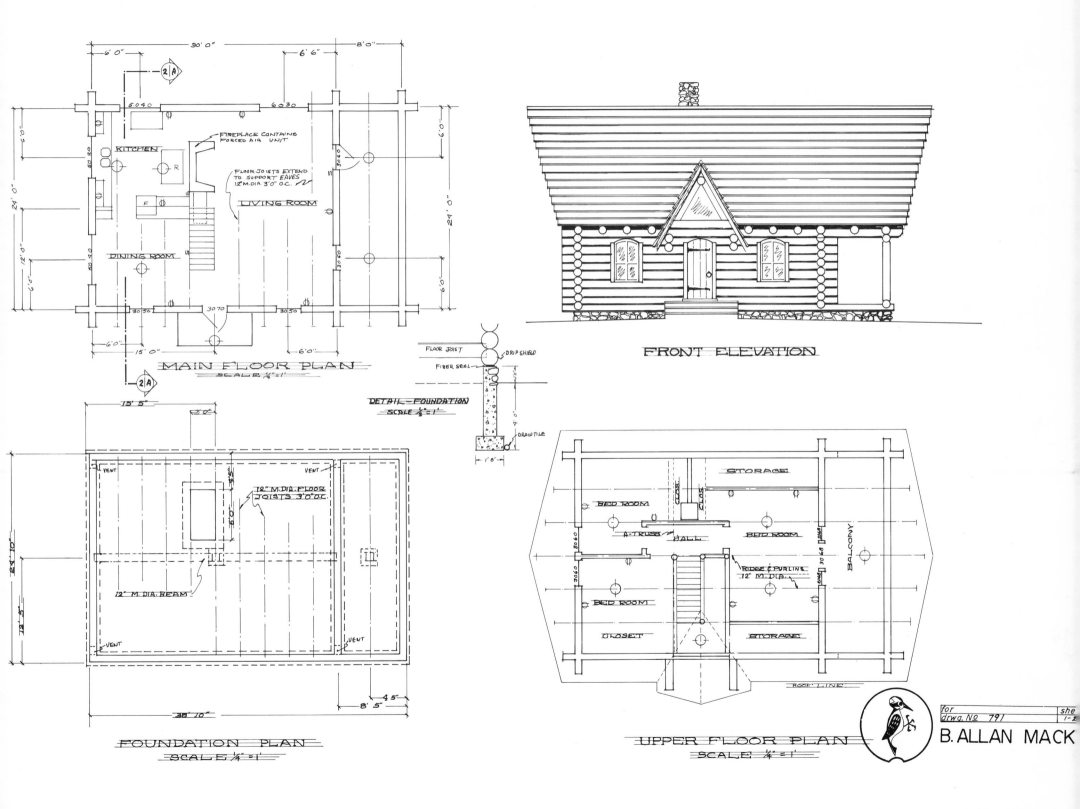

MAIN FLOOR PLAN
SCALE ¼"=1'

30'0"
6'0"
8'0"
6'6"
6'0"
24'0"
12'0"
6'0"
6'0"
29'0"
6040
6030
KITCHEN
6020
R
F
FIREPLACE CONTAINS FORCED AIR UNIT
FLOOR JOISTS EXTEND TO SUPPORT EAVES 12" M. DIA. 3'0" O.C.
LIVING ROOM
3060
3060
DINING ROOM
6050
3050
3070
3050
6'0"
15'0"
6'0"

2|A

DETAIL - FOUNDATION
SCALE ½"=1'
FLOOR JOIST
DRIP SHIELD
FIBER SEAL
DRAIN TILE
1'8"

FRONT ELEVATION

FOUNDATION PLAN
SCALE ¼"=1'
15'5"
3'0"
VENT
VENT
12" M. DIA. FLOOR JOISTS 3'0" O.C.
3'5"
6'0"
12" M. DIA. BEAM
24'10"
12'5"
VENT
VENT
4'5"
8'5"
38'10"

UPPER FLOOR PLAN
SCALE ¼"=1'
STORAGE
BED ROOM
CLOS.
CLOS.
A-TRUSS
HALL
BED ROOM
BALCONY
3060
3060
3060
RIDGE & PURLINE 12" M. DIA.
5040
3060
BED ROOM
CLOSET
STORAGE
ROOF LINE

for
drwg. No 791
she
1-2

B. ALLAN MACK

4

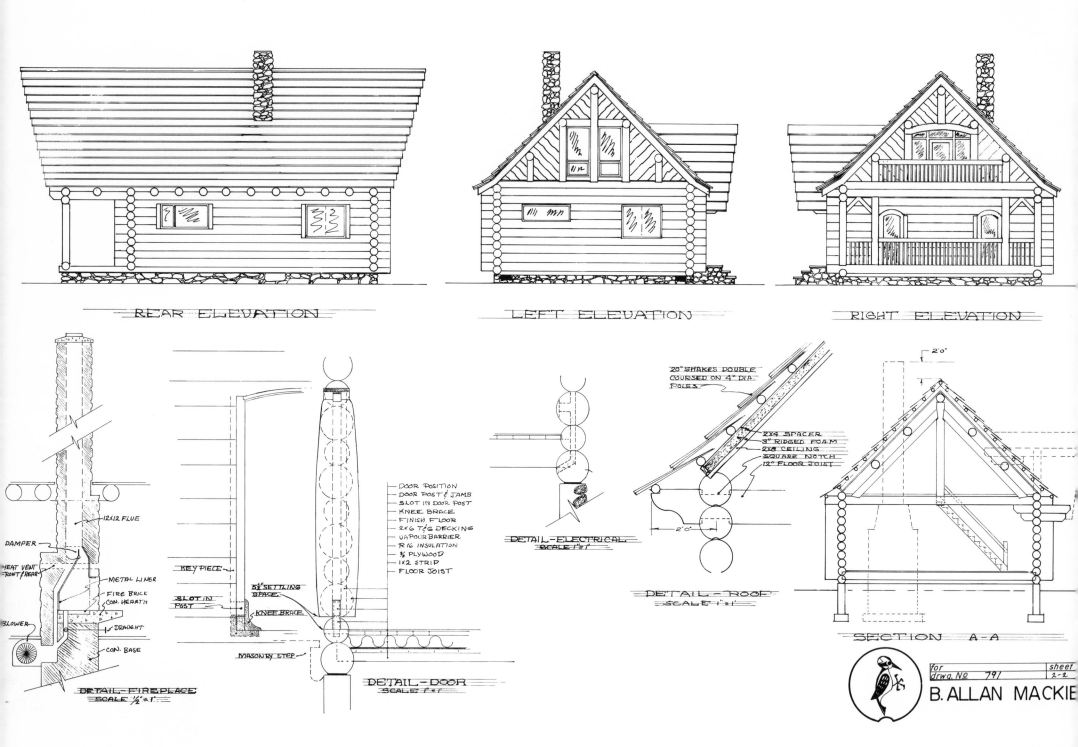

REAR ELEVATION

LEFT ELEVATION

RIGHT ELEVATION

DETAIL-FIREPLACE
SCALE ½"=1'

12X12 FLUE

DAMPER

HEAT VENT
FRONT & REAR

METAL LINER

FIRE BRICK

CON. HEARTH

BLOWER

DRAUGHT

CON. BASE

KEY PIECE

SLOT IN POST

MASONRY STEP

5½" SETTLING SPACE.

KNEE BRACE

DOOR POSITION
DOOR POST & JAMB
SLOT IN DOOR POST
KNEE BRACE
FINISH FLOOR
2x6 T&G DECKING
VAPOUR BARRIER.
R 16 INSULATION
¾ PLYWOOD
1x2 STRIP
FLOOR JOIST

DETAIL-DOOR
SCALE 1"=1'

DETAIL-ELECTRICAL
SCALE 1"=1'

20" SHAKES DOUBLE
COURSED ON 4" DIA.
POLES

2x4 SPACER
3" RIDGED FOAM
2X8 CEILING
SQUARE NOTCH
12" FLOOR JOIST

DETAIL-ROOF
SCALE 1"=1'

2'0"

2'0"

SECTION A-A

for
drwg. No 791

sheet
2-2

B. ALLAN MACKIE

#792 Lookout House   *Square feet: 948*

This house was designed for a promontory overlooking an isolated lake in central British Columbia.

During certain parts of the year, there is a lot of wildlife to be observed from this ridge and, although all the larger animals are driven off by hunting pressures during the otherwise wonderful autumn in that country, the stars hold a steady light in the extremely clear skies. In the distance, mountains which border the rim of the landscape, often seem close enough to touch, and have not yet been driven off although their lakes and rivers have been dammed, flooded, drained, and turned around.

This particular house will be used as a guest house when the main house is finished.

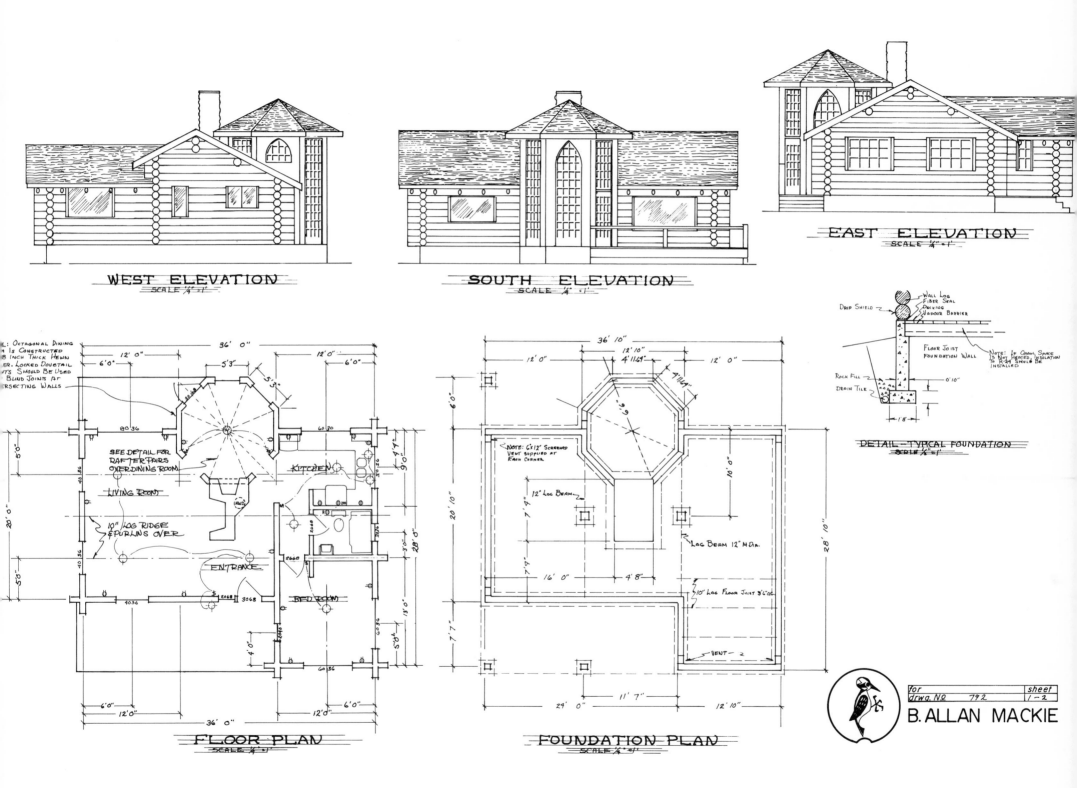

WEST ELEVATION
SCALE ¼"=1'

SOUTH ELEVATION
SCALE ¼"=1'

EAST ELEVATION
SCALE ¼"=1'

FLOOR PLAN
SCALE ¼"=1'

FOUNDATION PLAN
SCALE ¼"=1'

DETAIL — TYPICAL FOUNDATION
SCALE ¼"=1'

LIVING ROOM

KITCHEN

SEE DETAIL FOR
RAFTER PAIRS
OVER DINING ROOM

10" LOG RIDGE
& PURLINS OVER

ENTRANCE

BED ROOM

NOTE: Octagonal Dining
Room Is Constructed
From 8 Inch Thick Hewn
Timber. Locked Dovetail
Joints Should Be Used
And Blind Joints At
Intersecting Walls

NOTE: 6"x12" Screened
Vent Supplied At
Each Corner

12" Log Beam

Log Beam 12" M.Dia.

10" Log Floor Joist 3'6"o.c.

VENT - 2

Wall Log
Fiber Seal
Decking
Vapour Barrier
Drip Shield
Floor Joist
Foundation Wall
NOTE: If Crawl Space
Is Not Heated, Insulation
To R-24 Should Be
Installed
Rock Fill
Drain Tile

for
drwg. No.   792

sheet
1 - 2

B. ALLAN MACKIE

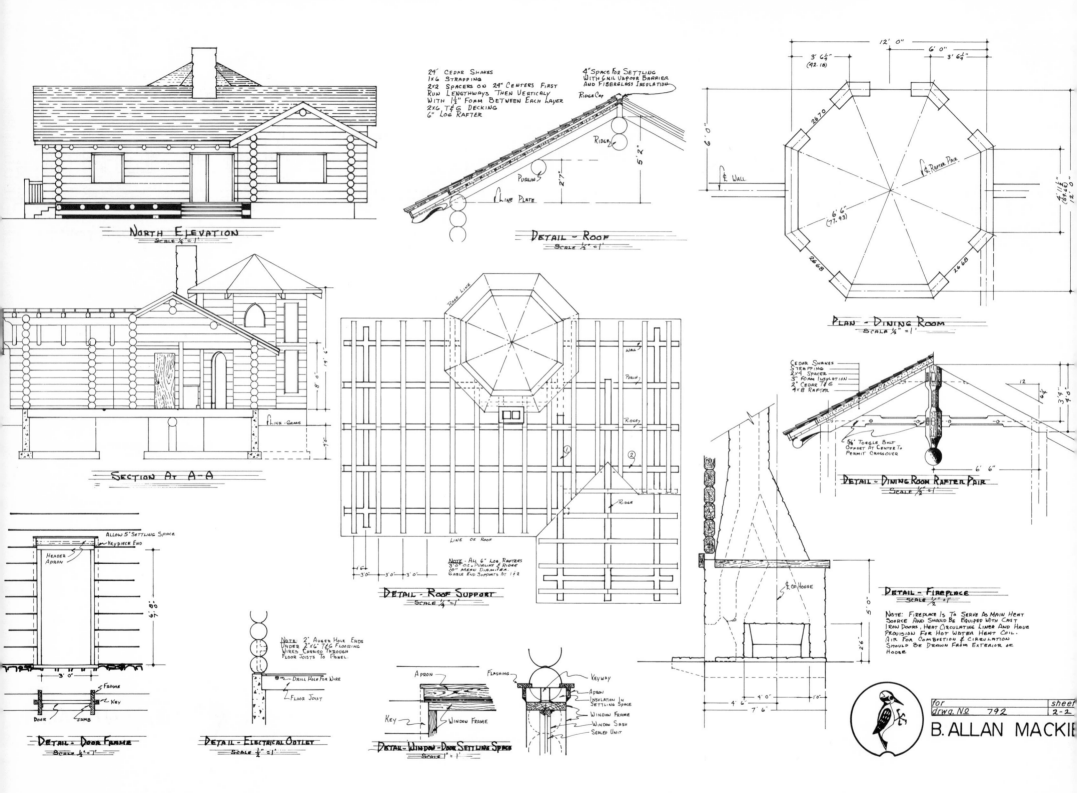

NORTH ELEVATION
Scale ¼" = 1'

24" CEDAR SHAKES
1x6 STRAPPING
2x2 SPACERS ON 24" CENTERS FIRST
RUN LENGTHWAYS THEN VERTICALLY
WITH 1½" FOAM BETWEEN EACH LAYER
2x6 T&G DECKING
6" LOG RAFTER

4" SPACE FOR SETTLING
WITH 6 MIL VAPOUR BARRIER
AND FIBERGLASS INSULATION

RIDGE CAP

RIDGE

PURLIN

LINE PLATE

DETAIL - ROOF
Scale ½" = 1'

PLAN - DINING ROOM
Scale ½" = 1'

SECTION AT A-A

CEDAR SHAKES
STRAPPING
2x4 SPACER
3" FOAM INSULATION
2" CEDAR T&G
4x8 RAFTER

⅝" TOGGLE BOLT
OFFSET AT CENTER TO
PERMIT CROSSOVER

DETAIL - DINING ROOM RAFTER PAIR
Scale ½" = 1'

DETAIL - ROOF SUPPORT
Scale ¼" = 1'

NOTE: ALL 6" LOG RAFTERS
3'-0" O.C. PURLINS & RIDGE
10" MEAN DIAMETER.
GABLE END SUPPORTS AT 1 & 2

LINE OF ROOF

DETAIL - FIREPLACE
Scale ½" = 1'

NOTE: FIREPLACE IS TO SERVE AS MAIN HEAT
SOURCE AND SHOULD BE EQUIPPED WITH CAST
IRON DOORS, HEAT CIRCULATING LINER AND HAVE
PROVISION FOR HOT WATER HEAT COIL.
AIR FOR COMBUSTION & CIRCULATION
SHOULD BE DRAWN FROM EXTERIOR OF
HOUSE

ALLOW 5" SETTLING SPACE
KEYPIECE END
HEADER
APRON

FRAME
KEY
DOOR   JAMB

DETAIL - DOOR FRAME
Scale ½" = 1'

NOTE: 2" AUGER HOLE ENDS
UNDER 2"x6" T&G FLOORING
WIRES CARRIED THROUGH
FLOOR JOISTS TO PANEL.

DRILL HOLE FOR WIRE

FLOOR JOIST

DETAIL - ELECTRICAL OUTLET
Scale ½" = 1'

APRON   FLASHING   KEYWAY
APRON
INSULATION IN
SETTLING SPACE
KEY   WINDOW FRAME
WINDOW FRAME
WINDOW SASH
SEALED UNIT

DETAIL - WINDOW - DOOR SETTLING SPACE
Scale 1" = 1'

for
drwg. No. 792

sheet
2-2

B. ALLAN MACKIE

#793   Square Feet: 1,100

This house is designed to supply the real human needs, with the least impact on resources.

This is a building which could be constructed for a very small amount of cash, and maintained for less than average costs.

The solar-tempered greenhouse could supply a large part of heat needs and, if the house is properly built, the fireplace could easily take care of the rest, even in —40° temperatures. The masonry floor and massive fireplace are to act as a heat sump.

Plumbing is incorporated in the fireplace so that an electric heating element in the hot water tank can protect the system during short absences.

The drain system is simple and could be made to include a heat extraction system ahead of the septic tank.

If a builder were to go to the additional effort of adding a heat

sump under the floor, which could have heat directed to it from the top of the greenhouse area by means of an air pump, then, if the heat were reused, in this way, very little additional heat from external sources would be required.

With the inclusion of wind or water power, the house could approach a very high degree of self-sufficiency.

I would urge the builder of this, or any house, to investigate further the means by which both self-support and human needs can be served by such things as indoor food-growing areas, in the composting of toilet and/or septic tank materials for garden use, and, of course, the many ways in which electrical gadgetry can be avoided in favour of a more natural, healthful, and non-energy using method. A good book to read, to get started into this new arena of building a real world right into the household, is "30 Energy-Efficient Houses You Can Build" by Alex Wade ($8.95 from Rodale Press.)

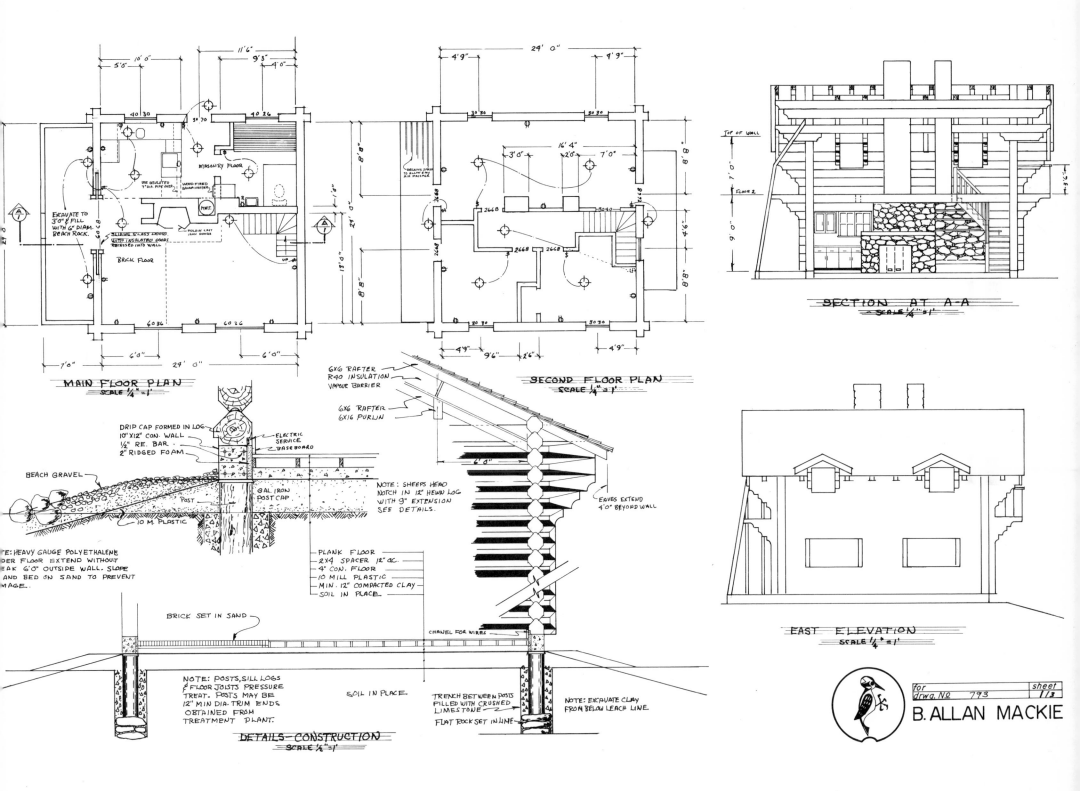

MAIN FLOOR PLAN
SCALE ¼" = 1'

EXCAVATE TO 3'0" & FILL WITH 6" DIAM. BEACH ROCK.

USE INSULATED 7" DIA. PIPE OVER WOOD FIRED SAUNA HEATER

MASONRY FLOOR

SLIDING GLASS DOORS WITH INSULATED DOORS RECESSED INTO WALL

BRICK FLOOR

FOLDIN CAST IRON DOORS

SECOND FLOOR PLAN
SCALE ¼" = 1'

DECKING SPACED TO ALLOW EASY AIR PASSAGE

SECTION AT A-A
SCALE ¼" = 1'

TOP OF WALL

FLOOR 2

EAST ELEVATION
SCALE ¼" = 1'

6X6 RAFTER
R40 INSULATION
VAPOUR BARRIER

6X6 RAFTER
6X16 PURLIN

DRIP CAP FORMED IN LOG
10" X 12" CON. WALL
½" RE. BAR
2" RIDGED FOAM

ELECTRIC SERVICE
BASEBOARD

BEACH GRAVEL

POST

GAL. IRON POST CAP

10 M. PLASTIC

NOTE: SHEEPS HEAD NOTCH IN 12" HEWN LOG WITH 9" EXTENSION SEE DETAILS.

EAVES EXTEND 4'0" BEYOND WALL

NOTE: HEAVY GAUGE POLYETHALENE UNDER FLOOR EXTEND WITHOUT BREAK 6'0" OUTSIDE WALL. SLOPE AND BED ON SAND TO PREVENT DAMAGE.

PLANK FLOOR
2X4 SPACER 12" OC.
4" CON. FLOOR
10 MILL PLASTIC
MIN. 12" COMPACTED CLAY
SOIL IN PLACE

BRICK SET IN SAND

CHANEL FOR WIRES

SOIL IN PLACE.

NOTE: POSTS, SILL LOGS & FLOOR JOISTS PRESSURE TREAT. POSTS MAY BE 12" MIN DIA. TRIM ENDS OBTAINED FROM TREATMENT PLANT.

TRENCH BETWEEN POSTS FILLED WITH CRUSHED LIMESTONE

FLAT ROCK SET IN LINE

NOTE: EXCAVATE CLAY FROM BELOW LEACH LINE

DETAILS - CONSTRUCTION
SCALE ½" = 1'

for
drwg. No 793
sheet
1/3

B. ALLAN MACKIE

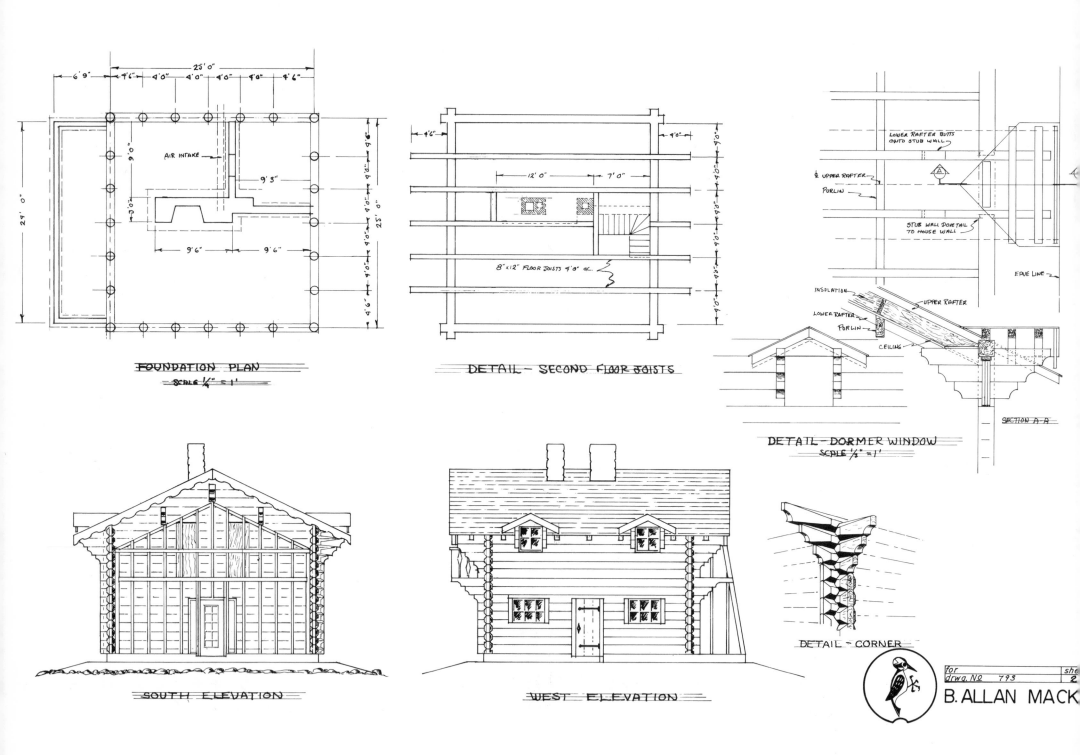

25' 0"
6' 9" 4' 6" 4' 0" 4' 0" 4' 0" 4' 0" 4' 6"

9' 0"

AIR INTAKE

9' 3"

3' 0"

25' 0"

9' 6" 9' 6"

9' 6" 9' 6" 9' 6" 9' 6" 9' 6" 9' 6"

FOUNDATION PLAN
SCALE ¼" = 1'

4' 6"   9' 0"

12' 0"   7' 0"

9' 0" 9' 0" 9' 6" 9' 0" 9' 0"

8" x 12" FLOOR JOISTS 4' 0" oc

DETAIL - SECOND FLOOR JOISTS

LOWER RAFTER BUTTS
ONTO STUB WALL

R UPPER RAFTER

PURLIN

STUB WALL DOVETAIL
TO HOUSE WALL

EAVE LINE

INSULATION
UPPER RAFTER
LOWER RAFTER
PURLIN
CEILING

SECTION A-A

DETAIL - DORMER WINDOW
SCALE ½" = 1'

SOUTH ELEVATION

WEST ELEVATION

DETAIL - CORNER

for
drwg. Nº 793

she
2

B. ALLAN MACK

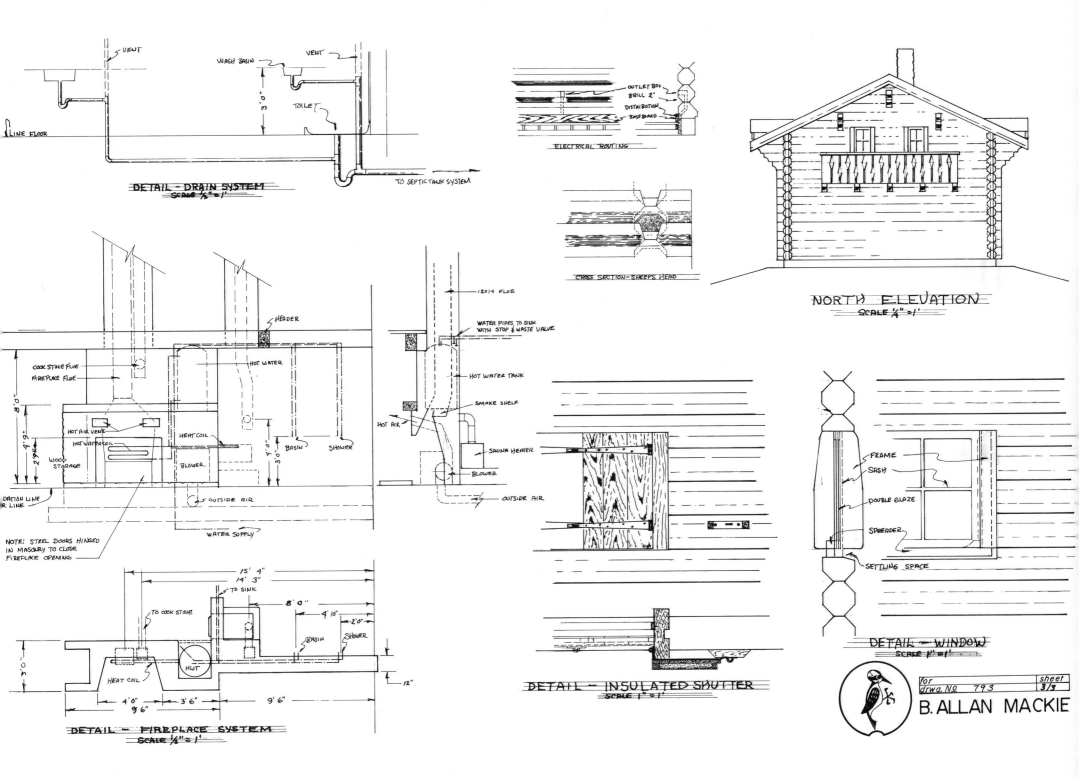

VENT

WASH BASIN VENT

3'0"

TOILET

LINE FLOOR

DETAIL - DRAIN SYSTEM
SCALE ½"=1'

TO SEPTIC TANK SYSTEM

OUTLET BOX
DRILL 2"
DISTRIBUTION
BASE BOARD

ELECTRICAL ROUTING

CROSS SECTION - SHEEPS HEAD

NORTH ELEVATION
SCALE ¼"=1'

HEADER

COOK STOVE FLUE
FIREPLACE FLUE

8'0"   4'9"   2'9"

HOT AIR VENTS
HOT WATER COIL

WOOD STORAGE

DATION LINE
R LINE

HOT WATER

HEAT COIL

BLOWER

7'0" 3'0"

BASIN   SHOWER

OUTSIDE AIR

NOTE: STEEL DOORS HINGED
IN MASONRY TO CLOSE
FIREPLACE OPENING

WATER SUPPLY

12×14 FLUE

WATER PIPES TO SINK
WITH STOP & WASTE VALVE

HOT WATER TANK

SMOKE SHELF

HOT AIR

SAUNA HEATER

BLOWER

OUTSIDE AIR

15'4"
14'3"

TO SINK
TO COOK STOVE

8'0"
4'10" 2'0"

BASIN   SHOWER

HEAT COIL   HWT

4'0"   3'6"   9'6"
9'6"

12"

DETAIL - FIREPLACE SYSTEM
SCALE ⅛"=1'

DETAIL - INSULATED SHUTTER
SCALE 1"=1'

FRAME

SASH

DOUBLE GLAZE

SPREADER

SETTLING SPACE

DETAIL - WINDOW
SCALE 1"=1'

for drwg. No 793   sheet 3/3

B. ALLAN MACKIE

#794

Square feet: 1,500

This is a house intended for a sloping location with an extensive view to the front. It is essentially a bachelor house with easy and uncrowded facilities.

The loft area is intended for visitors, as is the basement accommodation.

The basement garage is meant for cold country locations. For this same reason, the front windows are perhaps a trifle smaller than would be preferred by some.

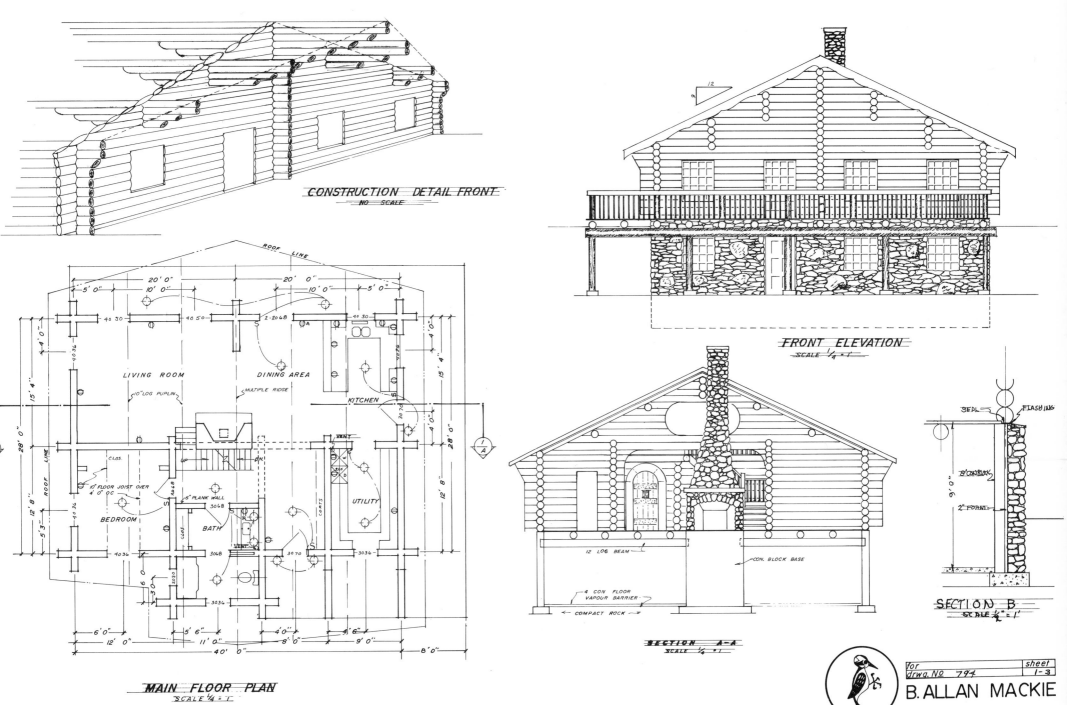

CONSTRUCTION DETAIL FRONT
NO SCALE

FRONT ELEVATION
SCALE ¼" = 1'

ROOF LINE

20' 0"   20' 0"
5' 0"   10' 0"   10' 0"   5' 0"

4050   4050   2-2068   4030

LIVING ROOM   DINING AREA

10"LOG PUPLIN   MULTIPLE RIDGE

KITCHEN

VENT

CLOS.

10' FLOOR JOIST OVER
4' 0" OC

6' PLANK WALL   UTILITY

3068

BEDROOM   BATH

VENT

4036   3068   3070   3036

6' 0"   5' 6"   4' 0"   4' 6"   9' 0"
12' 0"   11' 0"   8' 0"   8' 0"
40' 0"

MAIN FLOOR PLAN
SCALE ¼" = 1'

SECTION A-A
SCALE ¼" = 1'

12 LOG BEAM

CON. BLOCK BASE

4 CON FLOOR
VAPOUR BARRIER

COMPACT ROCK

SEAL   FLASHING

8"CON.BLOCK

2" FORM

SECTION B
SCALE ½" = 1'

for
drwg. No 794   sheet
                     1-3

B. ALLAN MACKIE

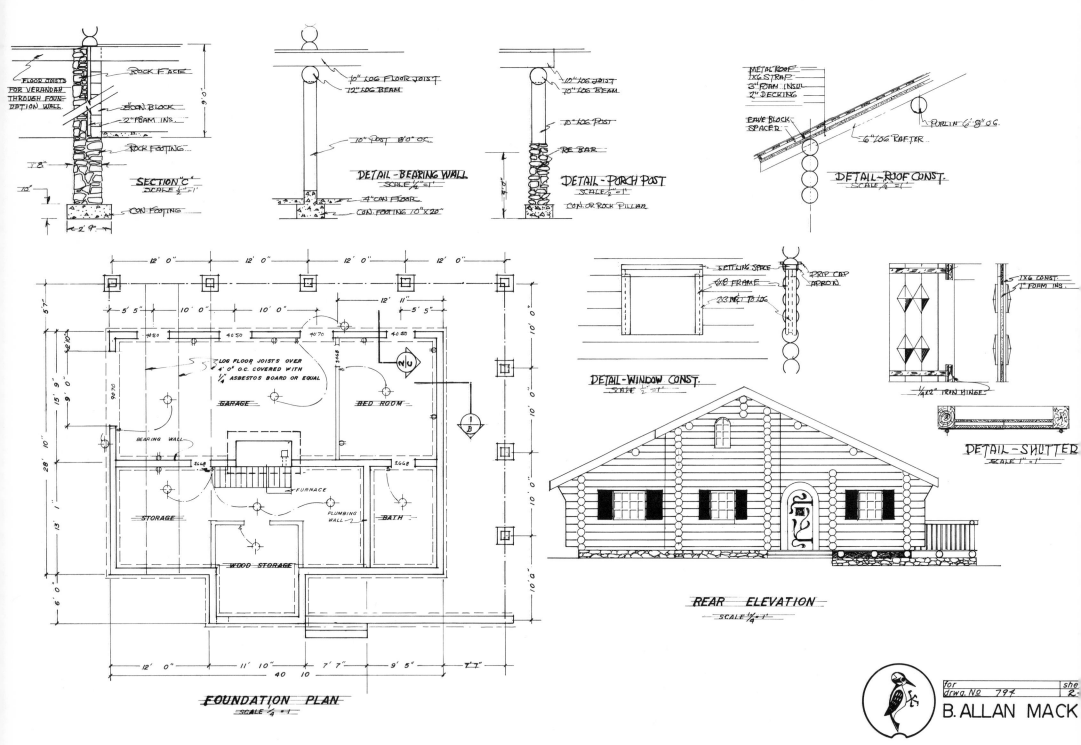

FLOOR JOISTS FOR VERANDAH THROUGH FOUNDATION WALL

ROCK FACE

9'·0"

FDN. BLOCK

2" FOAM INS.

ROCK FOOTING

1'·8"

SECTION "C"
SCALE 1/2"=1'

10"

CON. FOOTING

2'·9"

10" LOG FLOOR JOIST

12" LOG BEAM

10" POST 8'·0" O.C.

DETAIL—BEARING WALL
SCALE 1/2"=1'

4" CON FLOOR

CON. FOOTING 10"X20"

10" LOG JOIST

10" LOG BEAM

10" LOG POST

RE BAR

DETAIL—PORCH POST
SCALE 1/2"=1'

CON. OR ROCK PILLAR

METAL ROOF
1X6 STRAP
3" FOAM INSUL
2" DECKING

EAVE BLOCK SPACER

PURLIN 6'·8" O.C.

6" LOG RAFTER

DETAIL—ROOF CONST.
SCALE 1/2"=1'

FOUNDATION PLAN

12'·0"   12'·0"   12'·0"   12'·0"

5'·5"   10'·0"   10'·0"   12'·11"   5'·5"

4050   4050   4070   4050

GARAGE   BED ROOM

LOG FLOOR JOISTS OVER 4'·0" O.C. COVERED WITH 1/4" ASBESTOS BOARD OR EQUAL

BEARING WALL

2668   2668

FURNACE

STORAGE   PLUMBING WALL   BATH

WOOD STORAGE

5'·7"   12'·10"   15'·9"   9'·0"   28'·10"   13'·1"   6'·0"

10'·0"   10'·0"   10'·0"   10'·0"

12'·0"   11'·10"   7'·7"   9'·5"   7'·7"

40   10

FOUNDATION PLAN
SCALE 1/4"=1'

SETTLING SPACE

6X8 FRAME

2X3 NKT TO LOG

DRIP CAP APRON

DETAIL—WINDOW CONST.
SCALE 1/2"=1'

1X6 CONST.
1" FOAM INS.

1/4"X2" IRON HINGE

DETAIL—SHUTTER
SCALE 1"=1'

REAR   ELEVATION
SCALE 1/4"=1'

for
drwg. No 794

she
2.

B. ALLAN MACK

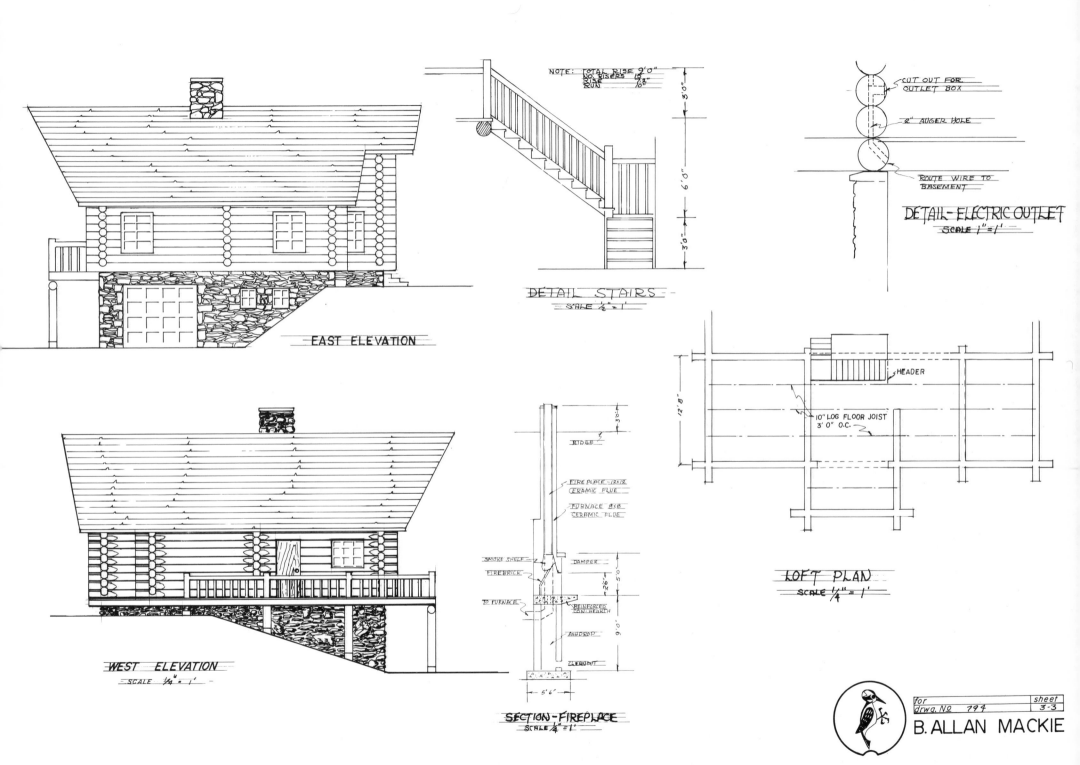

EAST ELEVATION

WEST ELEVATION
SCALE ¼" = 1'

NOTE: TOTAL RISE 9'0"
NO. RISERS 15
RISE 7½"
RUN 10½"

3'0"

6'0"

3'0"

DETAIL STAIRS
SCALE ½" = 1'

CUT OUT FOR
OUTLET BOX

2" AUGER HOLE

ROUTE WIRE TO
BASEMENT

DETAIL - ELECTRIC OUTLET
SCALE 1" = 1'

HEADER

12'8"

10" LOG FLOOR JOIST
3'0" O.C.

LOFT PLAN
SCALE ¼" = 1'

3'0"

RIDGE

FIRE PLACE - 12x12
CERAMIC FLUE

FURNACE 8x8
CERAMIC FLUE

SMOKE SHELF

FIREBRICK

DAMPER

26'0"

5'0"

TO FURNACE

REINFORCED
CON. HEARTH

ASHDROP

9'0"

CLEANOUT

5'6"

SECTION - FIREPLACE
SCALE ¼" = 1'

for
drwg. No. 794

sheet
3-3

B. ALLAN MACKIE

#795

Square feet: 2,000

This is a very comfortable family home in Banff, Alberta. The house was designed and built by a Forest Ranger of that area and, while I have taken minor liberties with the floorplan, the house is very much that same excellent example.

There are a great many really good log houses in Alberta. "Pete's place," they'll tell you, in Banff, is just down the road a bit: the boyhood log home of Premier Peter Lougheed. The log homes, churches, halls,

libraries, are everywhere and I feel that Albertans could be most proud of the high standard of workmanship and concept that they have brought to the art.

This particular home is generous in all its rooms, having a good traffic flow, and while there are only two large upstairs bedrooms, the house is on a sloped lot and basement bedrooms are freely lighted and of easy access.

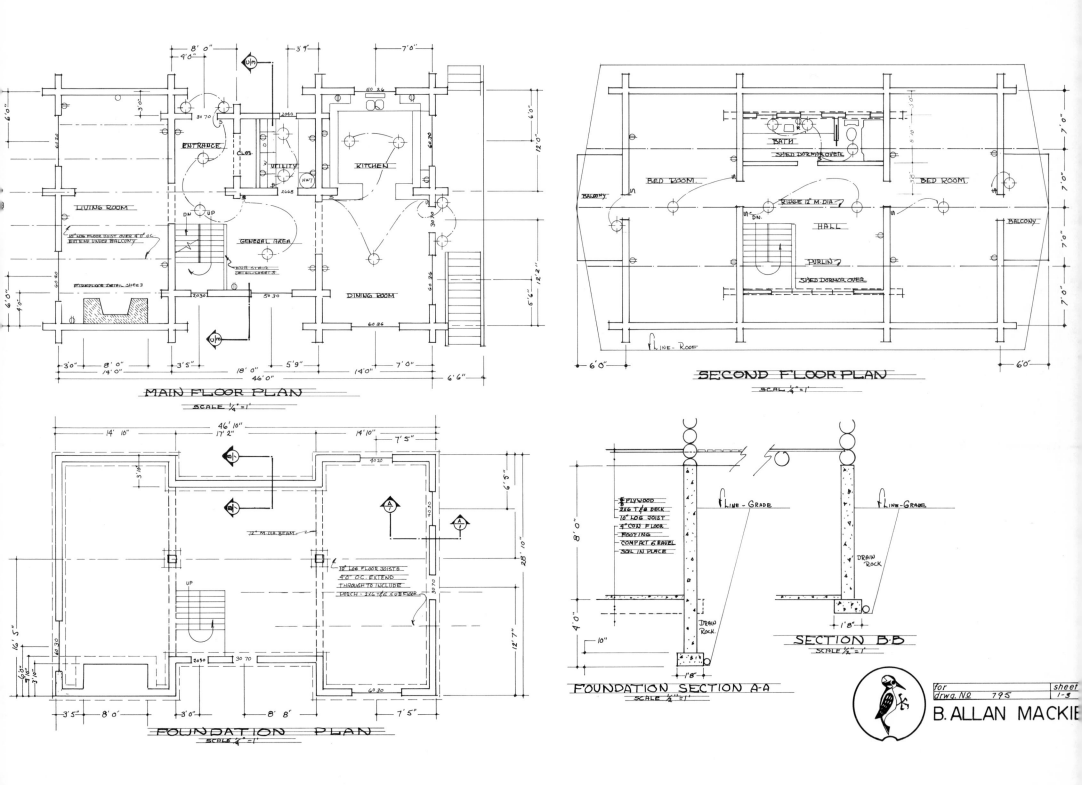

MAIN FLOOR PLAN
SCALE ¼"=1'

SECOND FLOOR PLAN
SCALE ¼"=1'

FOUNDATION PLAN
SCALE ¼"=1'

FOUNDATION SECTION A-A
SCALE ½"=1'

SECTION B-B
SCALE ½"=1'

for drwg. No 795 sheet 1-3

B. ALLAN MACKIE

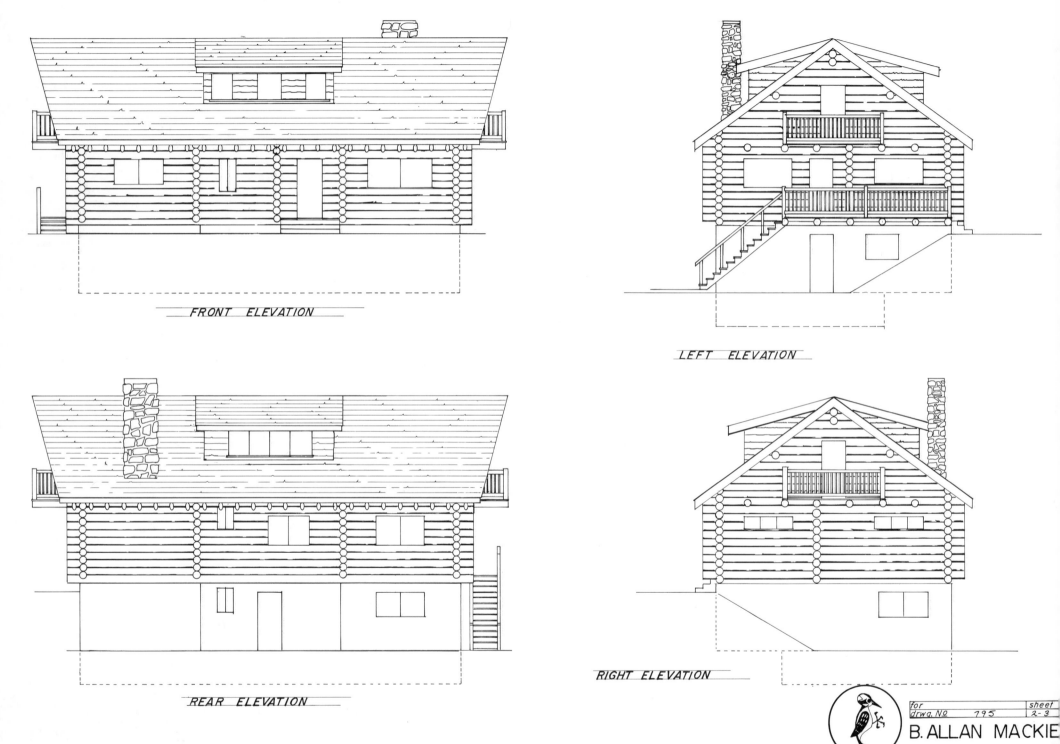

FRONT ELEVATION

LEFT ELEVATION

REAR ELEVATION

RIGHT ELEVATION

for drwg. No. 795 sheet 2-3

B. ALLAN MACKIE

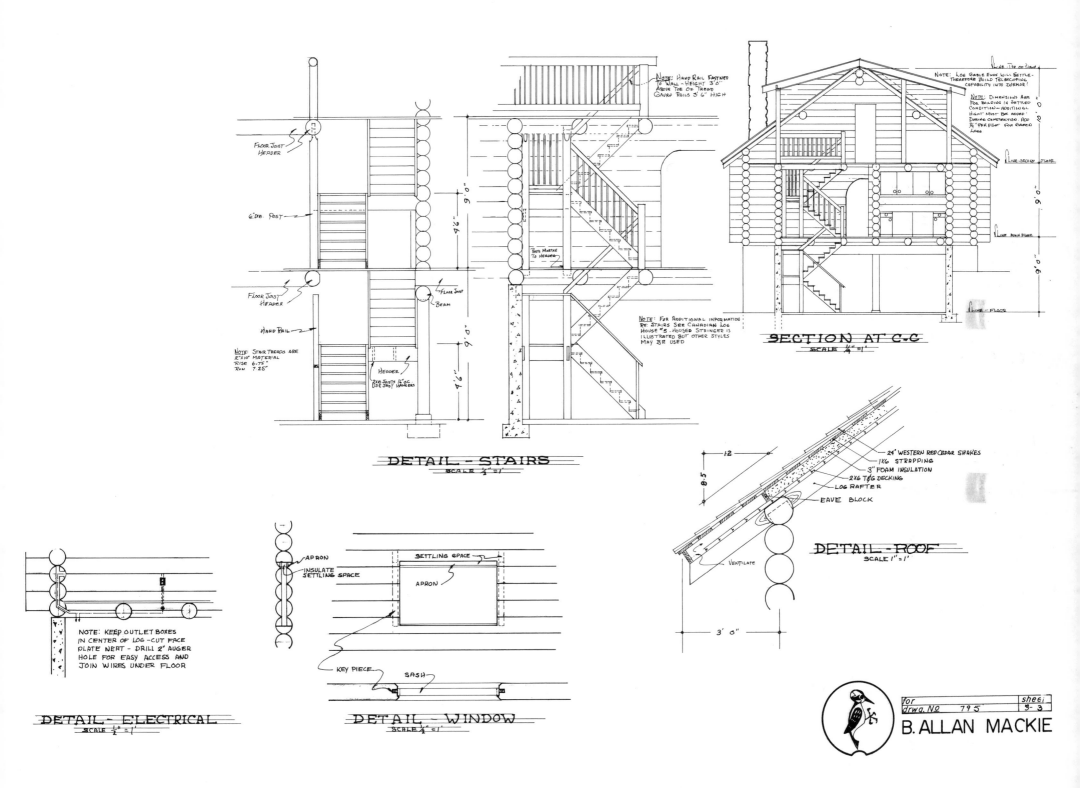

NOTE: Hand Rail Fastened To Wall - Height 3'0" Above Toe of Tread Guard Rails 3'6" High

NOTE: Dimensions Are For Building In Settled Condition - Additional Hight Must Be Added During Construction. Add ¾" Per Foot For Radial Loss

Floor Joist Header

6" DIA. Post

Floor Joist Header

Hand Rail

NOTE: Stair Treads Are 2"x10" Material Rise 6.75" Run 7.25"

9'0"
9'6"
9'0"
9'6"

Floor Joist

Beam

Header

2x10 Joists 16" o.c. Use Joist Hangers

Posts Mortise To Header

NOTE: For Additional Information Re: Stairs See Canadian Log House #5. Housed Stringer Is Illustrated But Other Styles May Be Used

DETAIL - STAIRS
SCALE ½" = 1'

NOTE: Log Gable Ends Will Settle - Therefore Build Telescoping Capability Into Dormer!

Line Top of Plate
Line Second Floor
Line Main Plate
Line Floor

9'0"
9'0"

SECTION AT C-C
SCALE ¼" = 1'

12
8.5

24" Western Red Cedar Shakes
1x6 Strapping
3" Foam Insulation
2x6 T&G Decking
Log Rafter
Eave Block

Ventilate

3'0"

DETAIL - ROOF
SCALE 1" = 1'

NOTE: KEEP OUTLET BOXES IN CENTER OF LOG - CUT FACE PLATE NEAT - DRILL 2" AUGER HOLE FOR EASY ACCESS AND JOIN WIRES UNDER FLOOR

DETAIL - ELECTRICAL
SCALE ½" = 1'

APRON
INSULATE SETTLING SPACE
SETTLING SPACE
APRON
KEY PIECE
SASH

DETAIL - WINDOW
SCALE ½" = 1'

for
drwg. No. 795
sheet
3-3

B. ALLAN MACKIE

#796 Coffee House

Square Feet: 1,784

This building was started in my own back yard, now the Mackie School of Log Building, primarily as a demonstration of Piece-sur-piece construction and simply for the joy of building in this medium and this design.

Travels across Canada have instilled in me a deep respect for the men who built the hewn timber-framed buildings, from Louisbourg in Cape Breton to Vancouver Island, British Columbia.

Preservation architects argue that the term Piece-sur-piece is incorrectly applied to this style of building since it means one piece (log) imposed on another. This may be so. But I'm not aware of this style of building having been constructed elsewhere and because of the important departure from the usual practice, I can understand the term being applied to differentiate between the two. The usual practice was to fill the spaces between the upright logs with rubble; in Canada, builders made an important switch from rubble(cold) to log (both warmer and more readily available). And so this new type of construction was called Piece-en-Piece or Piece-sur-piece, differentiating it from the former traditional colombage.

Whatever the case, everybody seems to know what it means and I like it simply because of the implicit tribute to those grand old builders that the sound evokes for me.

These buildings and the technique have a lot to recommend them. First, they can be built almost any size or shape. They can be constructed of predominantly short logs. They can be adapted to a great variety of materials and styles. And the material can be handled by one person using standard equipment.

This Coffee House is not large. But it contains a great deal of useable space. The present floor plan is designed to utilize the building as a lounge and hall, but the space could be divided into almost any proportions the builder wished.

The building is exceedingly strong and, I feel, when it is finished, it will become exceedingly beautiful. However, like most log houses, this one required a great deal of work and, while I do not think the amount of work is any greater than a round log building of a similar size, I do recommend that anyone attempting it should carefully assess his resources: a strong back, his ability to swing a broad-axe, and his available time. But again, that's true of any building.

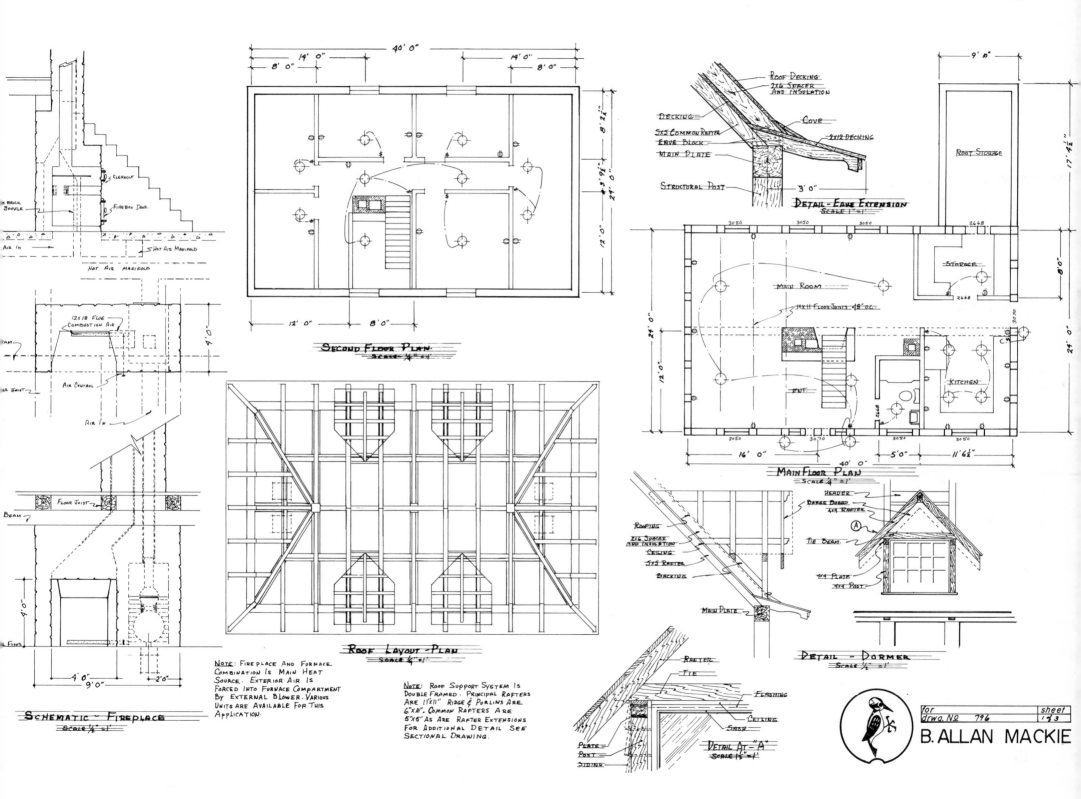

SECOND FLOOR PLAN
Scale ¼"=1'

ROOF LAYOUT-PLAN
Scale ⅛"=1'

SCHEMATIC-FIREPLACE
Scale ½"=1'

DETAIL-EAVE EXTENSION
Scale 1"=1'

MAIN FLOOR PLAN
Scale ¼"=1'

DETAIL-DORMER
Scale ½"=1'

DETAIL AT "A"
Scale 1½"=1'

NOTE: Fireplace And Furnace Combination Is Main Heat Source. Exterior Air Is Forced Into Furnace Compartment By External Blower. Various Units Are Available For This Application.

NOTE: Roof Support System Is Double Framed. Principal Rafters Are 11"x11" Ridge & Purlins Are 6"x8". Common Rafters Are 5"x5" As Are Rafter Extensions For Additional Detail See Sectional Drawing.

for drwg. No. 796   sheet 1 of 3

B. ALLAN MACKIE

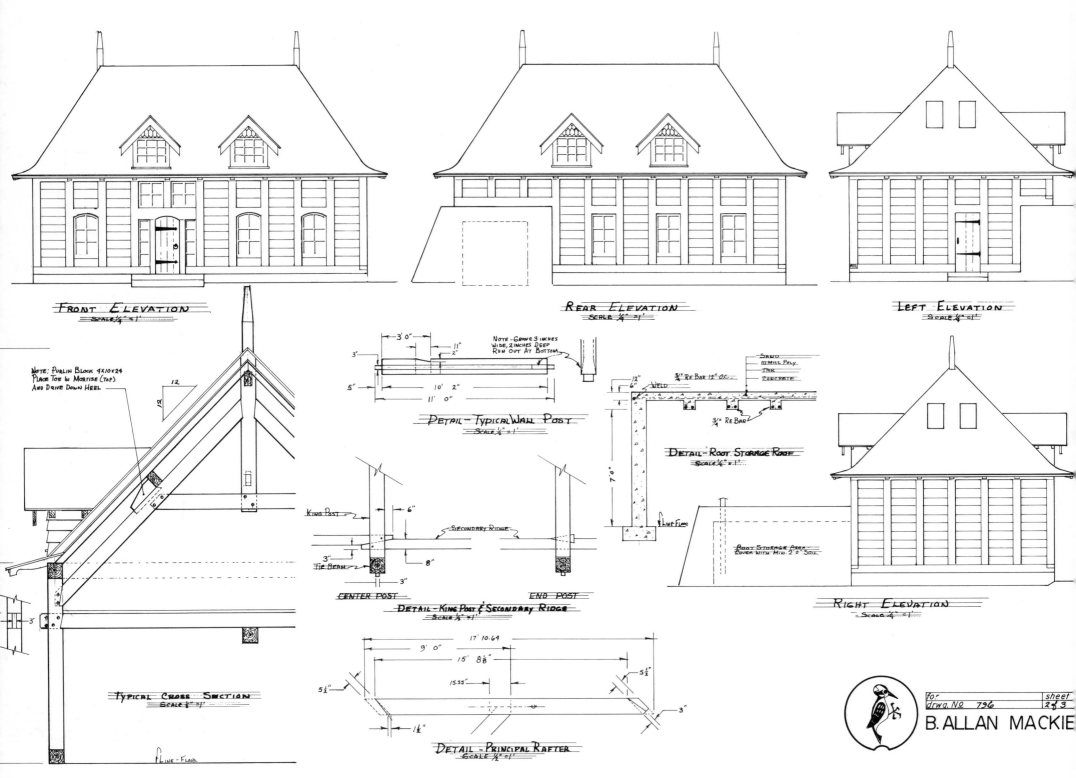

24

FRONT ELEVATION
SCALE ¼" = 1'

REAR ELEVATION
SCALE ¼" = 1'

LEFT ELEVATION
SCALE ¼" = 1'

RIGHT ELEVATION
SCALE ¼" = 1'

NOTE: PURLIN BLOCK 4X10X24
PLACE TOE IN MORTISE (TOP)
AND DRIVE DOWN HEEL

12
12

TYPICAL CROSS SECTION
SCALE ¼" = 1'

↓ LINE—FLOOR

3'

3' 0"
11"
2"
3"
5"
10' 2"
11' 0"

NOTE—GROVE 3 INCHES
WIDE, 2 INCHES DEEP
RUN OUT AT BOTTOM

DETAIL—TYPICAL WALL POST
SCALE ½" = 1'

KING POST
6"
SECONDARY RIDGE
3"
TIE BEAM
8"
3"
CENTER POST
END POST

DETAIL—KING POST & SECONDARY RIDGE
SCALE ½" = 1'

17' 10.64
9' 0"
15' 8 ½"
15.55"
5 ½"
5 ½"
5 ½"
1 ½"
3"

DETAIL—PRINCIPAL RAFTER
SCALE ½" = 1'

12"
6"
SAND
6 MILL POLY
TAR
CONCRETE
¾" RE BAR 12" OC.
WELD
¾" RE BAR
7' 0"

DETAIL—ROOT STORAGE ROOF
SCALE ¼" = 1'

↓ LINE FLOOR

ROOT STORAGE AREA
COVER WITH MIN 2'0 SOIL

for:
drwa. N⁰ 796
sheet
2 of 3

B. ALLAN MACKIE

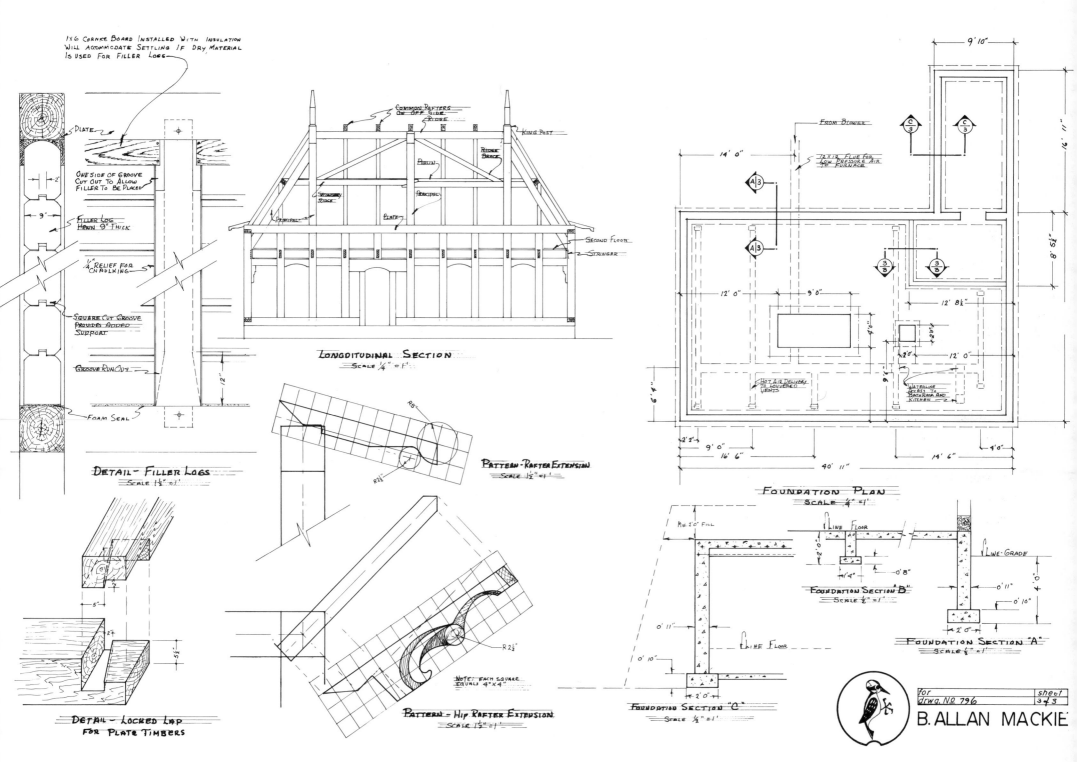

1x6 Cornice Board Installed With Insulation Will Accommodate Settling If Dry Material Is Used For Filler Logs

Plate

One Side Of Groove Cut Out To Allow Filler To Be Placed

Filler Log Hewn 9" Thick

1/4" Relief For Chaulking

Square Cut Groove Provides Added Support

Groove Run Out

Foam Seal

9"

12"

DETAIL - FILLER LOGS
Scale 1½"=1'

Common Rafters On Off Side
Ridge
King Post
Secondary Ridge
Ridge Brace
Purlin
Principal
Principal
Plate
Second Floor
Stringer

LONGDITUDINAL SECTION
Scale ¼"=1'

R5"

R2½"

PATTERN - RAFTER EXTENSION
Scale 1½"=1'

DETAIL - LOCKED LAP
FOR PLATE TIMBERS

5"
2"
5½"
3"

R 2½"

Note: Each Square Equals 4"x4"

PATTERN - HIP RAFTER EXTENSION
Scale 1½"=1'

9'10"
16'11"
14'0"
From Blower
12x12 Flue For Low Pressure Air Furnace

8'8"

A|3
A|3
C 3
C 3
3 B
3 B

12'0"
9'0"
12'8½"
2'0"
12'0"
9'6"
4'0"
6'4"
Hot Air Delivery To Louvered Vents
Waterline Across To Bathroom And Kitchen
2'2"
9'0"
16'6"
14'6"
4'0"
40'11"

FOUNDATION PLAN
Scale ¼"=1'

Min 2'0" Fill
Line Floor
2'0"
1'4"
0'8"
0'11"
Line Floor
0'11"
0'10"
2'0"

FOUNDATION SECTION "B"
Scale ½"=1'

Line-Grade
0'11"
0'10"
2'0"

FOUNDATION SECTION "A"
Scale ½"=1'

FOUNDATION SECTION "C"
Scale ½"=1'

for
drwg. No 796

sheet
3/3

B. ALLAN MACKIE

26

#797

Square feet: 2,100

This is a large house and expensive to build.

In addition to the 2,100 square feet of floor which contains kitchen, dining room, living room, 4 bedrooms with baths, closets and other facilities, there is a small personal den, a large entrance hall, and a combination swimming pool-greenhouse addition that is attached directly to the house.

It is basically the design and personal fantasy of a couple for whom cash flow is not the immediate concern now or in future, but whose concerns lie with the raising of their family and the enjoyment of life in the countryside. They understood the implications of sprawl both in construction and in maintenance, and decided to go with their personal dream. They did, however, include several items to ensure protection in times when electricity or fuel supplies might be cut off.

The main source of heat will be a wood-fired hot water system that will distribute heat to the main part of the house and will also maintain the pool which is intended for use in a cold-country winter as well as for summer training.

The inevitable greenhouse-effect of the pool area will also be used as a heat source, and this, in turn, will be complemented by solar collectors in the roof of the pool section. Heat transfer from the swimming pool roof will be built into the main hot water system and will operate by gravity as well as by electric power. The heating system will operate without power, however, and the fireplaces can maintain internal temperatures in the event of power outages.

The house is large and complicated to build, and a good set of working drawings should be developed for any particular site upon which its construction is contemplated. The original house is located on a gentle north slope and faces a panoramic view to the north.

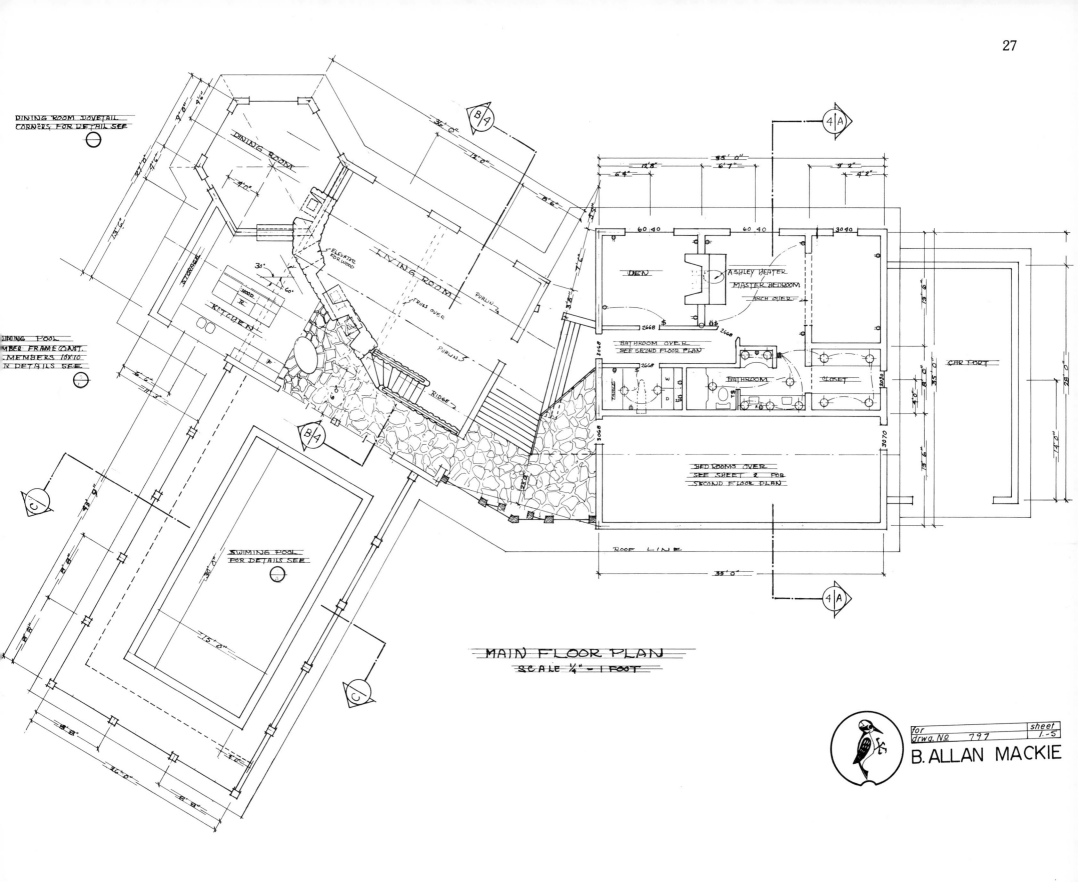

DINING ROOM DOVETAIL
CORNERS FOR DETAIL SEE ⊖

DINING ROOM

B/A

LIVING ROOM

ELEVATOR
FOR WOOD

TRUSS OVER

STORAGE

KITCHEN

PURLIN

PURLIN

RIDGE

B/A

DINING POOL
MBER FRAME CONST.
MEMBERS 10×10
R DETAILS SEE ⊖

C

SWIMING POOL
FOR DETAILS SEE ⊖

C

DEN

ASHLEY HEATER

MASTER BEDROOM

ARCH OVER

2668

2668

BATHROOM OVER
SEE SECOND FLOOR PLAN

2668

BATHROOM

CLOSET

BED ROOMS OVER
SEE SHEET 2 FOR
SECOND FLOOR PLAN

ROOF LINE

CAR PORT

4/A

4/A

35'0"

MAIN FLOOR PLAN
SCALE ¼" = 1 FOOT

for
drwg. No. 797

sheet
1.-5

B. ALLAN MACKIE

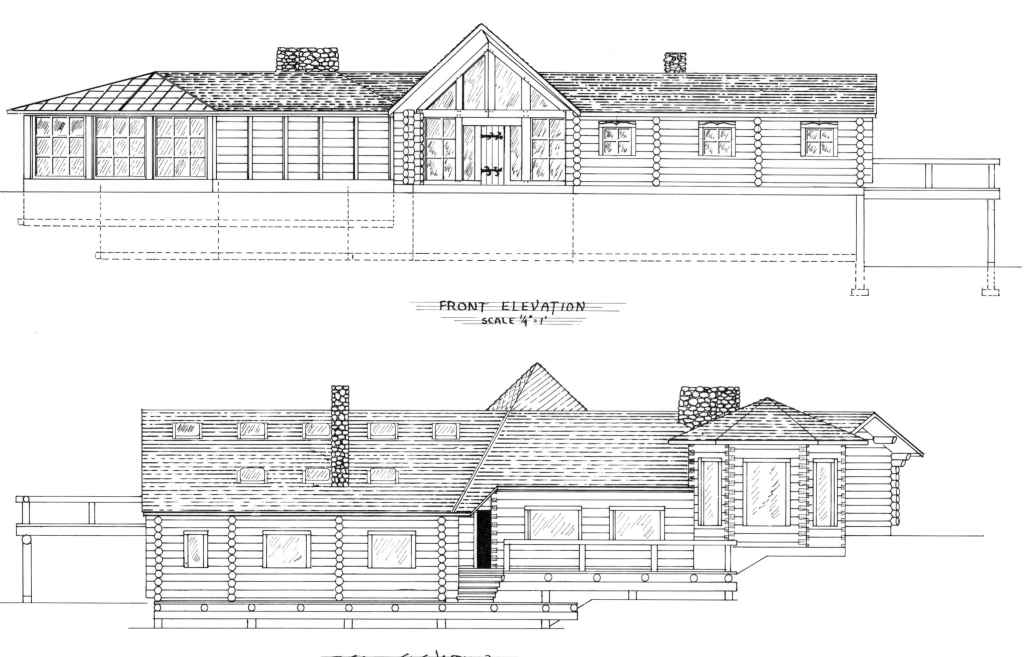

FRONT ELEVATION
SCALE ¼"=1'

REAR ELEVATION
SCALE ¼"=1'

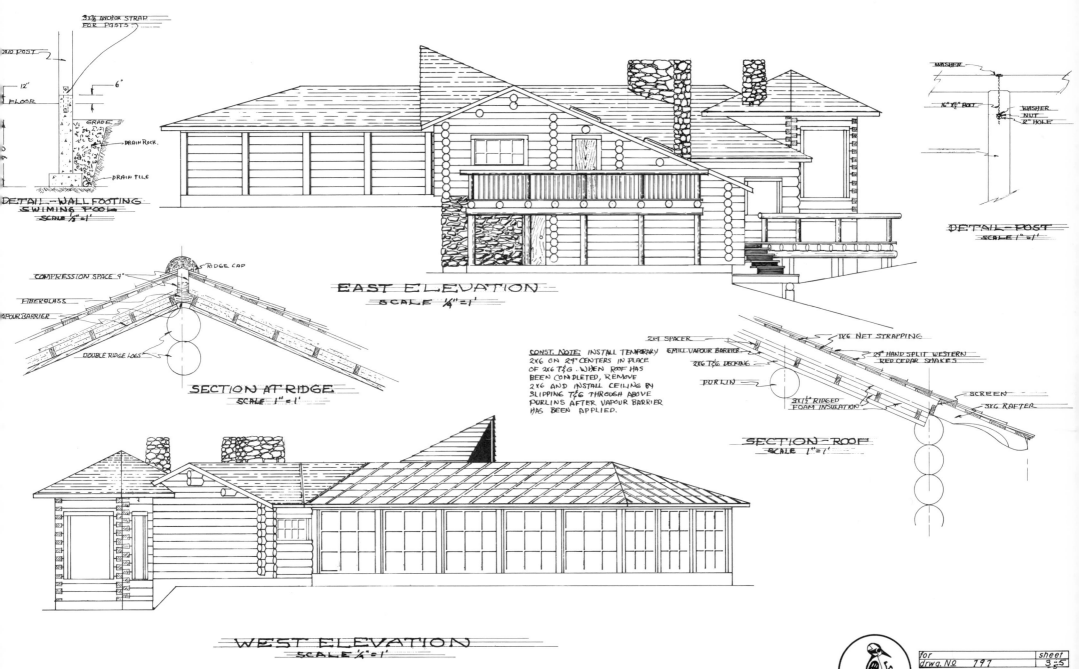

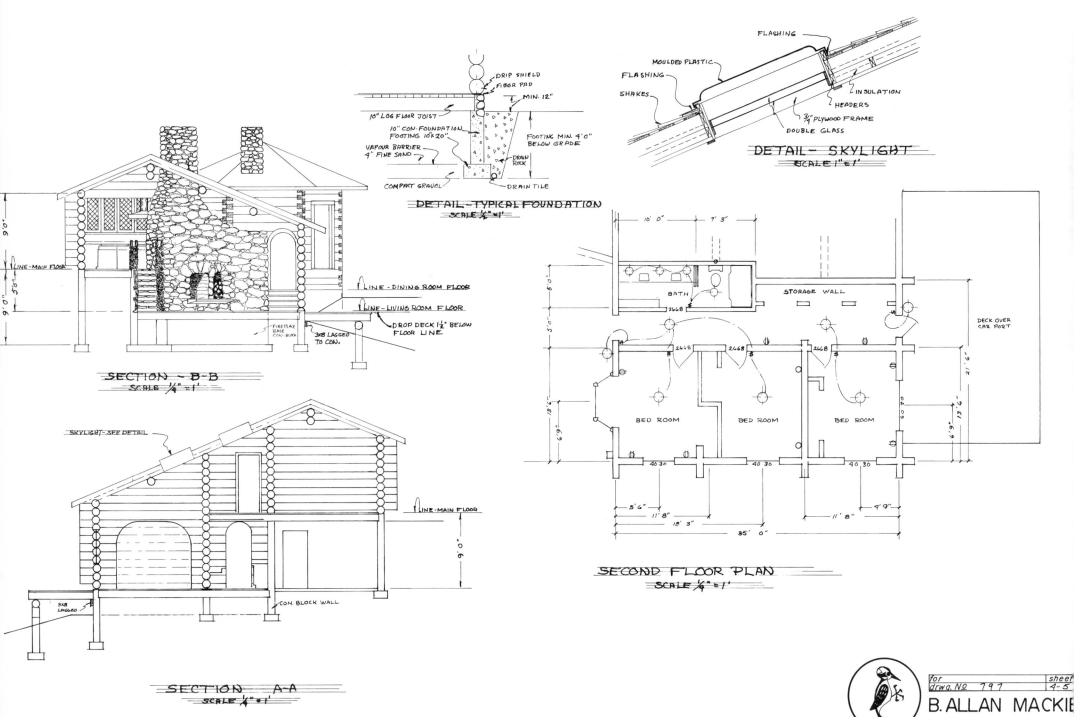

DETAIL- SKYLIGHT
SCALE 1"=1'

FLASHING
MOULDED PLASTIC
FLASHING
SHAKES
INSULATION
HEADERS
3/4" PLYWOOD FRAME
DOUBLE GLASS

DRIP SHIELD
FIBER PAD
MIN. 12"
10" LOG FLOOR JOIST
10" CON. FOUNDATION
FOOTING 10"x20"
VAPOUR BARRIER
4" FINE SAND
FOOTING MIN. 4'0"
BELOW GRADE
DRAIN ROCK
COMPACT GRAVEL
DRAIN TILE

DETAIL-TYPICAL FOUNDATION
SCALE 1/2"=1'

LINE-MAIN FLOOR
LINE - DINING ROOM FLOOR
LINE-LIVING ROOM FLOOR
DROP DECK 1 1/2" BELOW
FLOOR LINE
FIREPLACE BASE CON. BLOCK
3x8 LAGGED TO CON.
9'0"
9'0"
5'0"

SECTION - B-B
Scale 1/4"=1'

SKYLIGHT-SEE DETAIL
LINE-MAIN FLOOR
9'0"
CON. BLOCK WALL
3x8 LAGGED

SECTION A-A
SCALE 1/4"=1'

SECOND FLOOR PLAN
SCALE 1/4"=1'

BATH
2668
STORAGE WALL
DECK OVER CAR PORT
2668 2668 2668
BED ROOM
BED ROOM
BED ROOM
40 30 40 30 40 30

10' 0" 7' 3"
5'0"
5'0"
13'6"
6'9"
21' 6"
13' 6"
6'9"
5'6" 11' 8" 9'9"
18' 3"
11' 8"
35' 0"

for drwg. No. 797   sheet 4-5
B. ALLAN MACKIE

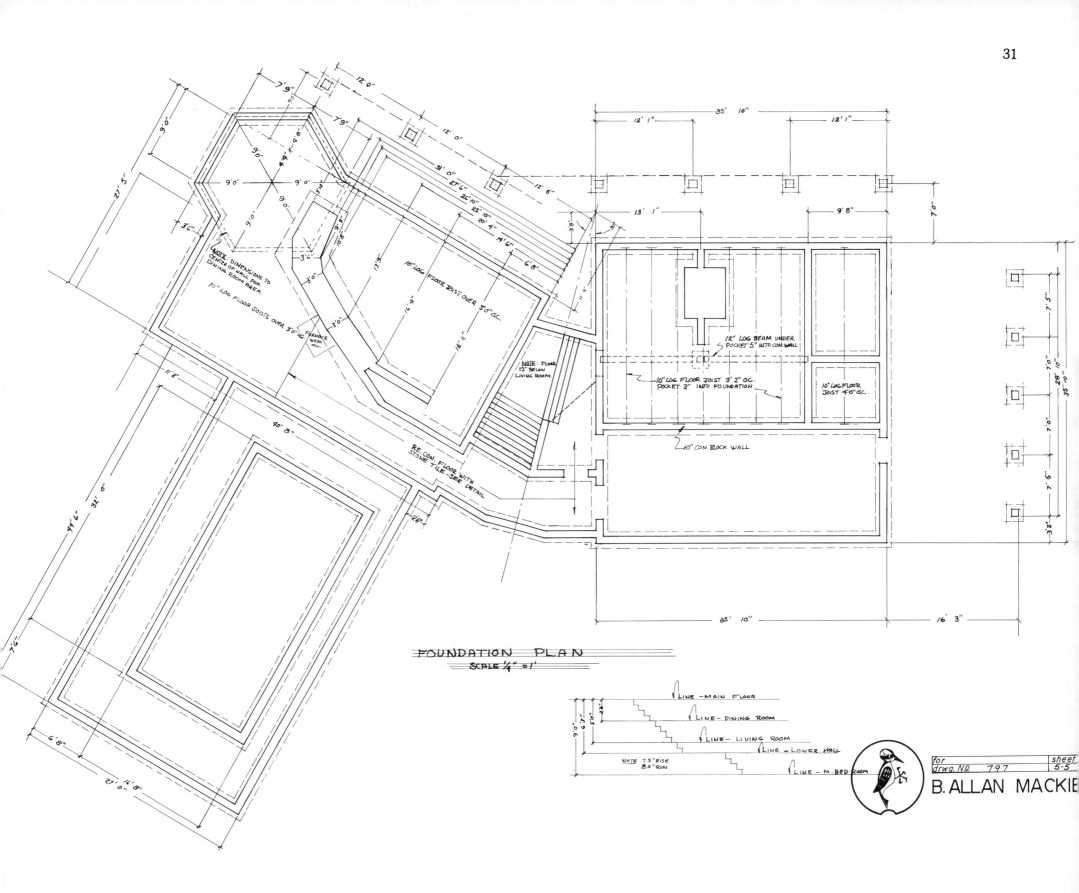

FOUNDATION PLAN
SCALE ¼" = 1'

NOTE: DIMENSIONS TO CENTER OF WALL FOR DINING ROOM AREA.

10" LOG FLOOR JOISTS OVER 3'0" O.C.

FURNACE WOOD OIL

10" LOG FLOOR JOIST OVER 3'0" O.C.

NOTE: FLOOR 15" BELOW LIVING ROOM.

RE. CON. FLOOR WITH STONE TILE - SEE DETAIL

12" LOG BEAM UNDER POCKET 5" INTO CON. WALL

10" LOG FLOOR JOIST 3' 2" O.C. POCKET 3" INTO FOUNDATION

10" LOG FLOOR JOIST 4'-0" O.C.

10" CON. BLOCK WALL

LINE - MAIN FLOOR
LINE - DINING ROOM
LINE - LIVING ROOM
LINE - LOWER HALL
NOTE 7.5" RISE 8.0" RUN
LINE - M. BED ROOM

for drwg. No 797 — sheet 5-5

B. ALLAN MACKIE

#798   *Square feet: 1,100*

This house, and several others in this book, were built, and the designs contributed, by Ed Campbell, an excellent log builder from Celista, near Kamloops, British Columbia.

This is a 2-bedroom house with a full basement, a straightforward and graceful accommodation.

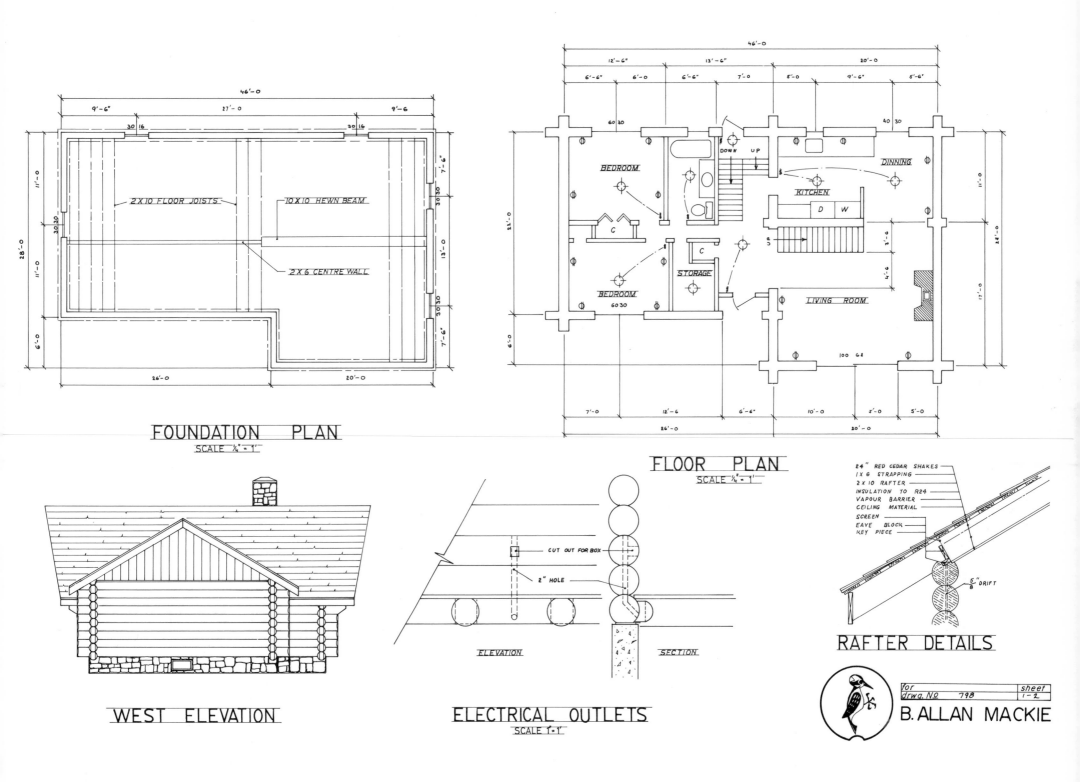

FOUNDATION PLAN
SCALE ¼" = 1'

FLOOR PLAN
SCALE ¼" = 1'

WEST ELEVATION

ELECTRICAL OUTLETS
SCALE 1" = 1'

RAFTER DETAILS

B. ALLAN MACKIE

34

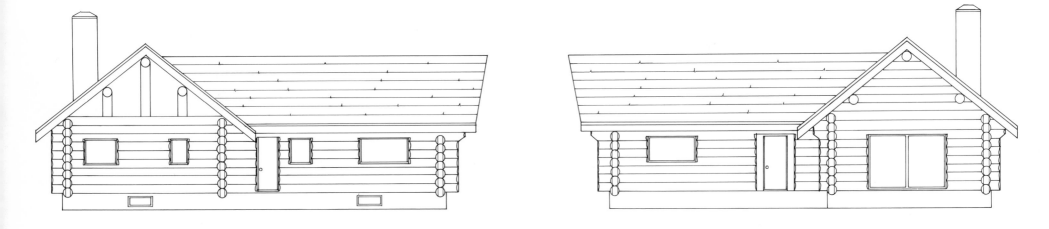

NORTH ELEVATION

SOUTH ELEVATION

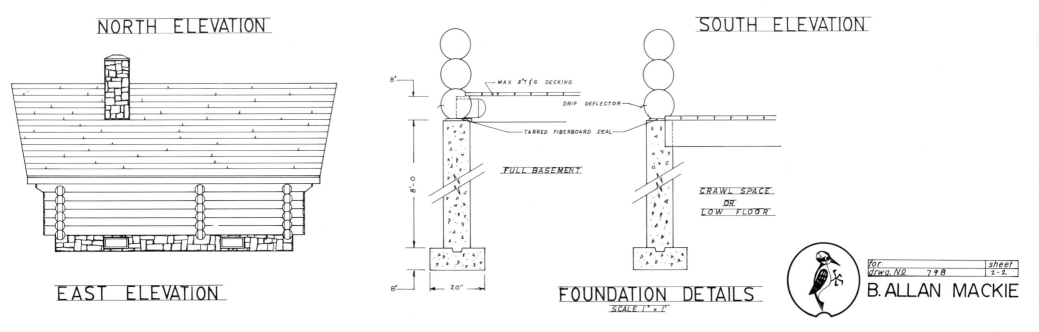

EAST ELEVATION

8"

MAX 8"T&G DECKING

DRIP DEFLECTOR

TARRED FIBERBOARD SEAL

FULL BASEMENT

8'-0

CRAWL SPACE
OR
LOW FLOOR

8"

20"

FOUNDATION DETAILS
SCALE 1" = 1'

for
drwg. No 798

sheet
2-2

B. ALLAN MACKIE

#799

Square feet: 1,232

Another good-sized, comfortable, 2-bedroom house, this one with a loft over the bedroom area for additional accommodation.

This simple plan is deceptive in size, the house is much larger than it, at first, appears. The dividing central wall provides wall and roof support as well as privacy to the bedroom area.

This room arrangement could adapt itself to almost any site.

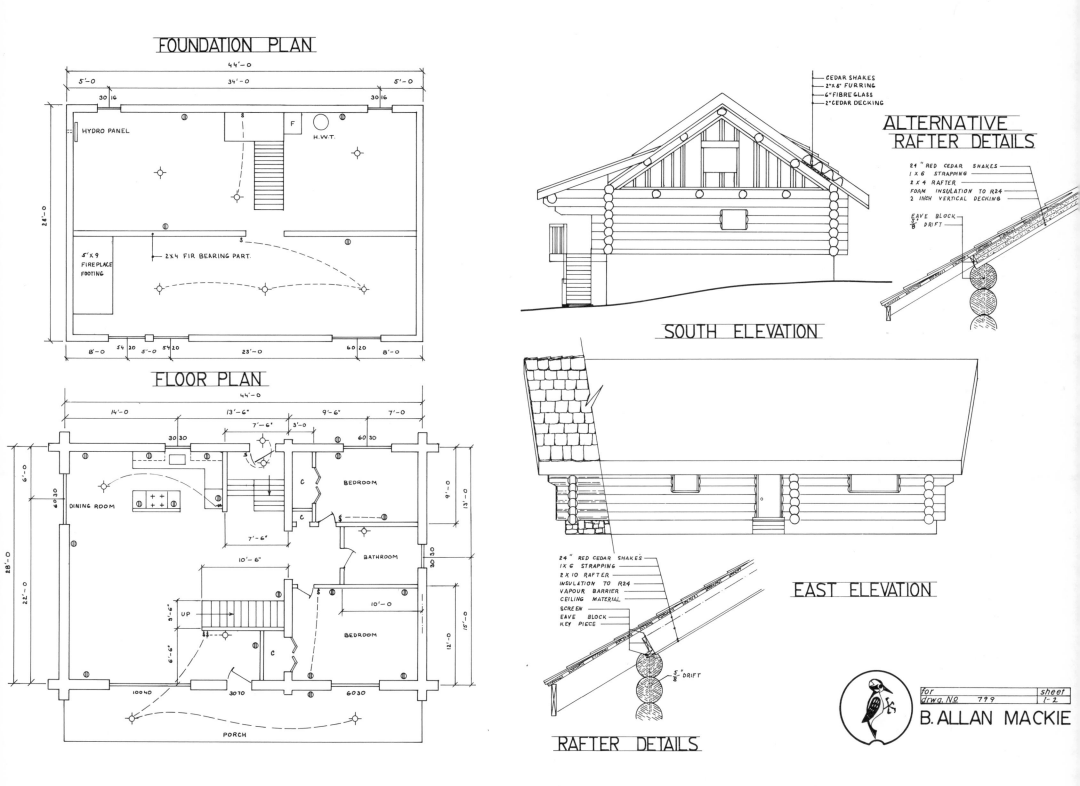

FOUNDATION PLAN

44'-0

5'-0 | 34'-0 | 5'-0

30 16 | 30 16

HYDRO PANEL

F
H.W.T.

28'-0

5'X9
FIRE PLACE
FOOTING

2X4 FIR BEARING PART.

8'-0 | 5'4 20 | 5'-0 | 5'4 20 | 23'-0 | 60 20 | 8'-0

FLOOR PLAN

44'-0

14'-0 | 13'-6" | 9'-6" | 7'-0

7'-6" | 3'-0

30 30 | 60 30

6'-0

6 030

DINING ROOM

BEDROOM

9'-0

13'-0

C

7'-6"

BATHROOM

30 30

28'-0

22'-0

10'-6"

10'-0

15'-0

12'-0

5'-6"
UP

6'-6"

BEDROOM

C

10 040 | 30 70 | 60 30

PORCH

SOUTH ELEVATION

CEDAR SHAKES
2"X 8" FURRING
6"FIBRE GLASS
2"CEDAR DECKING

ALTERNATIVE RAFTER DETAILS

24 " RED CEDAR SHAKES
1 X 6 STRAPPING
2 X 4 RAFTER
FOAM INSULATION TO R24
2 INCH VERTICAL DECKING

EAVE BLOCK
5/8 DRIFT

EAST ELEVATION

24 " RED CEDAR SHAKES
1 X 6 STRAPPING
2 X 10 RAFTER
INSULATION TO R24
VAPOUR BARRIER
CEILING MATERIAL
SCREEN
EAVE BLOCK
KEY PIECE

5/8 "DRIFT

RAFTER DETAILS

for
drwg. No   799

sheet
1 - 2

B. ALLAN MACKIE

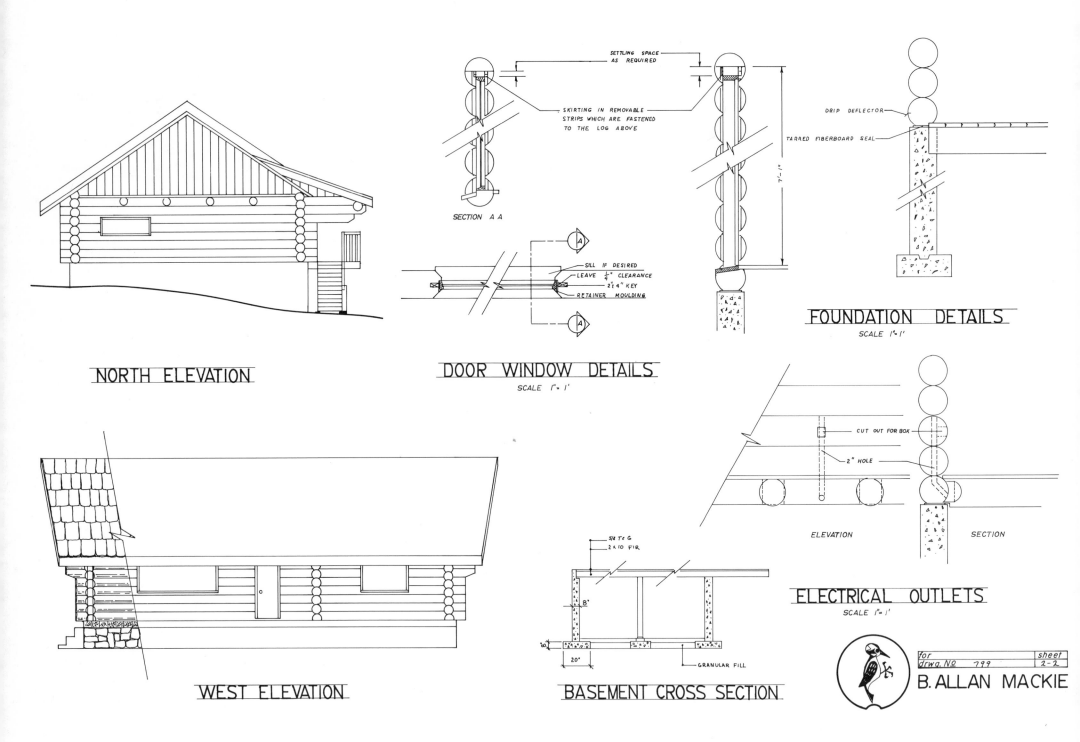

NORTH ELEVATION

SECTION A A

DOOR WINDOW DETAILS
SCALE 1"= 1'

SETTLING SPACE
AS REQUIRED

SKIRTING IN REMOVABLE
STRIPS WHICH ARE FASTENED
TO THE LOG ABOVE

SILL IF DESIRED
LEAVE 1/4" CLEARANCE
2" x 4" KEY
RETAINER MOULDING

DRIP DEFLECTOR
TARRED FIBERBOARD SEAL

FOUNDATION DETAILS
SCALE 1"= 1'

WEST ELEVATION

BASEMENT CROSS SECTION

5/8 T & G
2 x 10 FIR

8"

20"

GRANULAR FILL

CUT OUT FOR BOX

2" HOLE

ELEVATION   SECTION

ELECTRICAL OUTLETS
SCALE 1"= 1'

for
drwg. No 799

sheet
2-2

B. ALLAN MACKIE

#7910   *Square feet: 320*

This is a guest house, a summer camp, or a practice house . . . the size and layout having proved to be practical for these purposes.

It is included here as an illustration of these types of building which

are most useful as a first building on a new site.

As with all buildings, a building permit will be required unless you live in a highly privileged region. And so, of course, full blueprints are available for this design, as with the others.

41

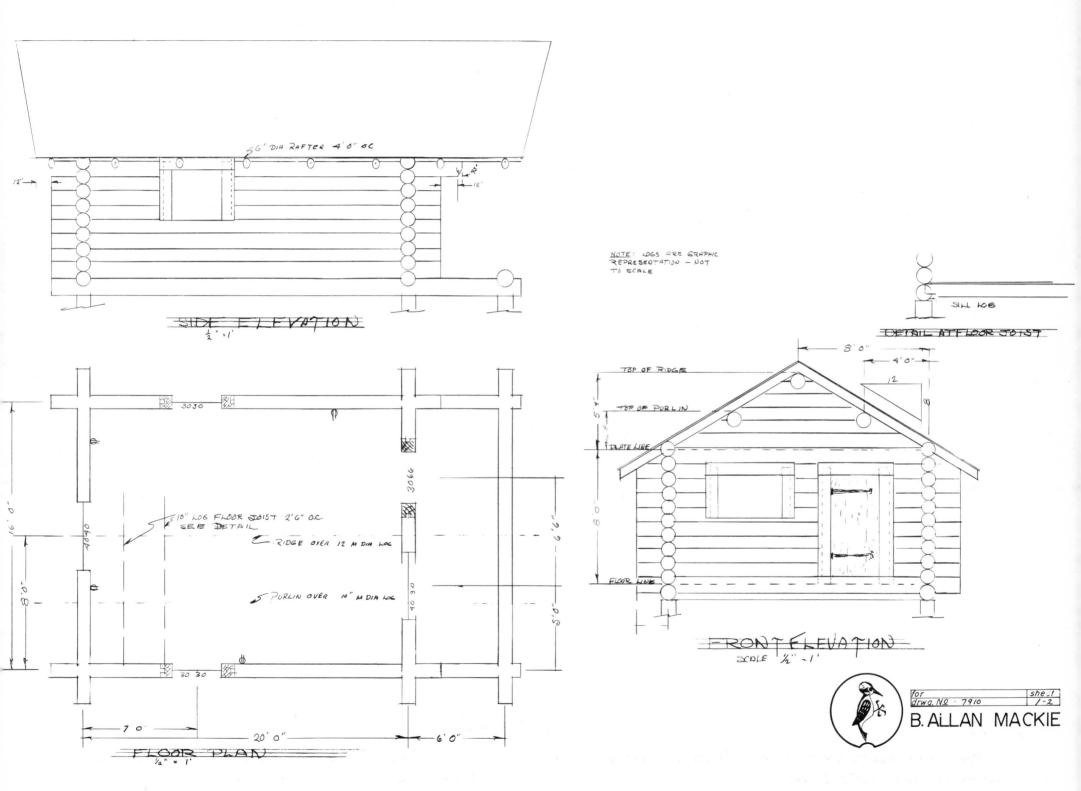

SIDE ELEVATION
½"=1'

5/6" DIA. RAFTER 4'0" OC

12"

12"

NOTE: LOGS ARE GRAPHIC REPRESENTATION — NOT TO SCALE

SILL LOG

DETAIL AT FLOOR JOIST

FLOOR PLAN
½"=1'

3030

3066

8×10" LOG FLOOR JOIST 2'6" O.C. SEE DETAIL

RIDGE OVER 12 M DIA LOG

PURLIN OVER 10" M DIA LOG

4040

4030

3030

16'0"

8'0"

5'0"

2'6"

7'0"

20'0"

6'0"

FRONT ELEVATION
SCALE ½"=1'

TOP OF RIDGE

TOP OF PURLIN

PLATE LINE

FLOOR LINE

8'0"

4'0"

12

8

5'4"

8'0"

for
drwg. No · 7910

sheet
1-2

B. ALLAN MACKIE

#7911

Square feet: 432

Another small but somewhat more sophisticated example than the previous one, of a practice house.

Well executed in construction, this will make an excellent camp or guest house, a particular joy to the young.

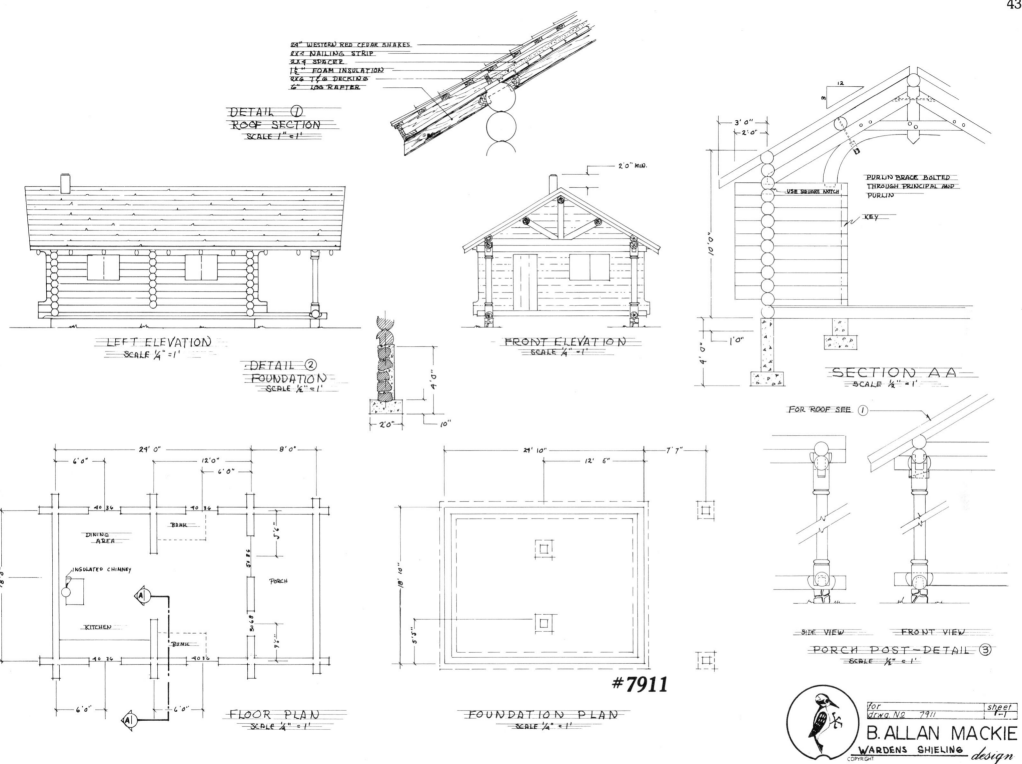

24" WESTERN RED CEDAR SHAKES
2X4 NAILING STRIP
2X4 SPACER
1½" FOAM INSULATION
2X6 T&G DECKING
6" LOG RAFTER

DETAIL ①
ROOF SECTION
SCALE 1"=1'

2'0" MIN.

LEFT ELEVATION
SCALE ¼"=1'

DETAIL ②
FOUNDATION
SCALE ½"=1'

4'0"

2'0"   10"

FRONT ELEVATION
SCALE ¼"=1'

3'0"
2'0"

12
3

10'0"

PURLIN BRACE BOLTED
THROUGH PRINCIPAL AND
PURLIN

USE SQUARE NOTCH

KEY

4'0"   1'0"

SECTION AA
SCALE ½"=1'

FOR ROOF SEE ①

SIDE VIEW   FRONT VIEW

PORCH POST-DETAIL ③
SCALE ½"=1'

29'0"   8'0"
6'0"   12'0"
6'0"

40 36   40 36

DINING
AREA   BDRM

INSULATED CHIMNEY

5' 6"
51 86

PORCH

56 68   9'2"

KITCHEN

BUNK

40 36   40 36

6'0"   6'0"

FLOOR PLAN
SCALE ¼"=1'

#7911

29'10"   7'7"
12' 5"

18'10"

5'3"

FOUNDATION PLAN
SCALE ¼"=1'

for
drwg No   7911   sheet
1-1

B. ALLAN MACKIE
WARDENS SHIELING design
COPYRIGHT

#7912

Square feet: 864

This, too, is really only a summer camp, although a building with a great deal more accommodation than the previous two shown.

While this is only a one-bedroom house, it will supply good, sub-stantial accommodation for two people and with the addition of a loft and full basement would be as large as many a $60,000 suburban home.

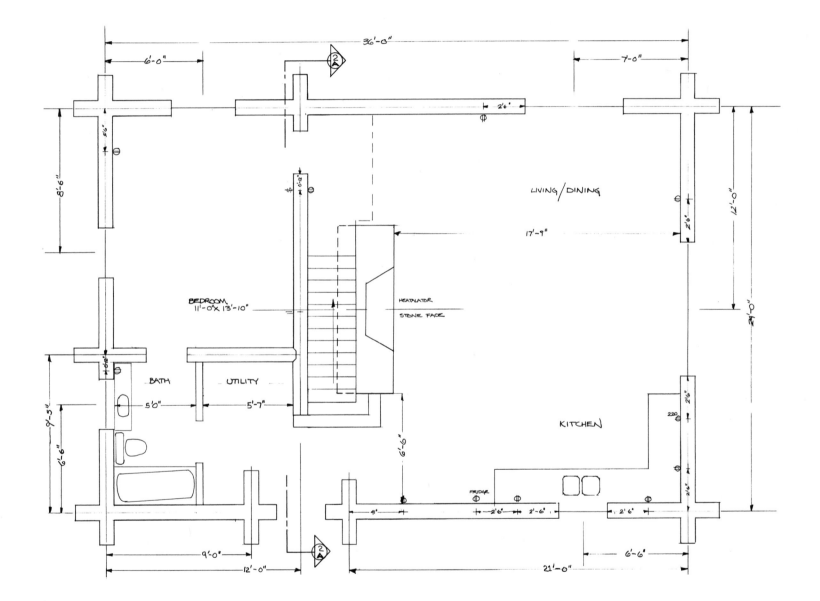

36'-0"

6'-0"

7'-0"

2'6"

8'-6"

LIVING/DINING

6'-0"

17'-9"

12'-0"

BEDROOM
11'-0"X 13'-10"

HEATALATOR
STONE FACE

2'6"

24'-0"

BATH

UTILITY

5'0"

5'-7"

KITCHEN

2'6"

9'-5"

220

6'-6"

6'-6"

FRIDGE

2'6"

4"

2'6"

2'-6"

2'6"

9'-0"

6'-6"

12'-0"

21'-0"

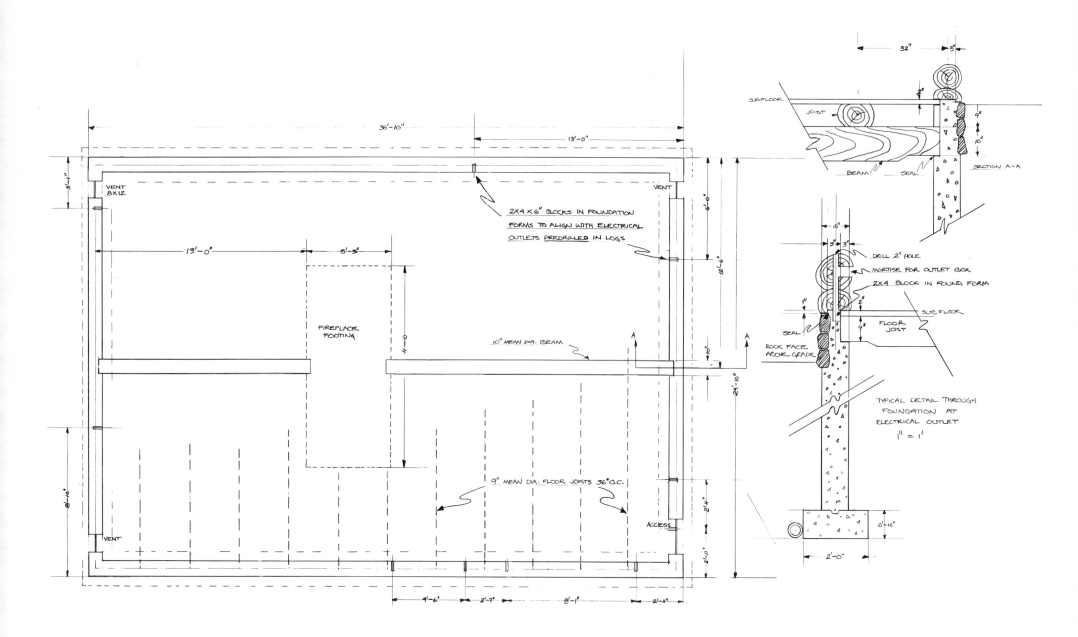

2X4X6" BLOCKS IN FOUNDATION
FORMS TO ALIGN WITH ELECTRICAL
OUTLETS PREDRILLED IN LOGS

VENT 8X12

VENT

VENT

FIREPLACE FOOTING

10" MEAN DIA. BEAM

9" MEAN DIA. FLOOR JOISTS 36" O.C.

ACCESS

VENT

36'-10"

13'-0"

13'-0"

5'-3"

4'-0"

5'-1"

6'-0"

12'-6"

10"

21'-10"

2'-4"

8'-10"

2'-11"

4'-6"

2'-7"

8'-1"

2'-11"

A

A

SECTION A-A

SUBFLOOR

JOIST

BEAM

SEAL

32"

3"

4"

9"

10"

DRILL 2" HOLE

MORTISE FOR OUTLET BOX

2X4 BLOCK IN FOUND. FORM

SUB FLOOR

FLOOR JOIST

SEAL

ROCK FACE ABOVE GRADE

10"

3"

3"

1"

2"

9"

TYPICAL DETAIL THROUGH
FOUNDATION AT
ELECTRICAL OUTLET

1" = 1'

0'-10"

2'-0"

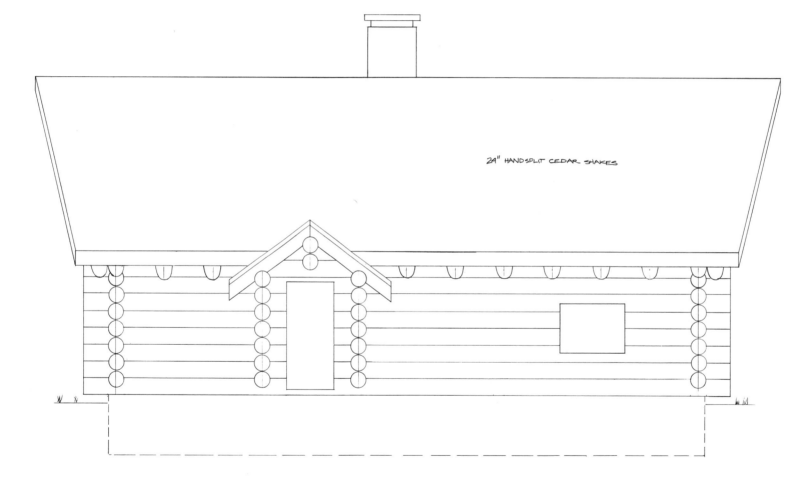

24" HANDSPLIT CEDAR SHAKES

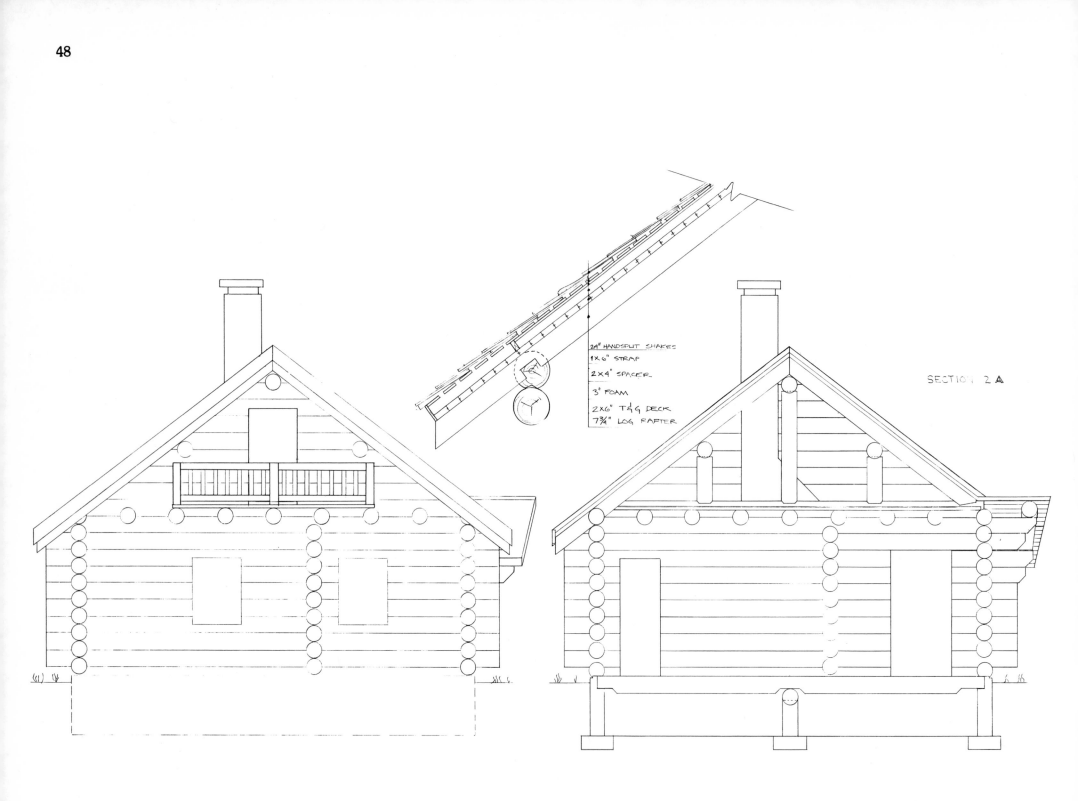

24" HANDSPLIT SHAKES
1×6" STRAP
2×4" SPACER
3" FOAM
2×6" T&G DECK
7¾" LOG RAFTER

SECTION 2 A

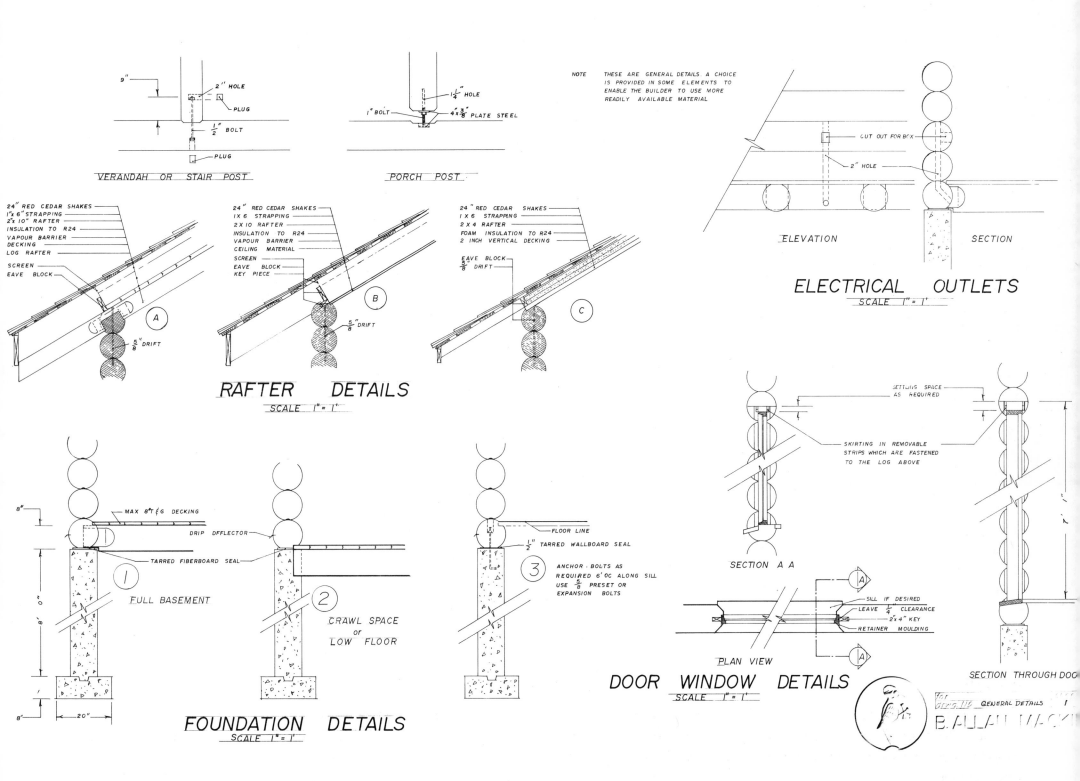

9"
2" HOLE
PLUG
½" BOLT
PLUG

VERANDAH OR STAIR POST

1¼" HOLE
1" BOLT
4"x 3/8" PLATE STEEL

PORCH POST

NOTE   THESE ARE GENERAL DETAILS. A CHOICE
IS PROVIDED IN SOME ELEMENTS TO
ENABLE THE BUILDER TO USE MORE
READILY AVAILABLE MATERIAL

CUT OUT FOR BOX
2" HOLE

ELEVATION   SECTION

ELECTRICAL OUTLETS
SCALE 1"= 1'

24" RED CEDAR SHAKES
1"x 6" STRAPPING
2"x 10" RAFTER
INSULATION TO R24
VAPOUR BARRIER
DECKING
LOG RAFTER
SCREEN
EAVE BLOCK
Ⓐ
5/8" DRIFT

24" RED CEDAR SHAKES
1 X 6 STRAPPING
2 X 10 RAFTER
INSULATION TO R24
VAPOUR BARRIER
CEILING MATERIAL
SCREEN
EAVE BLOCK
KEY PIECE
Ⓑ
5/8" DRIFT

24" RED CEDAR SHAKES
1 X 6 STRAPPING
2 X 4 RAFTER
FOAM INSULATION TO R24
2 INCH VERTICAL DECKING
EAVE BLOCK
5/8 DRIFT
Ⓒ

RAFTER DETAILS
SCALE 1"= 1'

SETTLING SPACE
AS REQUIRED

SKIRTING IN REMOVABLE
STRIPS WHICH ARE FASTENED
TO THE LOG ABOVE

8"
MAX 8" T&G DECKING
DRIP DEFLECTOR
TARRED FIBERBOARD SEAL
Ⓘ
FULL BASEMENT

Ⓞ
8'
1'
8"   20"

Ⓐ

Ⓩ
CRAWL SPACE
or
LOW FLOOR

FLOOR LINE
½" TARRED WALLBOARD SEAL
Ⓩ
ANCHOR BOLTS AS
REQUIRED 6' OC ALONG SILL
USE 5/8 PRESET OR
EXPANSION BOLTS

SECTION A A

SILL IF DESIRED
LEAVE ¼" CLEARANCE
2"x 4" KEY
RETAINER MOULDING

PLAN VIEW

FOUNDATION DETAILS
SCALE 1"= 1'

DOOR WINDOW DETAILS
SCALE 1"= 1'

SECTION THROUGH DOO

GENERAL DETAILS
B. ALLAN MACK

#7913

Square feet: 1,288

This is a good-sized home intended for a steep location.

It is designed for wood heating and as a further step toward self-support, there is provision for the storage of vegetables as well as the wood supply.

This will be a very handsome looking home that can be built with a reasonable amount of work, considering the size and quality of the accommodation.

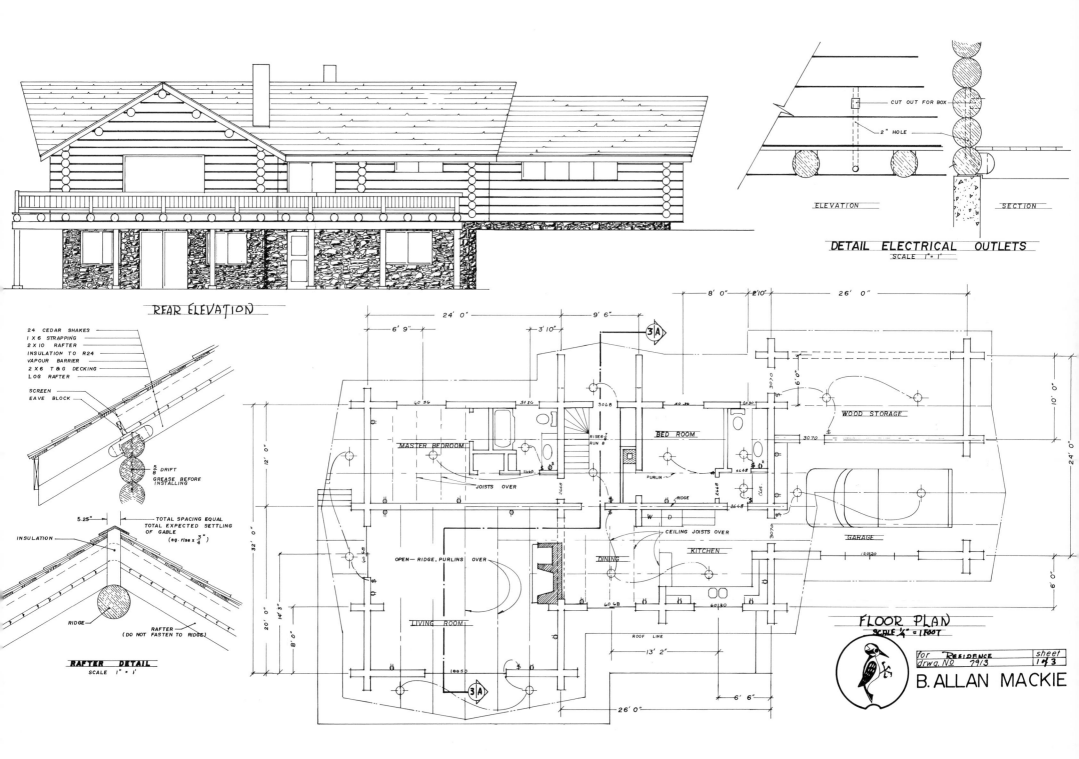

REAR ELEVATION

DETAIL ELECTRICAL OUTLETS
SCALE 1"= 1'

RAFTER DETAIL
SCALE 1" = 1'

FLOOR PLAN
SCALE ¼" = 1 FOOT

B. ALLAN MACKIE

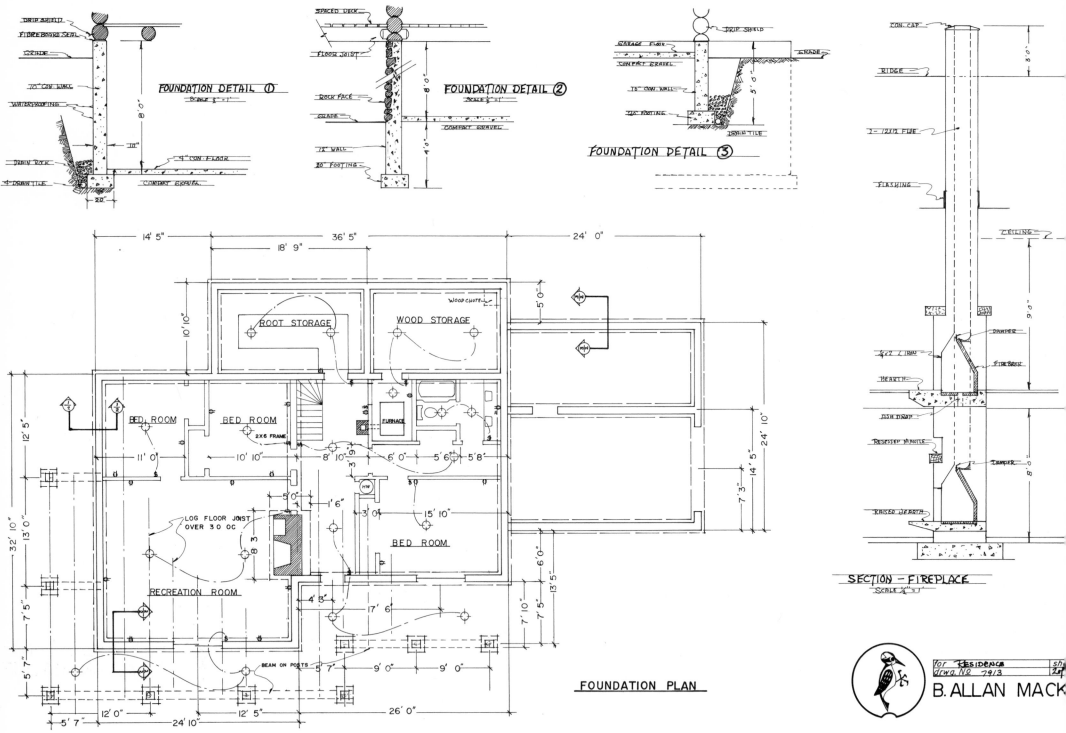

DRIP SHIELD
FIBREBOARD SEAL
GRADE
10" CON WALL
WATERPROOFING

DRAIN ROCK
4" DRAIN TILE
20"
COMPACT GRAVEL
4" CON FLOOR
8' 0"
10"

FOUNDATION DETAIL ①
SCALE ¾" =1'

SPACED DECK
FLOOR JOIST
ROCK FACE
GRADE
COMPACT GRAVEL
12" WALL
20" FOOTING
8' 0"
4' 0"

FOUNDATION DETAIL ②
SCALE ¾" =1'

DRIP SHIELD
GARAGE FLOOR
COMPACT GRAVEL
10" CON WALL
12" FOOTING
DRAIN TILE
GRADE
5' 0"

FOUNDATION DETAIL ③

CON. CAP
RIDGE
2 - 12X12 FLUE
FLASHING
CEILING
DAMPER
4X2 L'IRON
FIREBRICK
HEARTH
ASH DROP
RECESSED MANTLE
DAMPER
RAISED HEARTH
3' 0"
9' 0"
8' 0"

SECTION - FIREPLACE
SCALE ½" =1'

14' 5"   18' 9"   36' 5"   24' 0"
5' 0"
10' 10"

ROOT STORAGE   WOOD STORAGE   WOOD CHUTE
m/n
m/n

12' 5"
13' 0"
32' 10"
7' 5"
5' 7"

BED ROOM   BED ROOM   FURNACE
2X6 FRAME
11' 0"   10' 10"   8' 10"   6' 0"   5' 6"   5'8"
3' 9"

HW

5' 0"   1' 6"   3' 0"   15' 10"

LOG FLOOR JOIST
OVER 3 0 OC
8' 3"

BED ROOM

RECREATION ROOM
4' 3"   17' 6"
BEAM ON POSTS   5' 7"   9' 0"   9' 0"

24' 10"
14' 5"
7' 3"
6' 0"
7' 10"
7' 5"
13' 5"

12' 0"   12' 5"
5' 7"   24' 10"   26' 0"

FOUNDATION PLAN

for RESIDENCE   sh
drwg. No 7913   74

B. ALLAN MACK

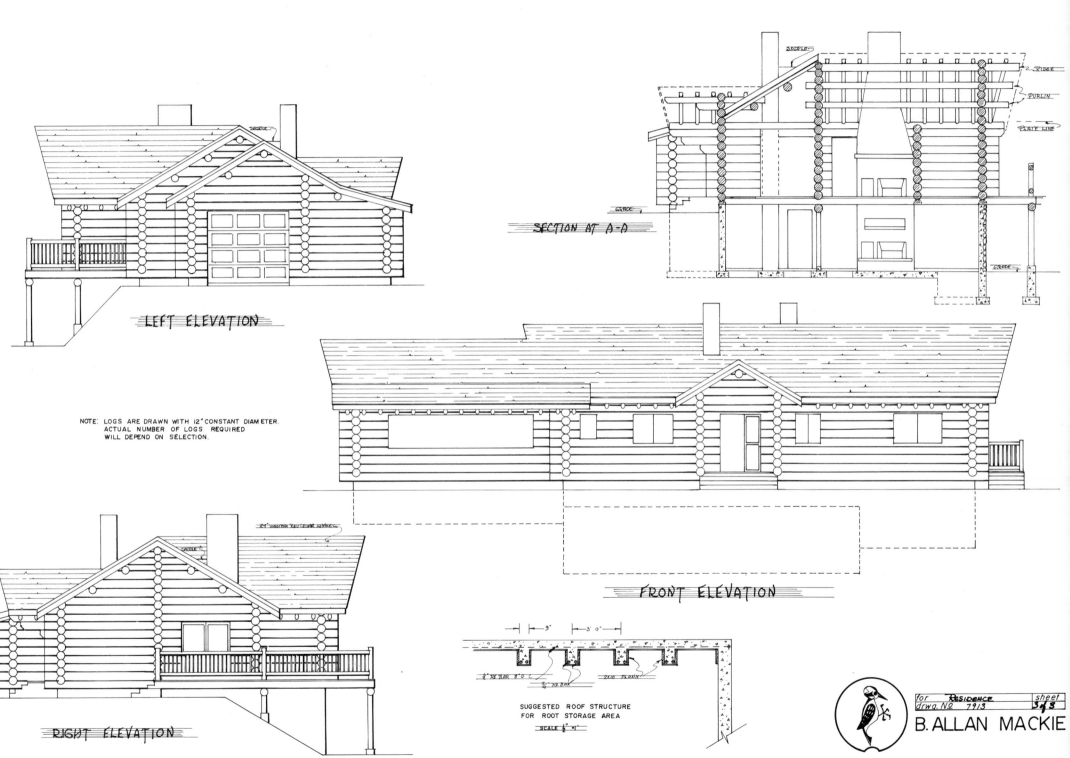

SECTION AT A-A

LEFT ELEVATION

NOTE: LOGS ARE DRAWN WITH 12" CONSTANT DIAMETER.
ACTUAL NUMBER OF LOGS REQUIRED
WILL DEPEND ON SELECTION.

FRONT ELEVATION

RIGHT ELEVATION

SUGGESTED ROOF STRUCTURE
FOR ROOT STORAGE AREA

SCALE ¼" = 1'

for   RESIDENCE   sheet
drwg. No 7913   3 of 3

B. ALLAN MACKIE

#7914   Square feet: 1,288

This is a house with style. It is another of Ed Campbell's designs. The house is located near Salmon Arm in British Columbia.

To me, Ed is an excellent builder by two measures: his homes are well executed and he puts them up with speed and efficiency. This, then, should perhaps be the description of the skills of any builder who undertakes this house which is of more than average difficulty to build, and,

consequently, more expensive.

The challenge lies in providing unhindered settling in the central portion. The builder should assess his understanding of log construction, his abilities and experience quite honestly, before attempting this design.

The house is well lighted, of course, and takes full advantage of an excellent outlook. It has a very good traffic pattern as well.

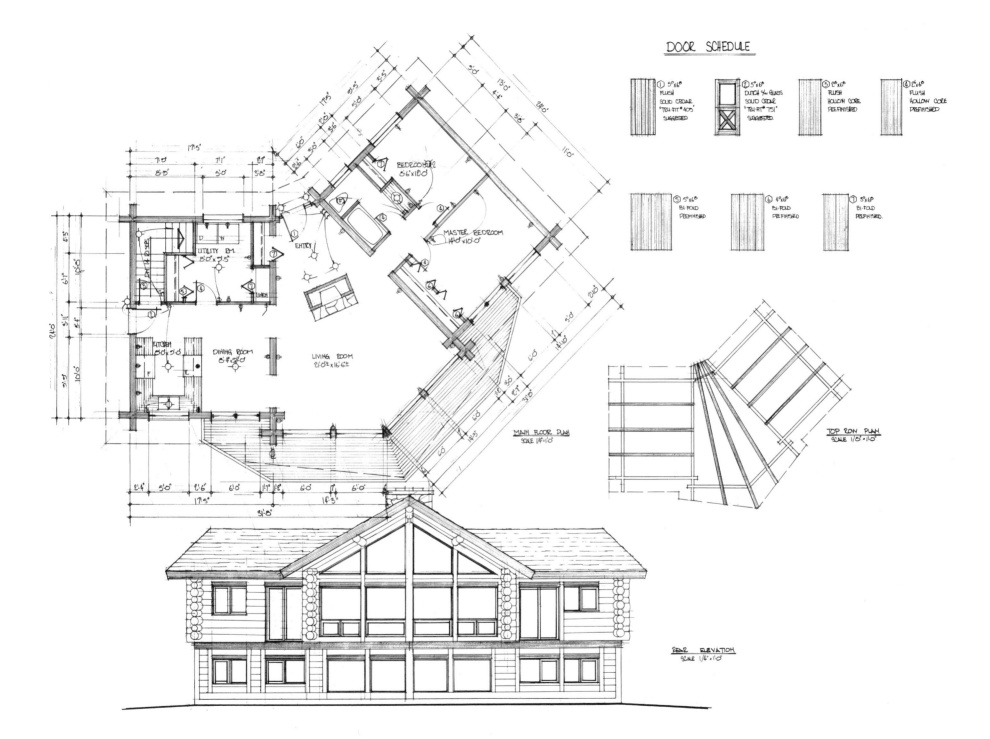

DOOR SCHEDULE

MAIN FLOOR PLAN
SCALE 1/4"=1'-0"

TOP ROW PLAN
SCALE 1/8"=1'-0"

REAR ELEVATION
SCALE 1/4"=1'-0"

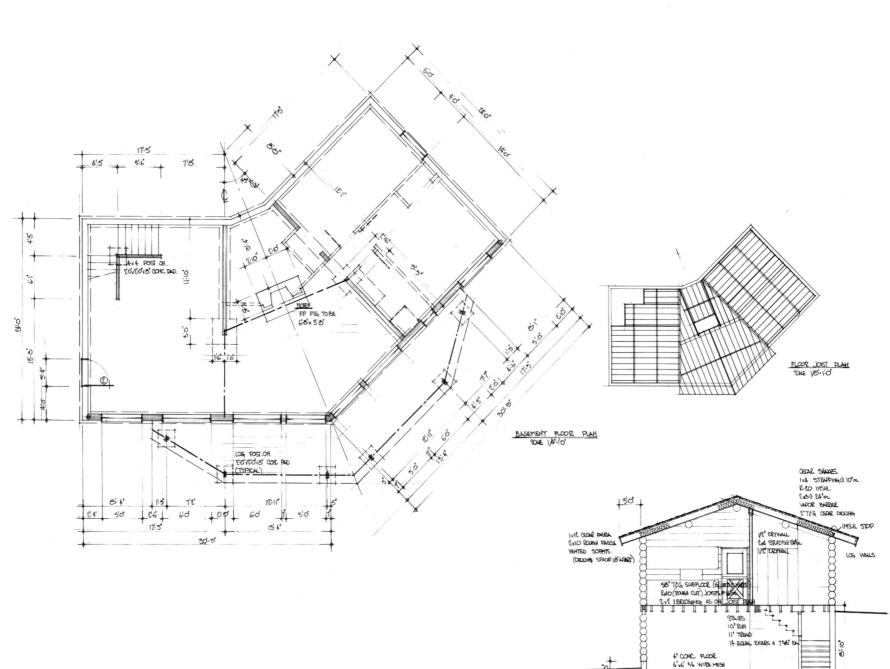

FLOOR JOIST PLAN
SCALE 1/8"=1'-0"

BASEMENT FLOOR PLAN
SCALE 1/4"=1'-0"

4×4 POST ON.
2'0"×2'0"×8" CONC. PAD.

NOTE:
F.P. FTG. TO BE
6'8"×3'8"

LOG POST ON.
2'0"×2'0"×8" CONC. PAD
(TYPICAL)

CEDAR SHAKES.
1×4 STRAPPING @ 10"o.c.
R-20 INSUL.
2×10 @ 24"o.c.
VAPOR BARRIER
1" T&G CEDAR DECKING

1×12 CEDAR FASCIA
2×10 ROUGH FASCIA
VENTED SOFFITS.
(DECKING SPACED 1/8" APART)

1/2" DRYWALL
2×4 STUDS @ 24"o.c.
1/2" DRYWALL

INSUL STOP

LOG WALLS

5/8" T&G SUBFLOOR (GLUED & NAILED)
2×10 (ROUGH CUT) JOISTS @ 16"o.c.
2×2 BRIDGING AS ON JOIST PLAN

STAIRS
10" RUN
11" TREAD
14 EQUAL RISERS @ 7 5/8" EA.

6" CONC. FLOOR.
6"×6" 6/6 WIRE MESH
5" COARSE GRAVEL

SECTION
SCALE 1/4"=1'-0"

NOTE: ALL PAD FTGS. TO BE
10" THICK UNLESS OTHER WISE NOTED.

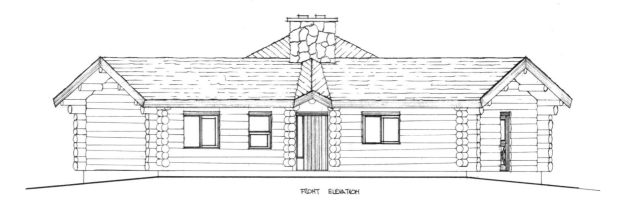

FRONT ELEVATION

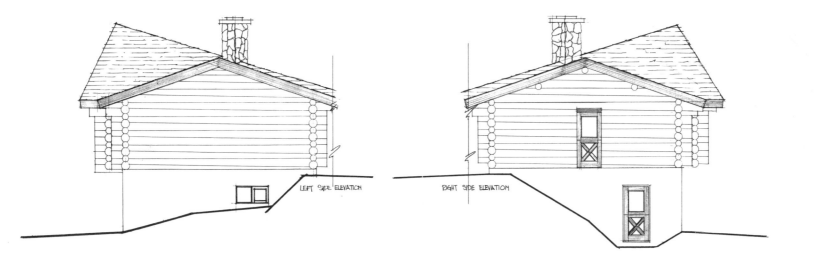

LEFT SIDE ELEVATION

RIGHT SIDE ELEVATION

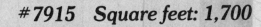

#7915 Square feet: 1,700

This is a truly straightforward and sensible house worthy of anyone's consideration.

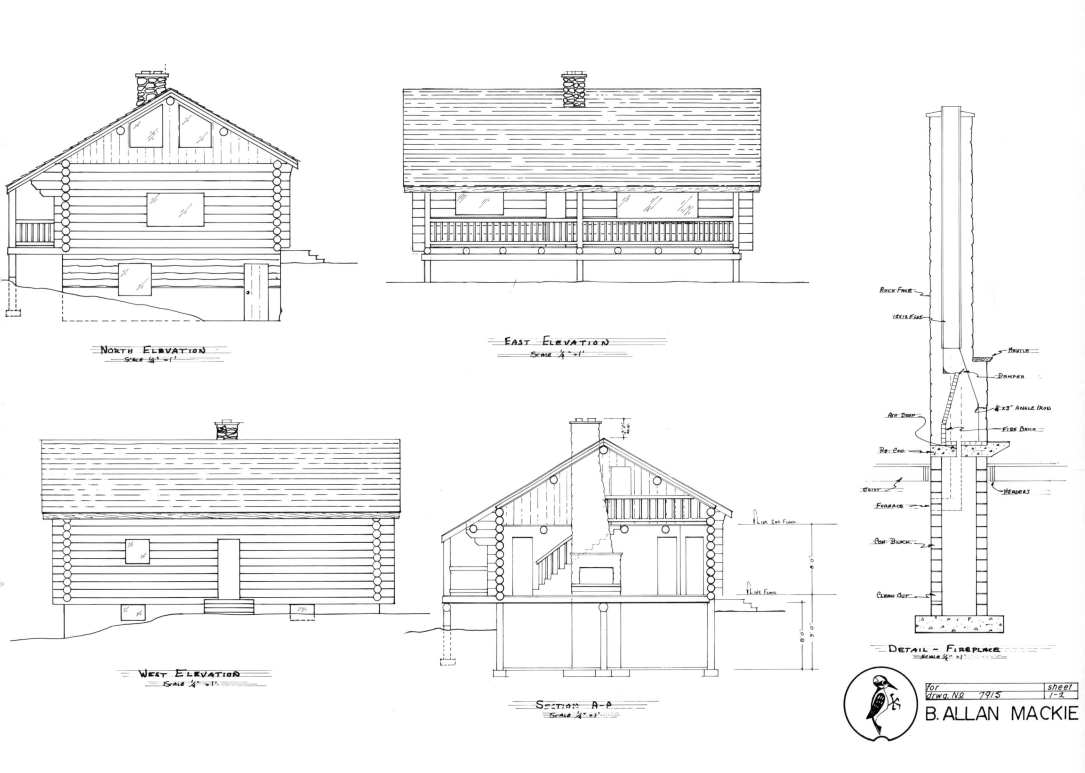

NORTH ELEVATION
Scale ¼" = 1'

EAST ELEVATION
Scale ¼" = 1'

WEST ELEVATION
Scale ¼" = 1'

SECTION A-A
Scale ¼" = 1'

DETAIL - FIREPLACE
Scale ½" = 1'

ROCK FACE
18x12 FLUE
MANTLE
DAMPER
4"x3" ANGLE IRON
ASH DROP
FIRE BRICK
RE. CON.
HEADERS
JOIST
FURNACE
CON. BLOCK
CLEAN OUT

Line 2nd Floor
Line Floor

for drwg. No. 7915   sheet 1-2

B. ALLAN MACKIE

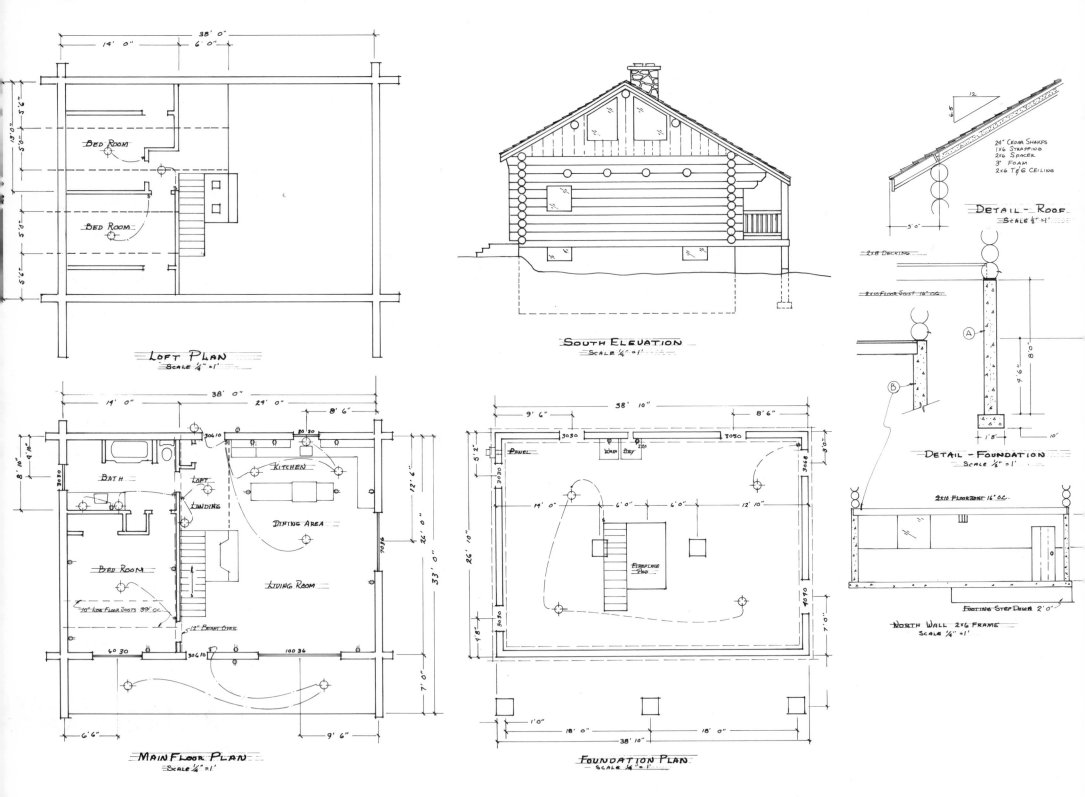

LOFT PLAN
Scale ¼" = 1'

SOUTH ELEVATION
Scale ¼" = 1'

DETAIL - ROOF
Scale ½" = 1'

24" CEDAR SHAKES
1x6 STRAPPING
2x6 SPACER
3" FOAM
2x6 T&G CEILING

2x8 DECKING

2x10 FLOOR JOIST 16" O.C.

DETAIL - FOUNDATION
Scale ½" = 1'

MAIN FLOOR PLAN
Scale ¼" = 1'

BATH   LOFT
        LANDING
BED ROOM
10" LIE FLOOR JOISTS 39" O.C.
12" BEAM OVER
KITCHEN
DINING AREA
LIVING ROOM

FOUNDATION PLAN
Scale ¼" = 1'

PANEL   WASH DRY
FIREPLACE PAD
FOOTING STEP DOWN 2'0"

2x10 FLOOR JOIST 16" O.C.

NORTH WALL 2x6 FRAME
Scale ¼" = 1'

#781   *Square feet: 1,290*

This design was often used, around the beginning of the century, for cottages and parks buildings.

I've just added a modern bathroom and an island kitchen for improved convenience.

Otherwise, I don't think this can be improved upon. It was no doubt put to the test of the centuries long before it came to a new familiarity in our parks.

FRONT ELEVATION

REAR ELEVATION

RIGHT ELEVATION

| for drwg. No. 781 | sheet 2-2 |

B. ALLAN MACKIE

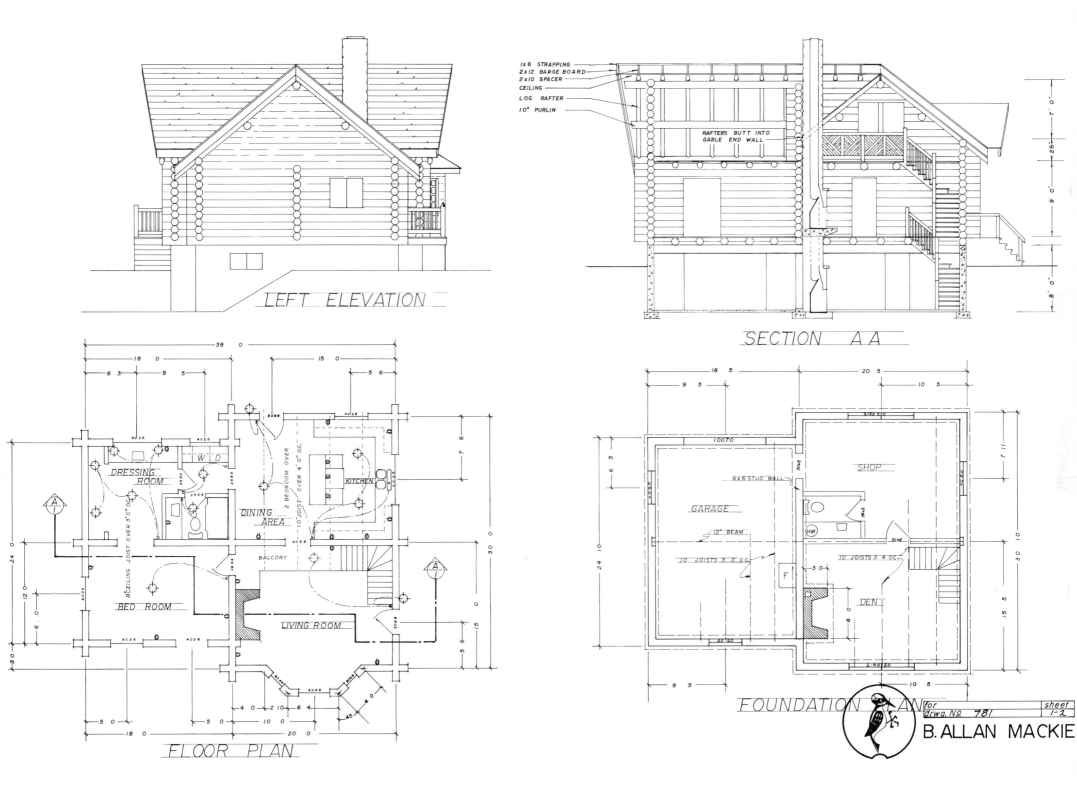

LEFT ELEVATION

SECTION A A

1x6 STRAPPING
2x12 BARGE BOARD
2x10 SPACER
CEILING
LOG RAFTER
10" PURLIN

RAFTERS BUTT INTO
GABLE END WALL

FLOOR PLAN

DRESSING ROOM
W D
DINING AREA
KITCHEN
2 BEDROOM OVER 4'0" OC
10 JOIST OVER 4'0" OC
8"CEILING JOIST OVER 3'0" OC
BED ROOM
BALCONY
LIVING ROOM

FOUNDATION PLAN

GARAGE
SHOP
6x6 STUD WALL
12" BEAM
10 JOISTS 3'0 OC
10 JOISTS 3'4 OC
HW
DEN
F

for
drwg. No. 781

sheet
1-2

B. ALLAN MACKIE

#782

Square feet: 1,088

This is a simple, well-functioning house that has been built successfully in a number of locations.

It provides adequate accommodation for a small family and could be altered easily by the addition of a few more floor joists over the living room to provide 3 or 4 upstairs bedrooms.

There is a particular economy in the plumbing set-up in this design, which saves a remarkable amount of money in construction. This is a point which should always be considered in any design. But the plumbing in this design is also in a good situation for cold-country protection and this, too, is a factor well worth some thought in any building.

While a full basement would provide more space, what I like about this house in its present form is that it is very simple and straightforward to build. It has no hidden problems with settling or with intersecting roofs. And at the same time, it is a good-looking house.

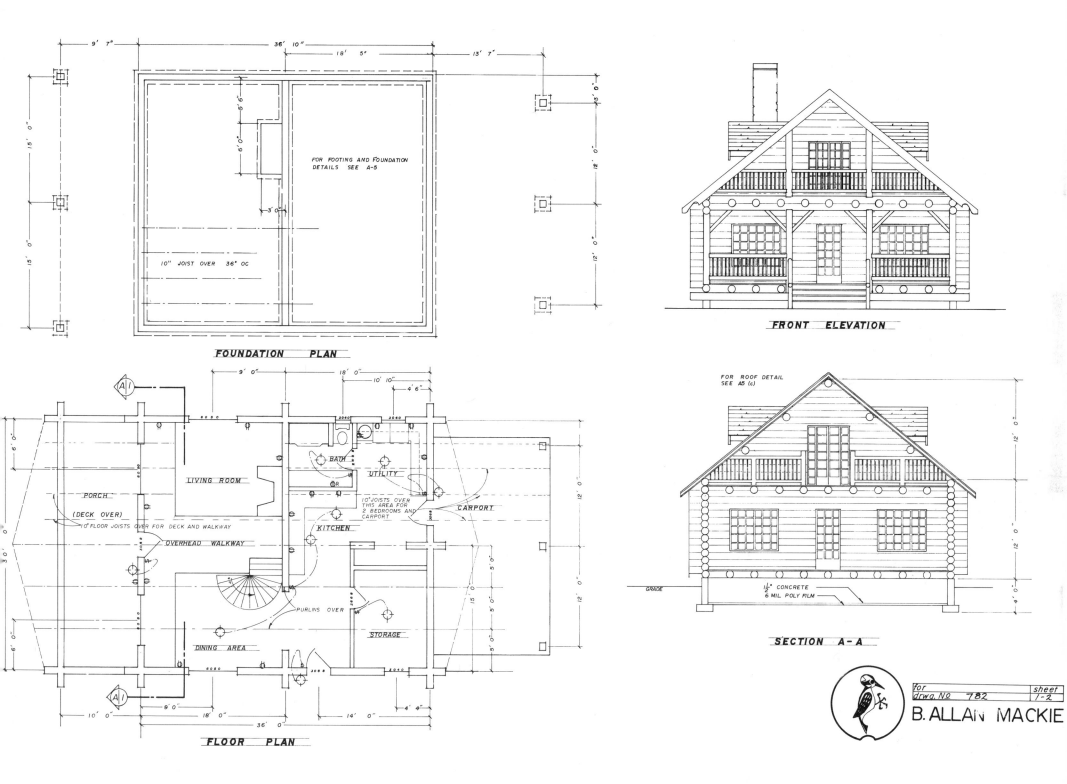

FOUNDATION PLAN

FOR FOOTING AND FOUNDATION
DETAILS SEE A-5

10" JOIST OVER 36" OC

FRONT ELEVATION

FOR ROOF DETAIL
SEE A5 (c)

SECTION A-A

GRADE

1½" CONCRETE
6 MIL POLY FILM

FLOOR PLAN

PORCH

(DECK OVER)

10" FLOOR JOISTS OVER FOR DECK AND WALKWAY

OVERHEAD WALKWAY

LIVING ROOM

BATH

UTILITY

10" JOISTS OVER
THIS AREA FOR
2 BEDROOMS AND
CARPORT

CARPORT

KITCHEN

PURLINS OVER

STORAGE

DINING AREA

for
drwg. No 782

sheet
1-2

B. ALLAN MACKIE

66

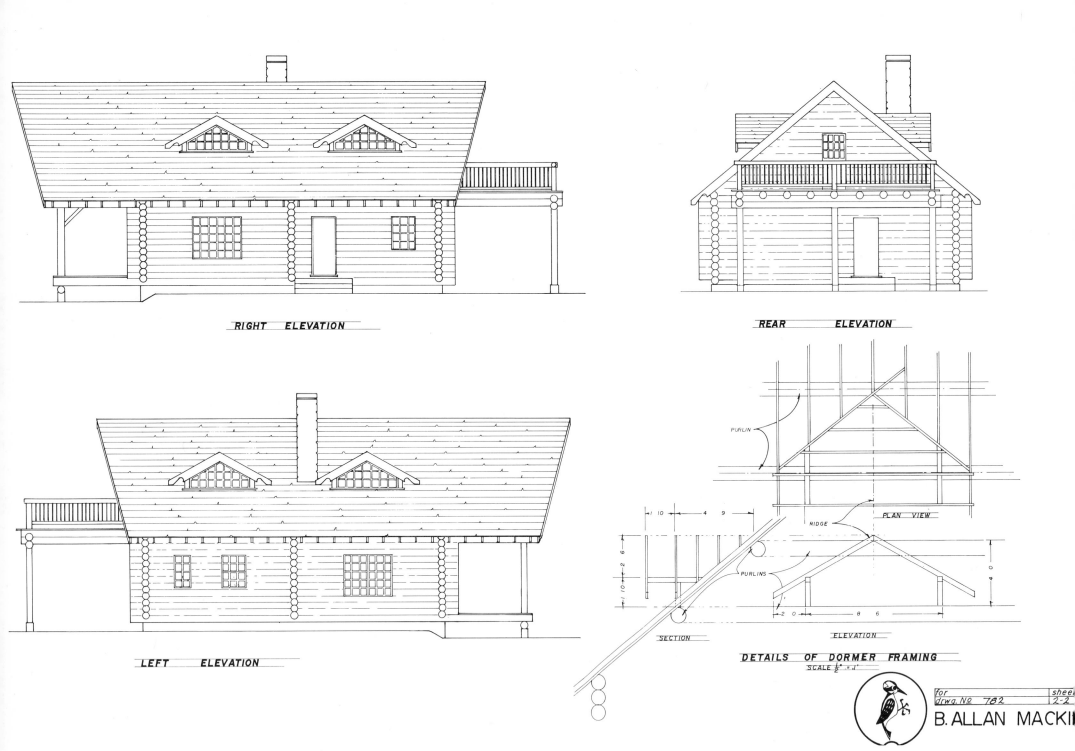

RIGHT ELEVATION

REAR ELEVATION

LEFT ELEVATION

PURLIN

PLAN VIEW

RIDGE

PURLINS

SECTION

ELEVATION

DETAILS OF DORMER FRAMING
SCALE ½" = 1'

for drwg. No 782   sheet 2-2

B. ALLAN MACKI

#783

Square feet: 1,500

I present here an old house design typical of the kinds of homes built by prosperous people around 1930. There seemed to have been an unusually large number of prosperous, high-living folk toward the end of the 1920s, who vanished with the Great Depression, leaving these homes and lodges, from British Columbia to Ontario.

These homes most often did not include bathrooms, halls, or protected entrances. Yet they were good and substantial houses which served their purpose well.

In this design, basement access is from the outside, which was common to that era, to facilitate the handling of bags of potatoes or of coal, whatever was needed for the winter ahead. A stairwell could be included in the interior but I leave that to the prospective builder. I like the house the way it is.

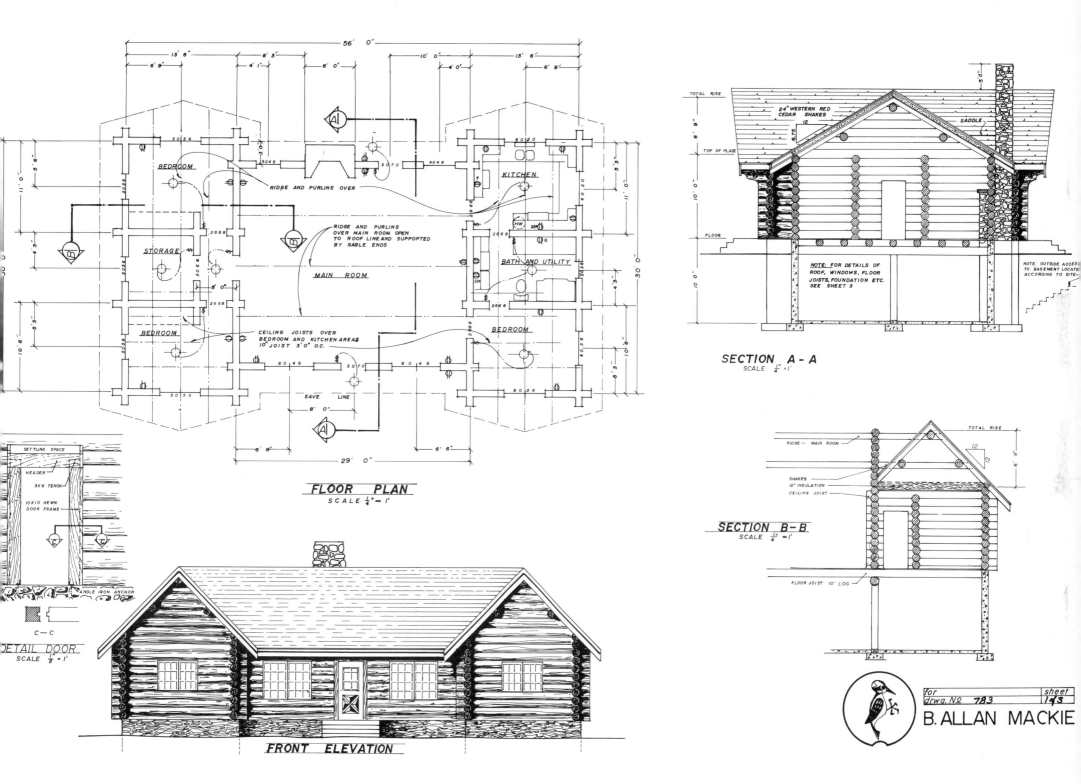

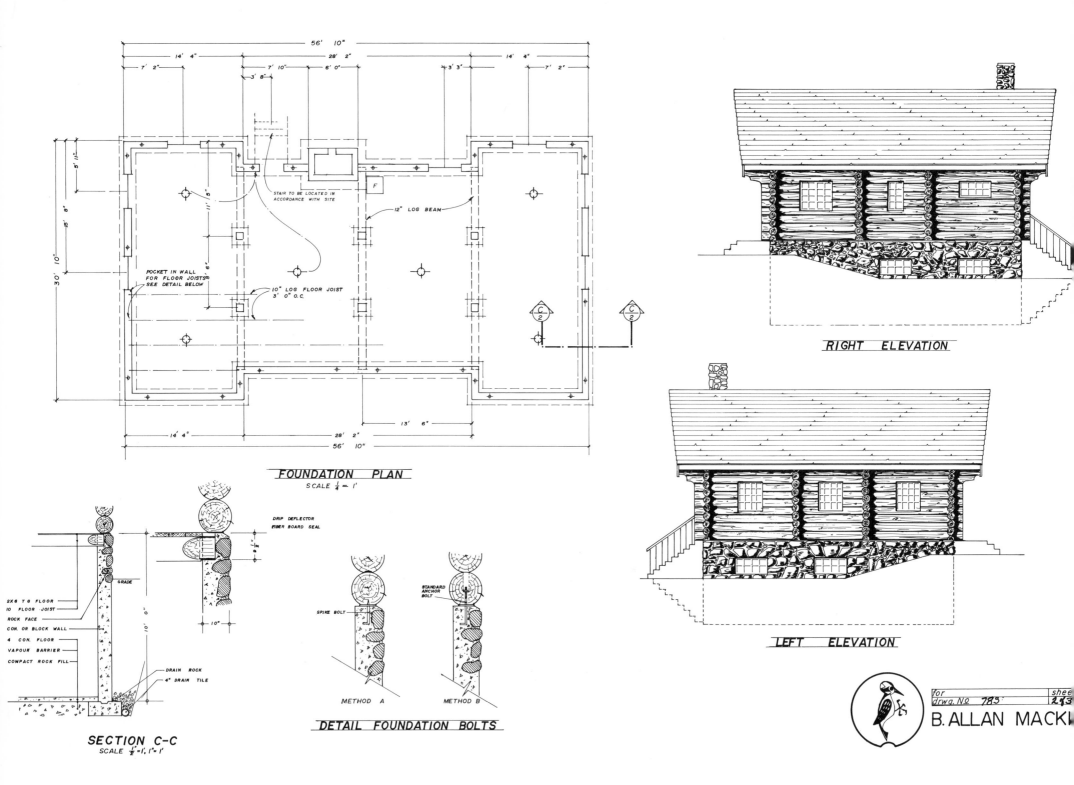

FOUNDATION PLAN
SCALE ¼ = 1'

56' 10"
14' 4"
28' 2"
14' 4"
7' 2"
7' 10"
6' 0"
3' 3"
7' 2"
3' 8"
5' 11"
10' 8"
30' 10"
11' 6"
6' 6"

POCKET IN WALL
FOR FLOOR JOISTS
SEE DETAIL BELOW

STAIR TO BE LOCATED IN
ACCORDANCE WITH SITE

12" LOG BEAM

10" LOG FLOOR JOIST
3' 0" O.C.

13' 6"
14' 4"
28' 2"
56' 10"

F

C 2

C 2

RIGHT ELEVATION

LEFT ELEVATION

SECTION C-C
SCALE ½ = 1, 1" = 1'

2X6 T & G FLOOR
10 FLOOR JOIST
ROCK FACE
CON. OR BLOCK WALL
4 CON. FLOOR
VAPOUR BARRIER
COMPACT ROCK FILL

GRADE

10' 0"

DRAIN ROCK
4" DRAIN TILE

DRIP DEFLECTOR
FIBER BOARD SEAL

10"

DETAIL FOUNDATION BOLTS

SPIKE BOLT

STANDARD
ANCHOR
BOLT

METHOD A

METHOD B

for
drwg. No 783

shee
273

B. ALLAN MACKI

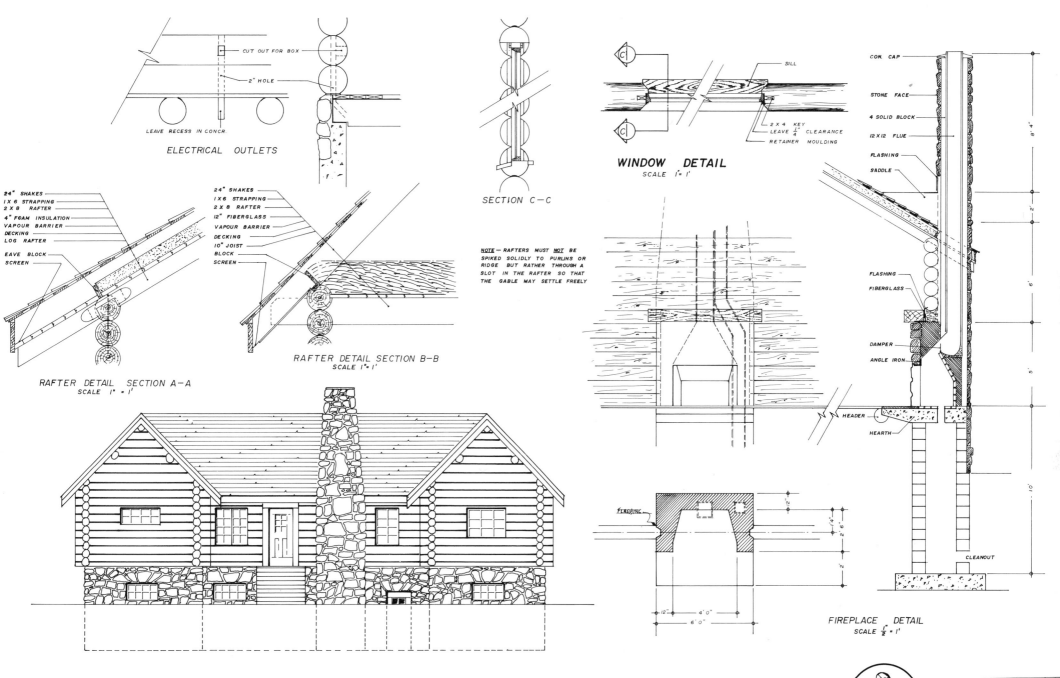

ELECTRICAL OUTLETS

CUT OUT FOR BOX
2" HOLE
LEAVE RECESS IN CONCR.

24" SHAKES
1 X 6 STRAPPING
2 X 8 RAFTER
4" FOAM INSULATION
VAPOUR BARRIER
DECKING
LOG RAFTER
EAVE BLOCK
SCREEN

RAFTER DETAIL SECTION A-A
SCALE 1" = 1'

24" SHAKES
1 X 6 STRAPPING
2 X 8 RAFTER
12" FIBERGLASS
VAPOUR BARRIER
DECKING
10" JOIST
BLOCK
SCREEN

RAFTER DETAIL SECTION B-B
SCALE 1" = 1'

SECTION C-C

WINDOW DETAIL
SCALE 1" = 1'

SILL
2 X 4 KEY
LEAVE 1/4" CLEARANCE
RETAINER MOULDING

NOTE — RAFTERS MUST NOT BE
SPIKED SOLIDLY TO PURLINS OR
RIDGE BUT RATHER THROUGH A
SLOT IN THE RAFTER SO THAT
THE GABLE MAY SETTLE FREELY

HEADER
HEARTH

CON. CAP
STONE FACE
4 SOLID BLOCK
12 X 12 FLUE
FLASHING
SADDLE
FLASHING
FIBERGLASS
DAMPER
ANGLE IRON
CLEANOUT

FLASHING

FIREPLACE DETAIL
SCALE 1/2" = 1'

12"   4'0"
6'0"

REAR ELEVATION

for drwg. No 783   sheet 3/3

B. ALLAN MACKIE

#784   *Square feet: 1,352*

This is a house with a low profile, intended to blend into the rolling landscape of Alberta. It does this very well and, at the same time, provides comfortable and gracious family living.

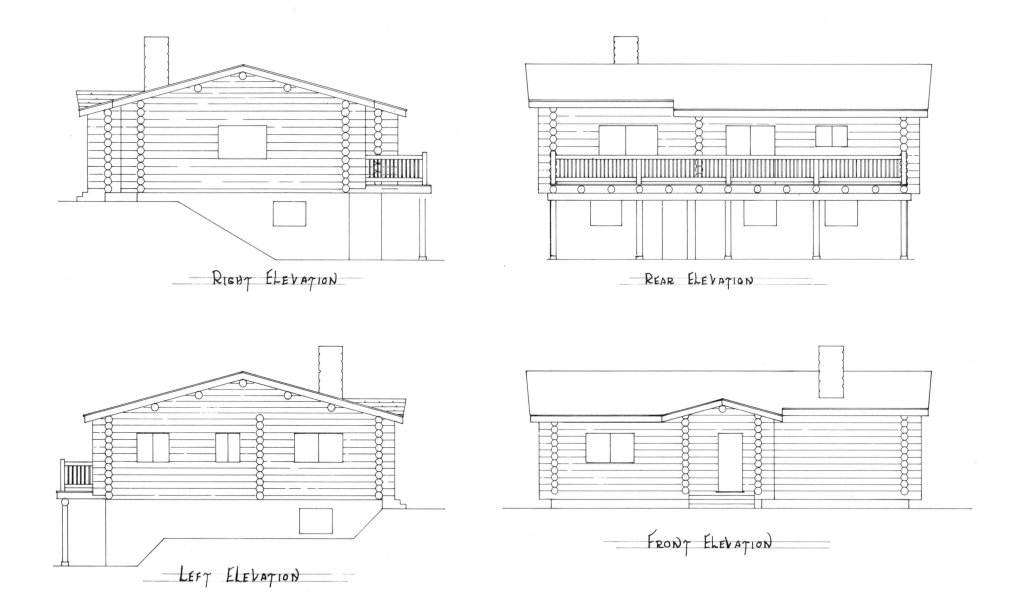

RIGHT ELEVATION

REAR ELEVATION

LEFT ELEVATION

FRONT ELEVATION

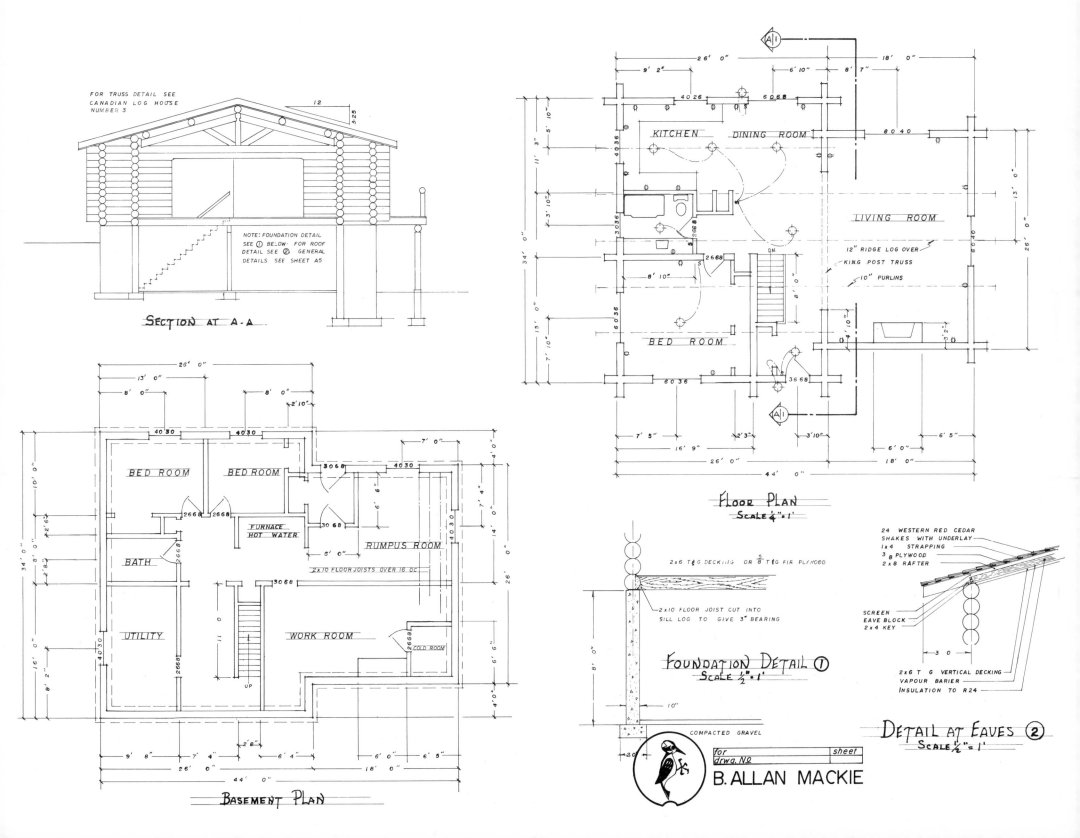

FOR TRUSS DETAIL SEE
CANADIAN LOG HOUSE
NUMBER 3

12
5·25

NOTE: FOUNDATION DETAIL
SEE ① BELOW. FOR ROOF
DETAIL SEE ② GENERAL
DETAILS SEE SHEET A5

SECTION AT A-A

KITCHEN   DINING ROOM

LIVING ROOM

12" RIDGE LOG OVER

KING POST TRUSS

10" PURLINS

BED ROOM

FLOOR PLAN
SCALE ¼"=1'

BED ROOM   BED ROOM

FURNACE
HOT WATER

RUMPUS ROOM

2x10 FLOOR JOISTS OVER 16 OC

BATH

UTILITY

WORK ROOM

COLD ROOM

UP

BASEMENT PLAN

2x6 T&G DECKING OR ⅝ T&G FIR PLYWOOD

2x10 FLOOR JOIST CUT INTO
SILL LOG TO GIVE 3" BEARING

FOUNDATION DETAIL ①
SCALE ½"=1'

COMPACTED GRAVEL

24 WESTERN RED CEDAR
SHAKES WITH UNDERLAY
1x4 STRAPPING
⅜ PLYWOOD
2x8 RAFTER

SCREEN
EAVE BLOCK
2x4 KEY

2x6 T G VERTICAL DECKING
VAPOUR BARIER
INSULATION TO R24

DETAIL AT EAVES ②
SCALE ½"=1'

for
drwg. No   sheet

B. ALLAN MACKIE

#771

Square feet: 1,540

This is a lush bachelor pad which could nicely accommodate two people. Unless the basement were made to provide further bedrooms, guests to this house would overnight elsewhere.

This is a well-designed home which suits its owners admirably, fulfilling the ideals and requirements for a well-to-do and sophisticated young couple who expect to get the most out of living, including luxury, grace, style, privacy, all in a breathtaking riverside setting with its own airstrip.

I very much admire people who build to their own tastes. To me, that's just another way of committing oneself to that environment. It's a statement: that you're never going to move away so why bother about the resale value of an inferior design. To me, this house says: this is me, this is how I live, I love it, and welcome to my world. I very much admire this couple for the things they dared, and achieved, with this house. Note, in particular, that it has no front door. They didn't want or need one; instead, they made their large main room open onto a delightful verandah, lawns, trees, and the river.

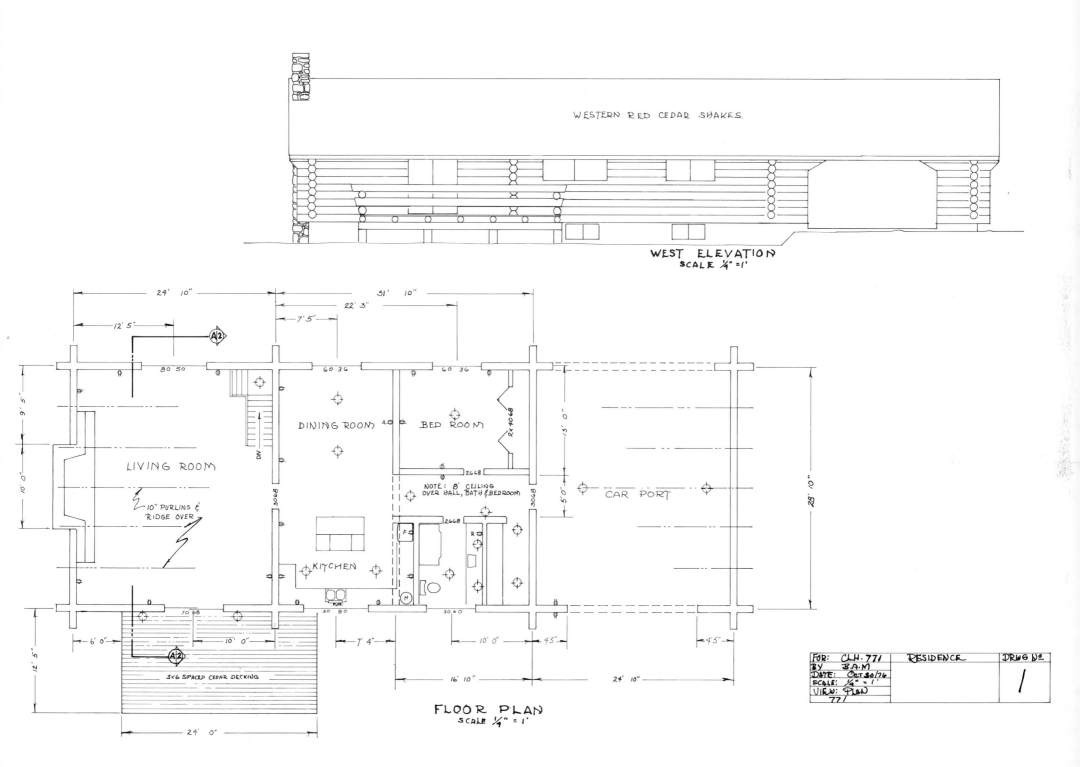

WESTERN RED CEDAR SHAKES.

WEST ELEVATION
SCALE ¼" = 1'

DINING ROOM

BED ROOM

2x 4068

LIVING ROOM

10" PURLINS &
RIDGE OVER

NOTE: 8' CEILING
OVER HALL, BATH & BEDROOM

CAR PORT

KITCHEN

3x6 SPACED CEDAR DECKING

FLOOR PLAN
SCALE ¼" = 1'

FOR: CLH·771   RESIDENCE   DRWG Nº
BY B.A.M
DATE: Oct.30/76
SCALE: ¼" = 1'
VIEW: PLAN
771

1

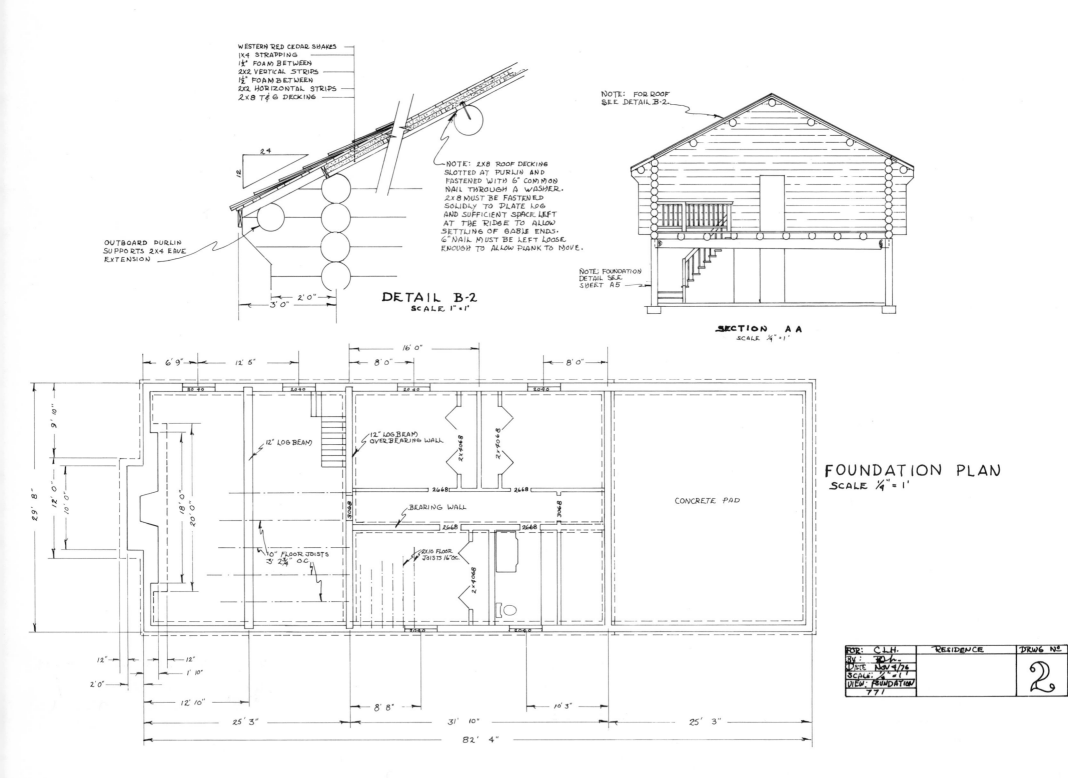

WESTERN RED CEDAR SHAKES
1X4 STRAPPING
1½" FOAM BETWEEN
2X2 VERTICAL STRIPS
1½" FOAM BETWEEN
2X2 HORIZONTAL STRIPS
2X8 T&G DECKING

24
12

NOTE: 2X8 ROOF DECKING
SLOTTED AT PURLIN AND
FASTENED WITH 6" COMMON
NAIL THROUGH A WASHER.
2X8 MUST BE FASTENED
SOLIDLY TO PLATE LOG
AND SUFFICIENT SPACE LEFT
AT THE RIDGE TO ALLOW
SETTLING OF GABLE ENDS.
6" NAIL MUST BE LEFT LOOSE
ENOUGH TO ALLOW PLANK TO MOVE.

OUTBOARD PURLIN
SUPPORTS 2X4 EAVE
EXTENSION

2'0"
3'0"

DETAIL B-2
SCALE 1"=1'

NOTE: FOR ROOF
SEE DETAIL B-2.

NOTE: FOUNDATION
DETAIL SEE
SHEET A5

SECTION AA
SCALE ¼"=1'

FOUNDATION PLAN
SCALE ¼"=1'

6'9"   12'5"   16'0"   8'0"
                    8'0"   8'0"

2040   2040   2040   2040

9'10"
12'0"
10'0"
29'8"
18'0"
20'0"

12" LOG BEAM

12" LOG BEAM
OVER BEARING WALL

2X4068
2X4068

2668   2668

3068   3068

BEARING WALL

10" FLOOR JOISTS
3' 2¾" O.C.

2X10 FLOOR
JOISTS 16" O.C.

2X4068

2668   2668

CONCRETE PAD

12"   12"
1'0"
2'0"
12'10"
25'3"   8'8"   31'10"   10'3"   25'3"
82'4"

FOR: CLH.	RESIDENCE	DRWG Nº
BY: RLH		
DATE: Nov 9/74		2
SCALE: ¼"=1'		
VIEW: FOUNDATION 771		

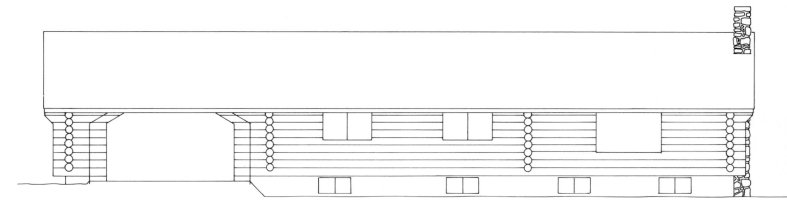

EAST ELEVATION

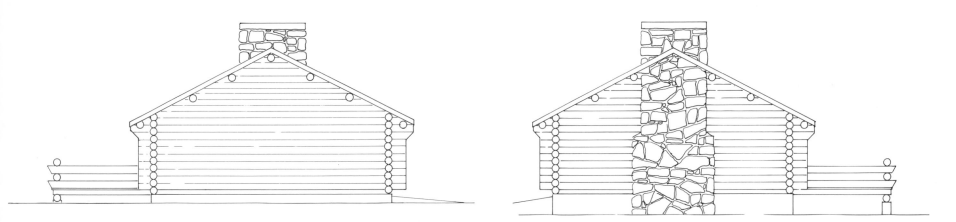

SOUTH ELEVATION

NORTH ELEVATION

FOR C.L.H. 771	RESIDENCE	DRWG. No
BY		
DATE NOV. 5/76		3
SCALE ¼"=1'		
VIEW ELEVATIONS 771		

#772

Square feet: 1,800

What kind of home does the Old Prospector build (a) when he strikes it rich, and (b) when he retires from roaming the hills.

Patrick James Carroll, who climaxed just such a career by becoming a major shareholder in Granisle Copper, built this house.

Situated on many hundreds of acres of rolling ranchland, this house can handle the full haying crew plus all the grandchildren and the greatgrandchildren. Yet, no matter how busy the rest of the household may be, Paddy and Beatrice could retire to their own quiet wing either for rest, or for work in their separate den and studio. The bedrooms faced onto peaceful ranch scenes, the den and studio fully faced the panorama of Richardson Lake with the Ootsa Dome beyond.

This house suffers from sprawl and I would urge anyone contemplating the building of this design to take particular care with the plumbing in the far corner of the bedroom wing.

But if stairs are to be avoided and privacy achieved, to suit the needs of senior citizens, this is the type of compromise which serves their needs. Some of those needs are emotional and, as Mrs. Carroll explained when I asked her why they chose to build with logs: "Whenever I reach my hand out and touch those walls, I can feel the tree as a living thing. I can imagine birdsongs the tree once knew, the beetles, the woodpeckers, the owls it must have had, the deer and moose, the bear and porcupine, that came to the tree . . . and I am back in the forest again, on the trail, with Paddy. It rejoices me and I never feel lonely."

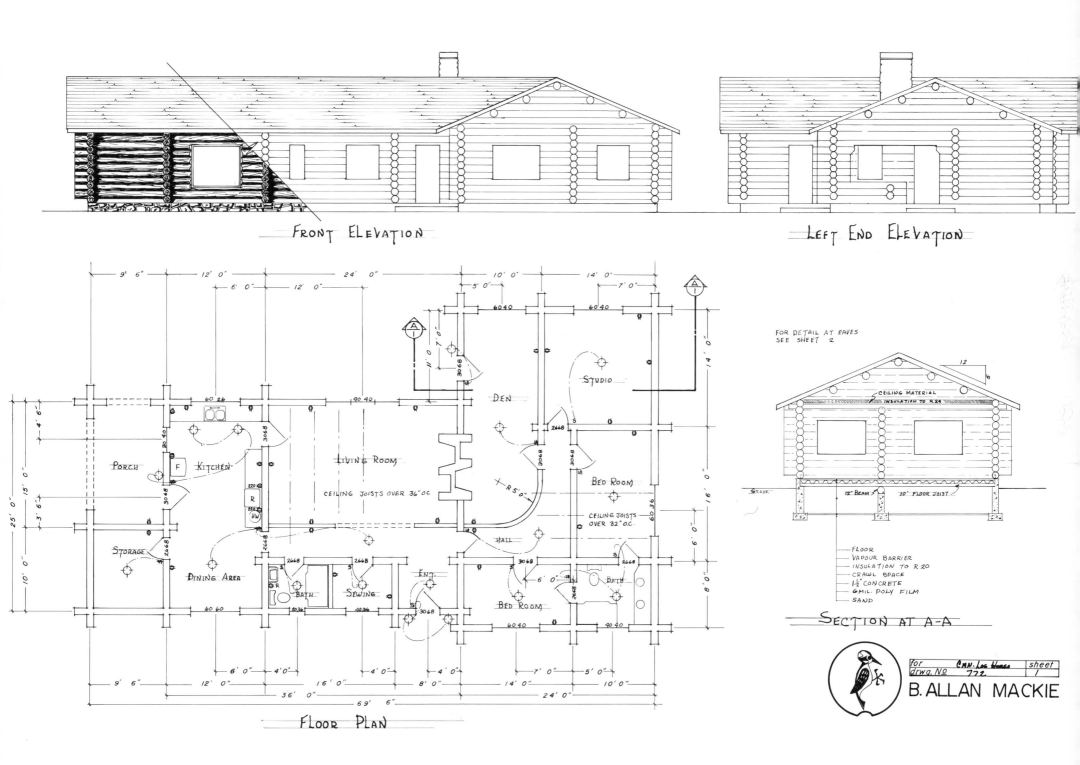

FRONT ELEVATION

LEFT END ELEVATION

FOR DETAIL AT EAVES
SEE SHEET 2

CEILING MATERIAL
INSULATION TO R24

GRADE

12" BEAM   10" FLOOR JOIST

FLOOR
VAPOUR BARRIER
INSULATION TO R 20
CRAWL SPACE
1½ CONCRETE
6 MIL. POLY FILM
SAND

SECTION AT A-A

6040   6040

Studio

Den

Living Room

Bed Room

CEILING JOISTS OVER 36" O.C.

CEILING JOISTS
OVER 32" O.C.

Porch   Kitchen

Storage

Dining Area   Bath   Sewing   Ent.   Bed Room   Bath

Hall

FLOOR PLAN

for   Cmn. Log House   sheet
drwg. No.   772   1

B. ALLAN MACKIE

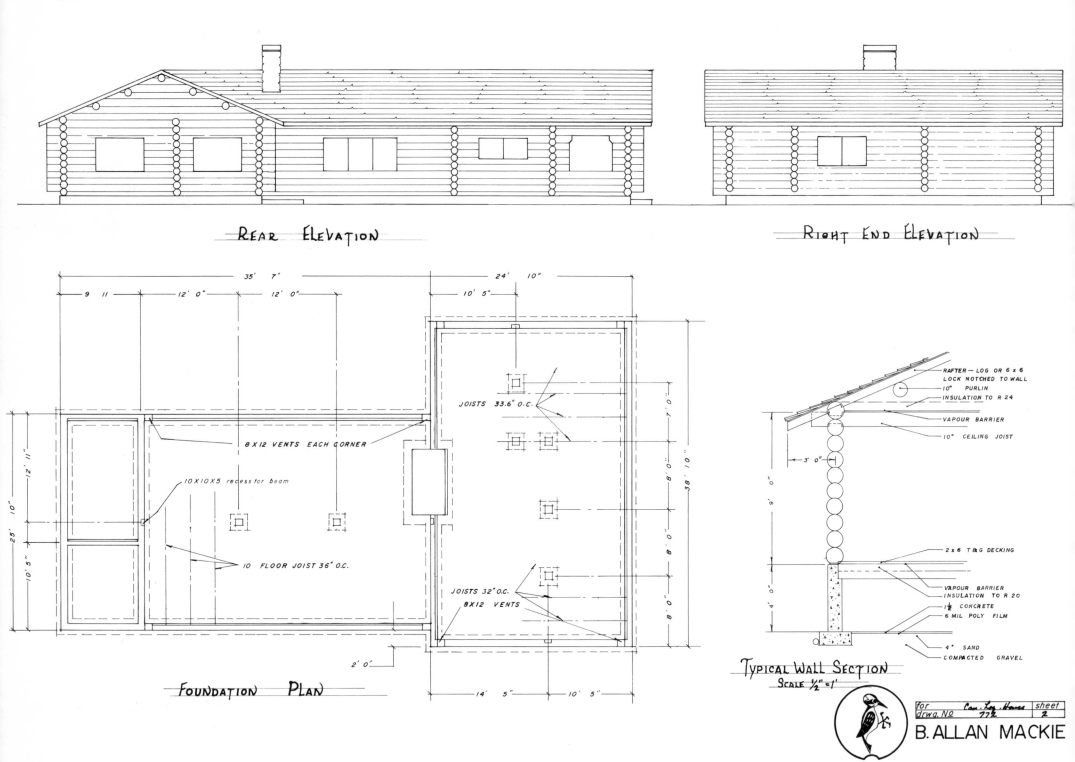

REAR ELEVATION

RIGHT END ELEVATION

FOUNDATION PLAN

35' 7"

9' 11"   12' 0"   12' 0"

24' 10"

10' 5"

JOISTS 33.6" O.C.

8 X 12 VENTS EACH CORNER

10 X 10 X 5 recess for beam

10 FLOOR JOIST 36" O.C.

JOISTS 32" O.C.
8 X 12 VENTS

12' 11"

25' 10"

10' 5"

2' 0"

14' 5"   10' 5"

7' 0"

8' 0"

8' 0"

8' 0"

38' 10"

TYPICAL WALL SECTION
SCALE ½"=1'

RAFTER — LOG OR 6 x 6
LOCK NOTCHED TO WALL
10" PURLIN
INSULATION TO R 24
VAPOUR BARRIER
10" CEILING JOIST

3' 0"

9' 0"

2 x 6 T & G DECKING

VAPOUR BARRIER
INSULATION TO R 20
1½ CONCRETE
6 MIL POLY FILM

4' 0"

4" SAND
COMPACTED GRAVEL

for   Can. Log. House   sheet
drwg. No   772   2

B. ALLAN MACKIE

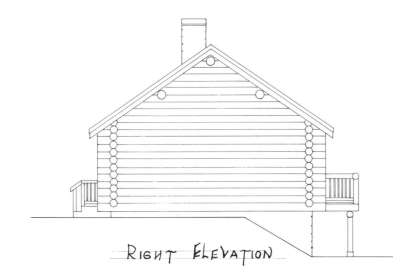

RIGHT ELEVATION

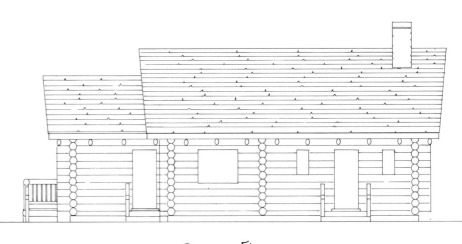

REAR ELEVATION

LEFT ELEVATION

#773   Square feet: 912

This design, although it is a sharp contrast to the previous one, is also a retirement home. I drew it after visiting the home of Harvey and Marie Webber of Terrace, on the invitation of their daughter-in-law who insisted it was the most perfect small house anyone could hope to see. It was so nicely built and furnished, I was inspired to incorporate a few mechanical aids which could enhance the usefulness of such a home for elderly occupants or for handicapped persons.

Design #773 incorporates an elevator which, of course, can be a broom closet if the builder doesn't want the elevator. But too often people believe an elevator to be enormously expensive and this is not necessarily the case, if you have mechanical skills. And the elevator can be a godsend to people confined to a wheelchair. I know a man who is an expert machinist and who built an elevator into his home, and another into his motor home, providing himself with a freedom he hasn't tasted in the 25 years he has been confined to a wheelchair with a broken back.

Stairs are also provided, of course. Workshop space is also included in the basement and an optional loft may be built over the living room area, for guests.

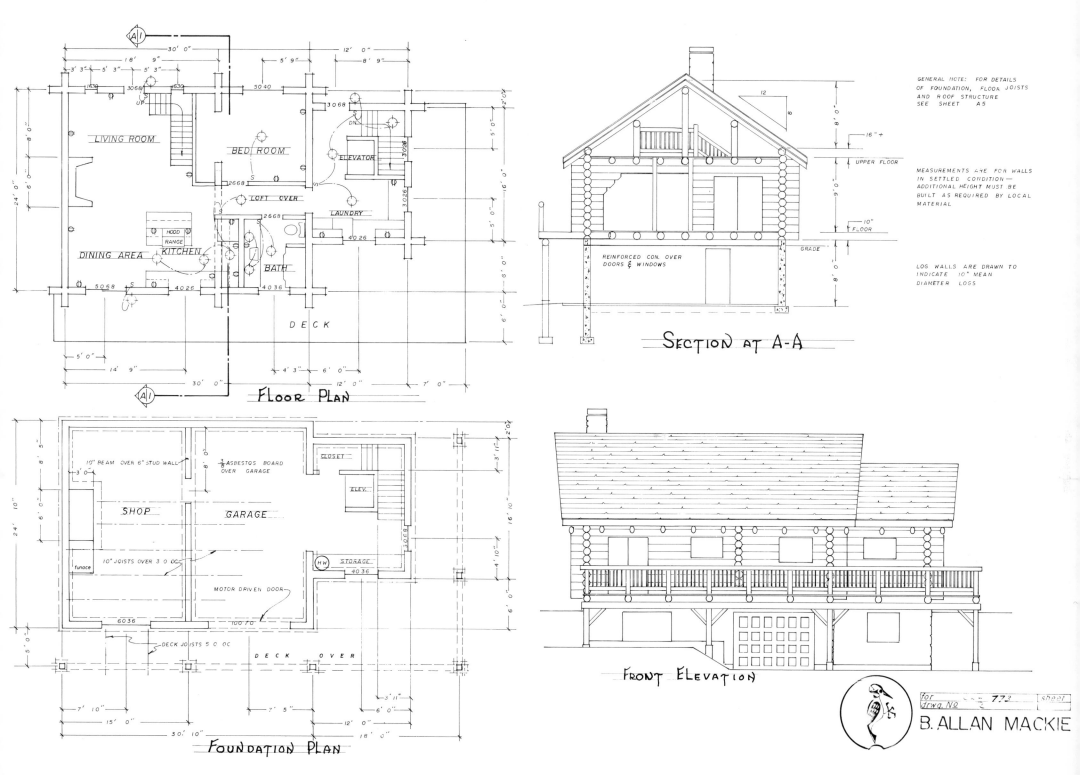

FLOOR PLAN

LIVING ROOM

BED ROOM

ELEVATOR

UP

DN.

LOFT OVER

LAUNDRY

HOOD RANGE

DINING AREA KITCHEN

BATH

DECK

SECTION AT A-A

GENERAL NOTE: FOR DETAILS OF FOUNDATION, FLOOR JOISTS AND ROOF STRUCTURE SEE SHEET A5

MEASUREMENTS ARE FOR WALLS IN SETTLED CONDITION — ADDITIONAL HEIGHT MUST BE BUILT AS REQUIRED BY LOCAL MATERIAL

LOG WALLS ARE DRAWN TO INDICATE 10" MEAN DIAMETER LOGS

UPPER FLOOR

FLOOR

GRADE

REINFORCED CON. OVER DOORS & WINDOWS

FOUNDATION PLAN

10" BEAM OVER 6" STUD WALL

¾ ASBESTOS BOARD OVER GARAGE

CLOSET

ELEV.

SHOP

GARAGE

funace

10" JOISTS OVER 3 0 OC

HW STORAGE

MOTOR DRIVEN DOOR

DECK JOISTS 5 0 OC

DECK OVER

FRONT ELEVATION

for drwg. No 773 sheet

B. ALLAN MACKIE

The Paul MacNab Cottage
Square feet: 540

#774

This design first appeared as a suggested floorplan for a guest cottage, shown in my book, BUILDING WITH LOGS. Many people have written to ask for the complete blueprints, over the years, but it was not until Paul MacNab had enrolled at the B. Allan Mackie School of Log Building that the blueprints were drawn, especially for him. Thus they came to be known that way.

This is a modest little building and yet it could serve very well as a home. With the porch railings and gable ends executed carefully, it could be a very pretty building, too.

It is shown in this design as being done in the Piece-en-piece method. Piece-en-piece houses are generally large and formal in design but, in this case, Paul wanted this technique and a small building. It could just as well be built with round logs as with hewn timbers, however. The blueprints serve both techniques.

I'd like to mention, here, that a blueprint is not a course in log building construction. Many people are dismayed when they see a blueprint. It may be their first sight of one. First, they may not know how to "read" one. Second, they say, "it does not show them how to build". Quite so. It should be borne in mind that a blueprint is a view of a house that is to be built. The actual building of it rests with the builder.

A blueprint provides:

* foundation plan
* floorplan
* 4 elevations (side views)
* a cross section (the house theoretically cut in half to show its construction)
* lot plan

If the building becomes more complicated in design, then a number of details would be included in its blueprint by way of explanation to the builder. But knowing how to build a log house is something that must come from the builder, not from the blueprint. This design, then, may be executed in either round log or in piece-en-piece, and any competent log builder will know how to achieve this design in either technique.

A builder may also know how to adapt a standard frame construction design, or your own pencil sketch, to log construction. But just a word of caution: there are fundamental principles of log construction which may not be ignored: cross-bracing being the most important, room sizes, settling, etc., being important too. These points will not have been taken into consideration if you adopt a standard house design or if you sketch something without being aware of those principles. So the builder should not be expected to take all the responsibilities of design, his domain is more properly the execution of a good design.

WEST ELEVATION

SOUTH ELEVATION

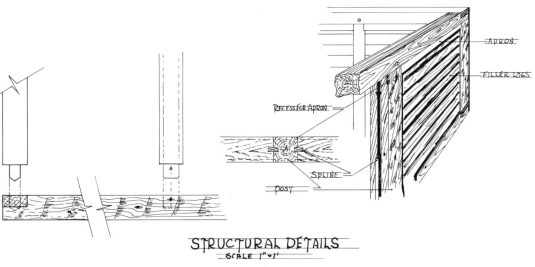

APRON

FILLER LOGS

RECESS FOR APRON

SPLINE

POST

STRUCTURAL DETAILS
SCALE 1"=1'

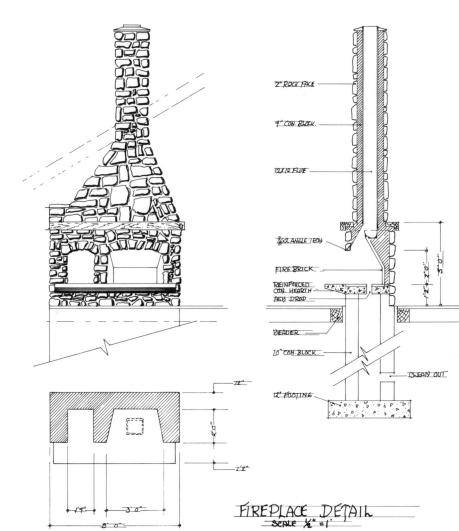

2" ROCK FACE

4" CON. BLOCK

12 X 12 FLUE

3 X 2 ANGLE IRON

FIRE BRICK

REINFORCED
CON. HEARTH

ASH DROP

HEADER

10" CON. BLOCK

CLEAN OUT

12" FOOTING

FIREPLACE DETAIL
SCALE ½"=1'

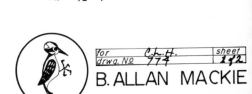

for C.H.
drwg. No 774   sheet 1/2

B. ALLAN MACKIE

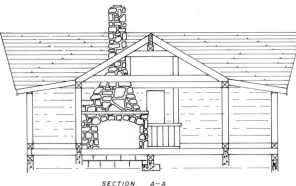

SECTION A—A
SCALE ¼" = I'

SOUTH ELEVATION

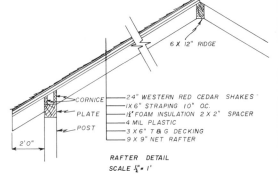

6 X 12" RIDGE

CORNICE — 24" WESTERN RED CEDAR SHAKES
— 1 X 6" STRAPING 10" OC.
PLATE — 1½" FOAM INSULATION 2 X 2" SPACER
— 4 MIL PLASTIC
POST — 3 X 6" T & G DECKING
— 9 X 9" NET RAFTER

2' 0"

RAFTER DETAIL
SCALE ¼" = I'

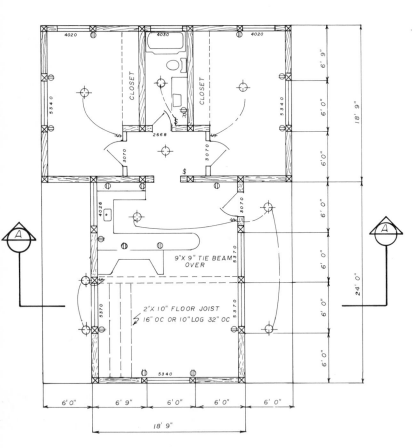

4020   4030   4020

CLOSET   CLOSET

5340   5340

2668

3070   3070

4026

3070

5370

9"X 9" TIE BEAM
OVER

5370

2"X 10" FLOOR JOIST
16" OC OR 10" LOG 32" OC

5370

5340

A   A

6' 0"   6' 9"   6' 0"   6' 0"   6' 0"

18' 9"

6' 9"   6' 0"   6' 0"   6' 0"   6' 0"   24' 0"

18' 9"

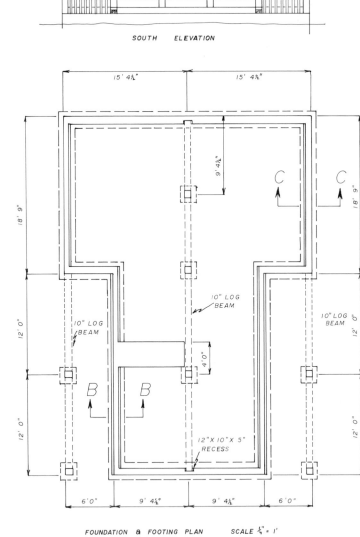

15' 4½"   15' 4½"

18' 9"

9' 4½"

C   C

12' 0"

10" LOG
BEAM

10" LOG
BEAM

10" LOG
BEAM

12' 0"

B   B

4' 0"

12' 0"

12"X 10"X 5"
RECESS

12' 0"

6' 0"   9' 4½"   9' 4½"   6' 0"

FOUNDATION & FOOTING PLAN   SCALE ¼" = I'

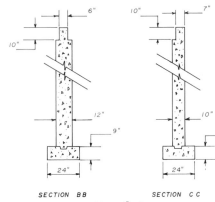

6"   10"

10"   7"

10"   12"   10"

9"   9"

24"   24"

SECTION BB   SECTION C C

SCALE ¼" = I'

for C.L.H.   sheet
drwg. No 774   212

B. ALLAN MACKIE

One last point, here: the true novice often asks if the blueprint shows exactly how to put in the wiring and the plumbing and the furnace system. It does not. As already explained, the blueprint shows where the plumbing and wiring should be installed, but for the skills involved the builder must obtain some instruction or perhaps seek out a copy of my books on how to build with logs. As for the furnace system, I don't presume to know the kind of heat the owners may wish to have and in fact, the installation of that system is best left to them or to the furnace man. In the case of solar heat, it may readily be seen that any number of adaptations are possible and so this is the choice of the owner.

One more caution is perhaps in order. Since there is a set of fundamentals to be carefully observed in good design for log construction, be sure that if you ask a draughtsman to prepare the blueprints that he understands these principles. At this time, most draughtsmen do not (although I certainly hope this state of affairs improves, as time goes on) and I've seen some of their designs in which perhaps 30 or 40 corners have been jotted down with no idea of the enormous cost in time and labour for creating 30 or 40 notches per round. I've seen architect-designed log structures intended for public use, with unbelievably long, unbraced walls ... fine for concrete ... but the whole wall could be pushed, rocked, and finally whip-lashed, just with one's hands, so flimsy and lacking in stability was the design. Log construction is special in very many ways. Its demands are also special. So I urge any novice builder or draughtsman to become knowledgeable about techniques. Learn how to build with logs. And then look to the blueprint to lead you to the final phase into construction of a log home.

Ask anyone who plunged into building, without study. Invariably they'll say, "I'd like to do this building all over again, now that I've learned by trial and error." Only by learning how to build, can this be avoided. Remember, then: the blueprint can't do that for you, but a good blueprint can assure you of a sound, graceful, and efficient design. That's important. But it's not the whole process. Virtually everything rests with the builder.

#775

This Ontario house is built of hewn logs. It is an extremely comfortable and hospitable home, although this has a lot to do with the owners, Hugh and Muriel MacMillan.

Square feet: 1,541

I have drawn the blueprints, in this case, with specific adaptations (a) for roundlog construction, and (b) for piece-en-piece construction with hewn logs as in the actual MacMillan home.

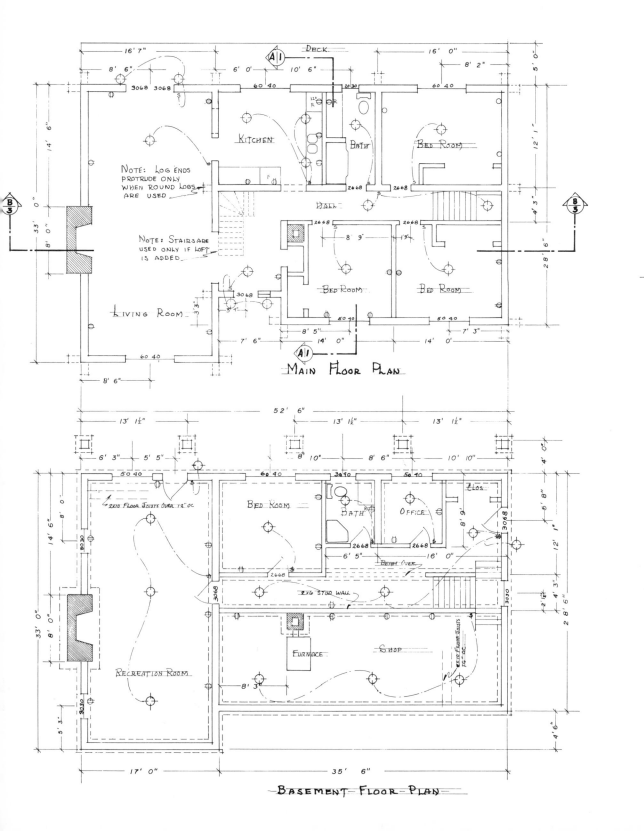

NOTE: Log ends
protrude only
when round logs
are used

NOTE: Stairs are
used only if loft
is added

Kitchen

Bath

Bed Room

Hall

Bed Room

Bed Room

Living Room

Deck

Main Floor Plan

Basement Floor Plan

2x10 Floor Joists over 12" OC

Bed Room

Bath

Office

Clos

Beam Over

2x6 Stud Wall

Furnace

Shop

2x10 Floor Joists 12" OC

Recreation Room

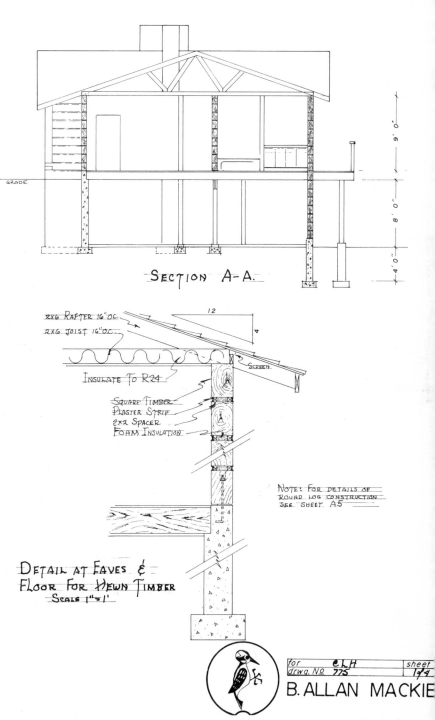

Section A-A.

Grade

2x6 Rafter 16" OC
2x6 Joist 16" OC

Screen

Insulate to R24

Square Timber
Plaster Strip
2x2 Spacer
Foam Insulation

Note: For details of
round log construction
see sheet A5

Detail at Eaves &
Floor For Hewn Timber
Scale 1"=1'

for CLH   sheet
drwg. No 775   1/4

B. ALLAN MACKIE

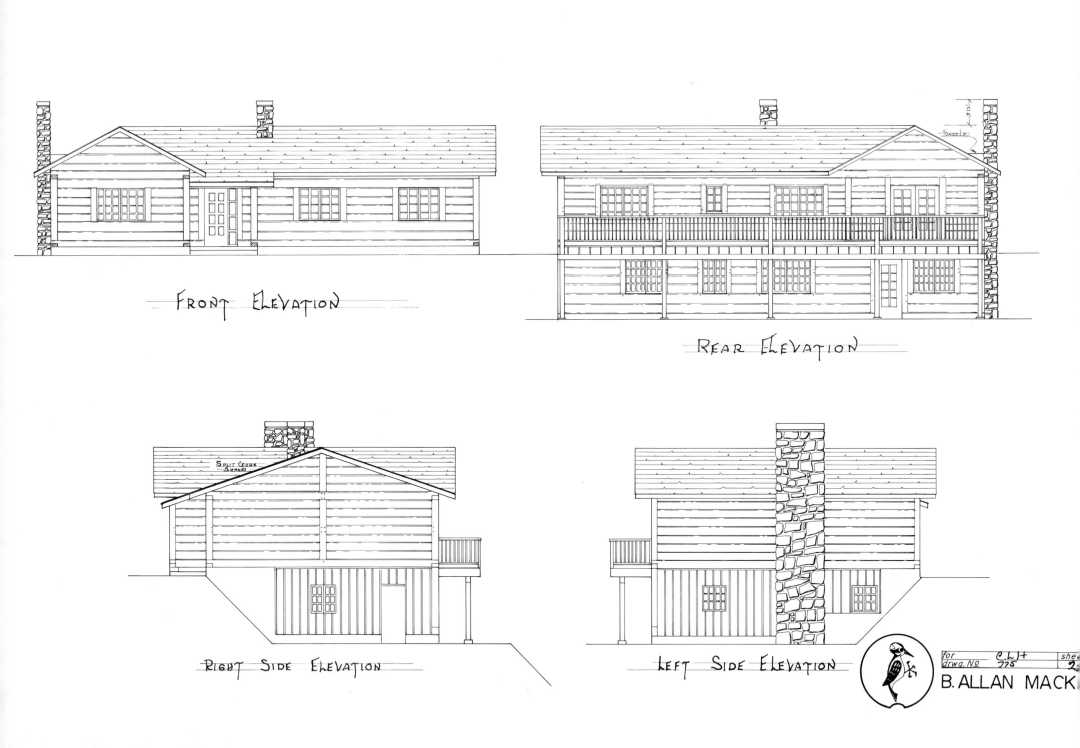

FRONT ELEVATION

REAR ELEVATION

RIGHT SIDE ELEVATION

LEFT SIDE ELEVATION

SPLIT CEDAR SHAKES

SADDLE

B. ALLAN MACK

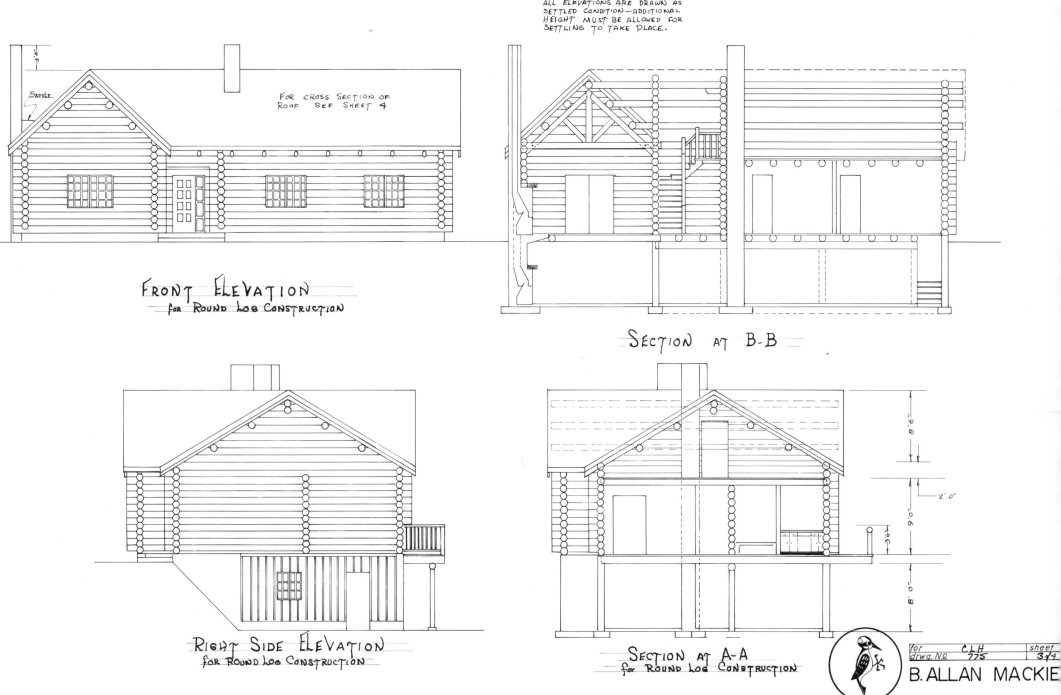

GENERAL NOTE: FOR TRUSS DETAIL
SEE CANADIAN LOG HOUSE VOL 3.
FOR FIREPLACE SECTION SEE SHEET 4.
ALL ELEVATIONS ARE DRAWN AS
SETTLED CONDITION—ADDITIONAL
HEIGHT MUST BE ALLOWED FOR
SETTLING TO TAKE PLACE.

FOR CROSS SECTION OF
ROOF SEE SHEET 4

Saddle

FRONT ELEVATION
for ROUND LOG CONSTRUCTION

SECTION AT B-B

RIGHT SIDE ELEVATION
for ROUND LOG CONSTRUCTION

SECTION AT A-A
for ROUND LOG CONSTRUCTION

8'6"

2'0"

9'0"

8'0"

| for | C L H | sheet |
| drwg. No | 775 | 3/4 |

B. ALLAN MACKIE

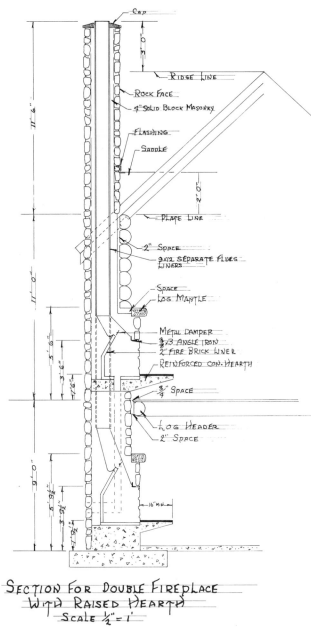

CAP

RIDGE LINE

ROCK FACE

4" SOLID BLOCK MASONRY

FLASHING

SADDLE

PLATE LINE

2" SPACE

9x12 SEPARATE FLUES LINERS

SPACE

LOG MANTLE

METAL DAMPER

3x3 ANGLE IRON

2" FIRE BRICK LINER

REINFORCED CON. HEARTH

3/4" SPACE

LOG HEADER

2" SPACE

16" MIN

SECTION FOR DOUBLE FIREPLACE
WITH RAISED HEARTH
SCALE ½" = 1'

11'6"

11'0"

5'6"

3'6"

6'0"

5'9½"

3'9½"

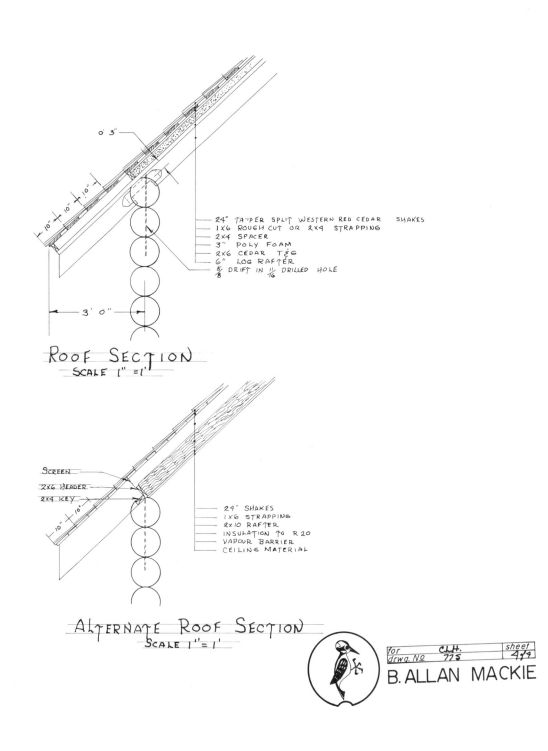

0'3"

10"

10"

3'0"

24" TAPER SPLIT WESTERN RED CEDAR SHAKES
1x6 ROUGH CUT OR 2x4 STRAPPING
2x4 SPACER
3" POLY FOAM
2x6 CEDAR T&G
6" LOG RAFTER
⅝ DRIFT IN 9/16 DRILLED HOLE

ROOF SECTION
SCALE 1" = 1'

SCREEN

2x6 HEADER

2x4 KEY

10"

10"

24" SHAKES
1x6 STRAPPING
2x10 RAFTER
INSULATION TO R20
VAPOUR BARRIER
CEILING MATERIAL

ALTERNATE ROOF SECTION
SCALE 1" = 1'

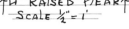

| for | C.H. | sheet |
| drwg. No | 775 | 474 |

B. ALLAN MACKIE

#776

Square feet: 1,744

Design #776 idealizes many people's dreams of a log house, I think, because it has been popular all across Canada.

It has a central fireplace, exposed stairway, lofty living room and exposed timber framing.

The upstairs provides extra bedrooms.

With the addition of a small entry hall at the back door, I think I would rather like this home for myself.

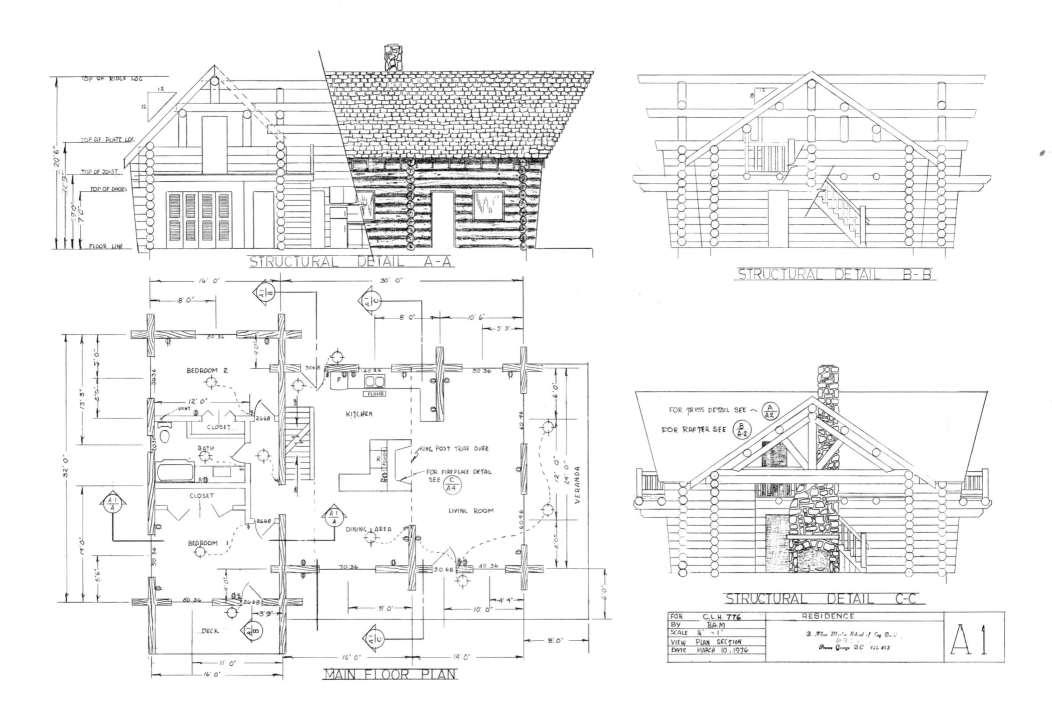

STRUCTURAL DETAIL A-A

STRUCTURAL DETAIL B-B

STRUCTURAL DETAIL C-C

MAIN FLOOR PLAN

BEDROOM 2

CLOSET

BATH

CLOSET

BEDROOM 1

KITCHEN

King Post Truss Over

FOR FIREPLACE DETAIL SEE C/A4

LIVING ROOM

DINING AREA

VERANDA

DECK

FOR TRUSS DETAIL SEE A/A-2

FOR RAFTER SEE B/A-2

FOR	C.L.H. 776	RESIDENCE	
By	B.A.M		A1
SCALE	¼" = 1'	B. Allan Mackie School of Log Building	
VIEW	PLAN SECTION	Prince George BC V2L 4S3	
DATE	MARCH 10, 1976		

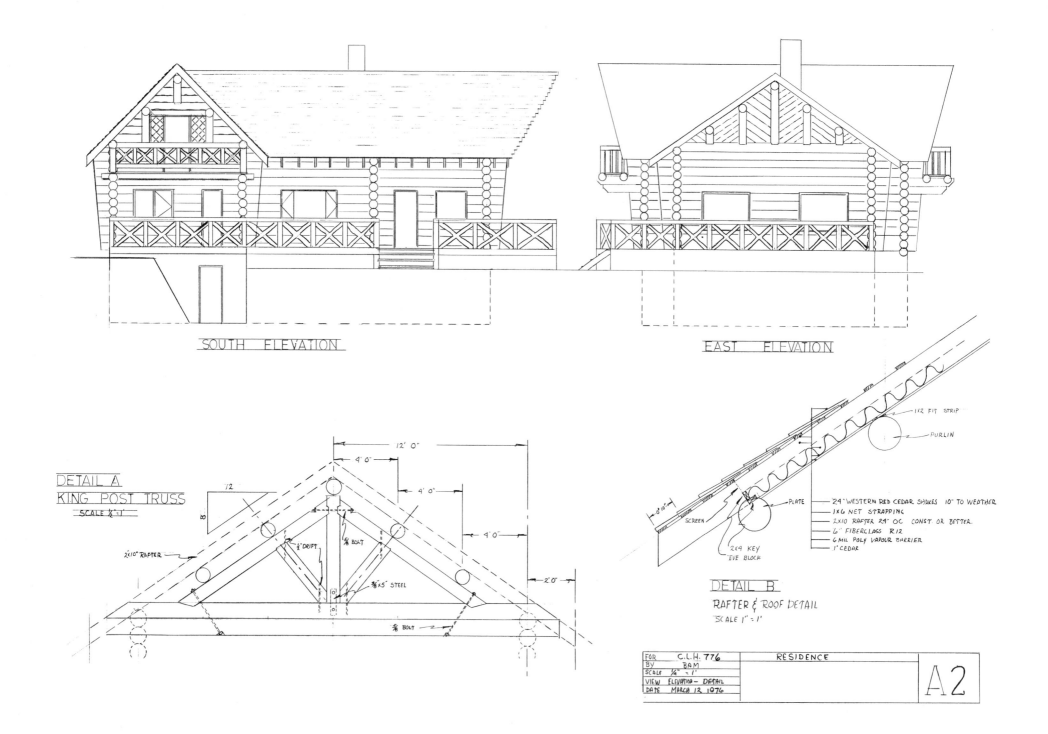

SOUTH ELEVATION

EAST ELEVATION

DETAIL A
KING POST TRUSS
SCALE ½" = 1'

12' 0"
4' 0"
4' 0"
4' 0"
2' 0"
12
8

2×10" RAFTER
½" DRIFT
⅝ BOLT
⅜"×5" STEEL
⅝ BOLT

1×2 FIT STRIP
PURLIN
PLATE
SCREEN
2×4 KEY
EVE BLOCK

24" WESTERN RED CEDAR SHAKES 10" TO WEATHER
1×6 NET STRAPPING
2×10 RAFTER 24" OC CONST OR BETTER.
6" FIBERGLASS R12
6 MIL POLY VAPOUR BARRIER
1" CEDAR

DETAIL B
RAFTER & ROOF DETAIL
SCALE 1" = 1'

FOR	C.L.H. 776	RESIDENCE	A2
BY	BAM		
SCALE	¼" = 1'		
VIEW	ELEVATION - DETAIL		
DATE	MARCH 12, 1976		

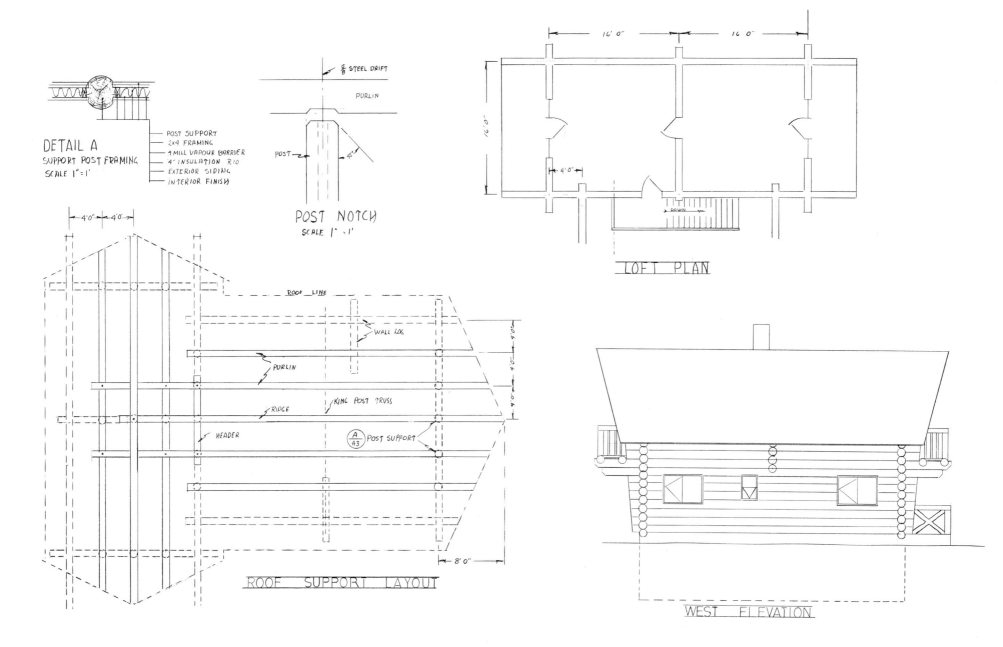

DETAIL A
SUPPORT POST FRAMING
SCALE 1"=1'

POST SUPPORT
2x4 FRAMING
4 MILL VAPOUR BARRIER
4" INSULATION R10
EXTERIOR SIDING
INTERIOR FINISH

⅝ STEEL DRIFT

PURLIN

POST

45°

POST NOTCH
SCALE 1" = 1'

16' 0"   16' 0"

16' 0"

4' 0"

DOWN

LOFT PLAN

4' 0"   4' 0"

ROOF LINE

WALL LOG

PURLIN

RIDGE   KING POST TRUSS

HEADER   A/A3 POST SUPPORT

4' 0" 4' 0" 4' 0"

8' 0"

ROOF SUPPORT LAYOUT

WEST ELEVATION

FOR	CLH·776	RESIDENCE	A3
BY	B.A.M		
SCALE	¼" = 1'		
VIEW			
DATE			

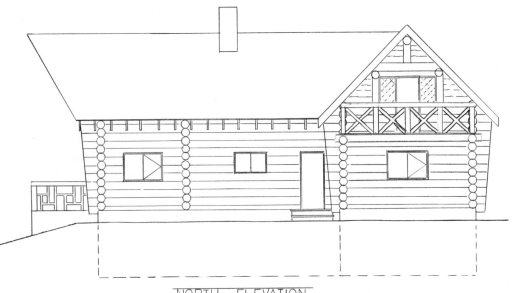

NORTH ELEVATION

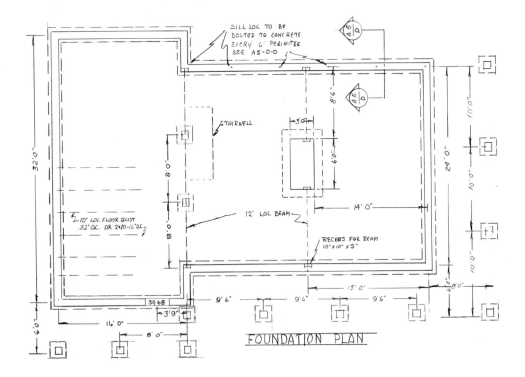

SILL LOG TO BE
BOLTED TO CONCRETE
EVERY 6' PERIMETER
SEE A5-D-D

STAIRWELL

2-10" LOG FLOOR JOIST
32" OC. OR 2X10-16"OC.

12" LOG BEAM

RECESS FOR BEAM
10"X10" X5"

32'0"

6'0"

16'0"

8'0"

3'9"

30 68

9'6"

9'6"

9'6"

15'0"

14'0"

8'0"

6'0"

10'0"

10'0"

24'0"

10'0"

8'0"

8'0"

3'0"

6'0"

FOUNDATION PLAN

FIREPLACE DETAIL C

SCALE ½"·1'

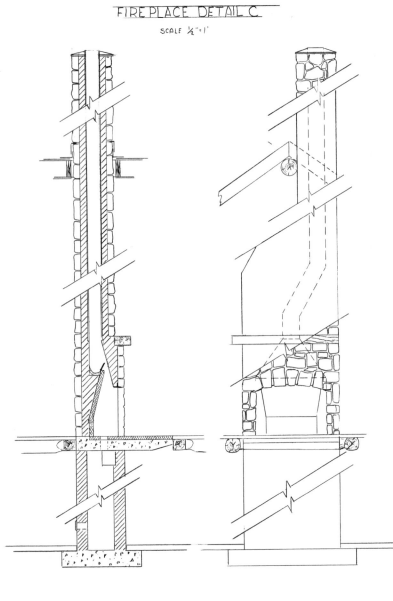

FOR	CLH 776		RESIDENCE	
BY	B.A.H			
SCALE	½" : 1'			A4
VIEW				
DATE	MARCH 14 1976			

#761

Square feet: 1,632

This was the home in which, as a young and unsuspecting 30-year-old, I imagined I'd be spending the rest of my life. I took great pains with it (to the best of my understanding at that time), and incorporated every feature which I believed to be important to the longterm survival of my family and my ranch.

There was a tremendous amount going for that ranch and for the house which is centred in its high, breathtaking fields. It is designed so that the family could function smoothly for six months at a stretch without a trip to a grocery store.

Uppermost in our minds, as we planned the house, was the idea that it should serve its occupants rather than the occupants serving the house through constant repairs, painting, polishing, or by submitting our free movement to any avoidable obstacles or inconvenience.

First of all it was large enough. Each member of the family had a room which could be entirely his or her own and that's important in real isolation (the nearest neighbour was 8 horseback miles away, the nearest village was 26 miles, the nearest town 70 miles). There was poor radio reception, no television, no telephone, and weekly mail pick-up at best, for newspapers or magazines. Each of us needed special space for making our own amusements in the way of reading, writing, or whatever.

We considered that isolation — solitude is a better word — a privilege. We were determined to make the house serve to provide the fullest appreciation of that idyllic experience. Thus, all supplies including firewood came under the ranch house roof. We believed that the better our plan, including the complete freedom from upstairs-downstairs, would prevent our having to depart for easier living in our old age. Now that old age isn't so tremendously far off, what wouldn't we give to be back in that ranch house again! But we had to become older to be wiser, it seemed.

So that isolation need not mean boredom, we arranged for all rooms but one to overlook the sweeping horizon and Nadina Mountain.

Climate, we thought, indicated the entry halls. These were incorporated into both the front and back door entries to afford double-door protection against the cold. The back entrance was further protected by the woodshed, permitting severely mudded boots to be kicked off or snow to be brushed off quite comfortably even before the first door was opened.

The kitchen was central, and was virtually a fortress. Its long walls were protected. It had the double-door access. And it had two window seats which could serve as bunks. No amount of cold, no blizzard, no furnace failures could ever catch us without an answer. And the kitchen was very large, as suits a working ranch.

The room which underwent the most drastic adaptation and became very unlike downtown design, was the so-called living room. Any ranch family knows that after they've packed 16 hours of living into their day, they're ready for something restful ... so it first of all shrank down into a retreat measuring 12 by 14, suited to quiet conversation, to reading, or to staring thoughtfully into the fireplace, meditating. In keeping with that deliberate effort to attain tranquillity, it faced away from the exciting sweep of mountain scenery and looked, instead, onto trees and quiet pastures.

I've talked in more detail about the Silloep Hills ranch house in my first book, BUILDING WITH LOGS. For now, I'd just like to say that I believe the method we used for finding out what kind of house we needed would serve anyone as a guide, even if their purposes were entirely different.

The patterns of our lives are indeed mysterious. The loss of this ranch and this home has been a deep wound but one friend, who knows us and the ranch very well, said the words which, in the end, comforted me: "It has worked for the best. If you hadn't left the ranch, you wouldn't have gone into teaching. If you hadn't gone into teaching, you wouldn't have taught log construction. And if you hadn't done that, then hundreds of other people would never have learned to build homes. Now, don't you think that was worth it?"

I have to agree, perhaps it is. But I still search for the mountain valley which I can call my own, as I did those Silloep Hills and the ranch house built of spruce.

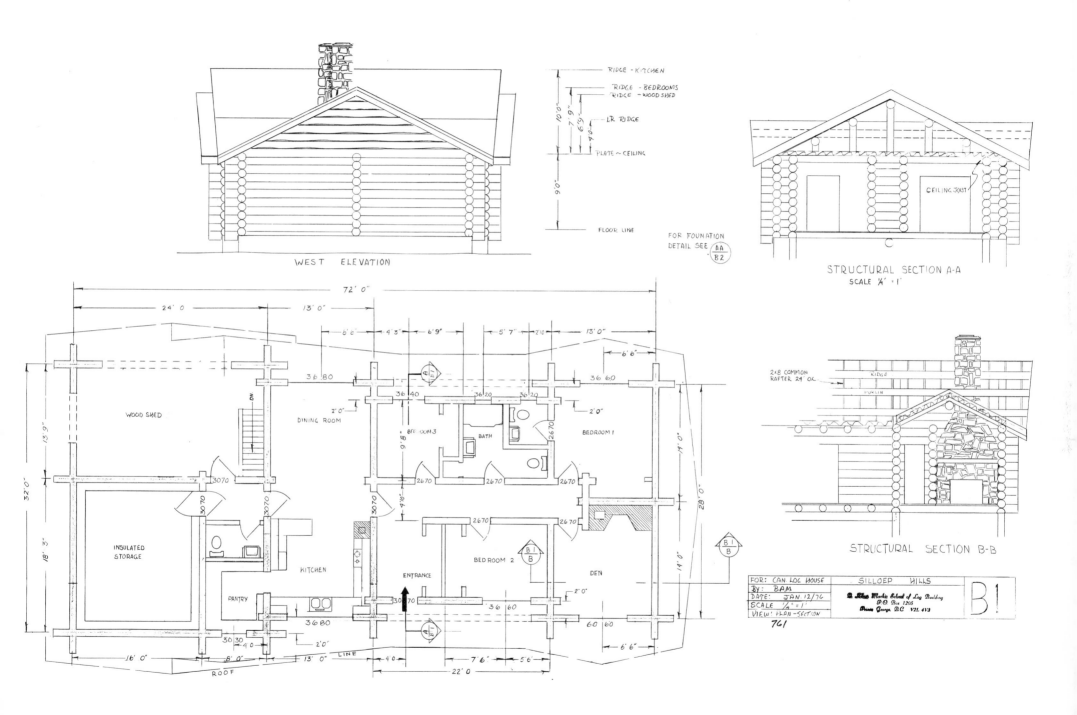

WEST ELEVATION

RIDGE - KITCHEN
RIDGE - BEDROOMS
RIDGE - WOOD SHED

L.R. RIDGE

10'0"
7'9"
6'9"
4'0"

PLATE ~ CEILING

9'0"

FLOOR LINE

FOR FOUNATION
DETAIL SEE AA/B2

STRUCTURAL SECTION A-A
SCALE ¼" = 1'

CEILING JOIST

STRUCTURAL SECTION B-B

2x8 COMMON
RAFTER 24" O.C.

RIDGE
PURLIN

72' 0"
24' 0"
13' 0"
6'6"
4'3"
6'9"
5'7"
2'10"
13' 0"
6'6"

WOOD SHED

15'9"

32'0"

18'3"

INSULATED
STORAGE

PANTRY

KITCHEN

DINING ROOM

DN

36 80

2'0"

3070

3070

3070

BEDROOM 3

9'8"

4'0"

BATH

2670

2670

2670

2670

2670

ENTRANCE

30 70

36 80

30 30
40

2'0"

BEDROOM 2

36 40

36 20

36 20

A/B1

B/B

B/B

BEDROOM 1

2'0"

36 60

2670

DEN

2'0"

36 60

60 60

6'6"

14'0"

28'0"

19'0"

A/B1

ROOF LINE
4'0"
7'6"
5'6"
13' 0"
22' 0"
16' 0"
8' 0"

ROOF

FOR: CAN LOG HOUSE   SILLOEP   HILLS
BY: BAM
DATE: JAN. 12/76
SCALE: ¼" = 1'
VIEW: PLAN - SECTION
761

B1

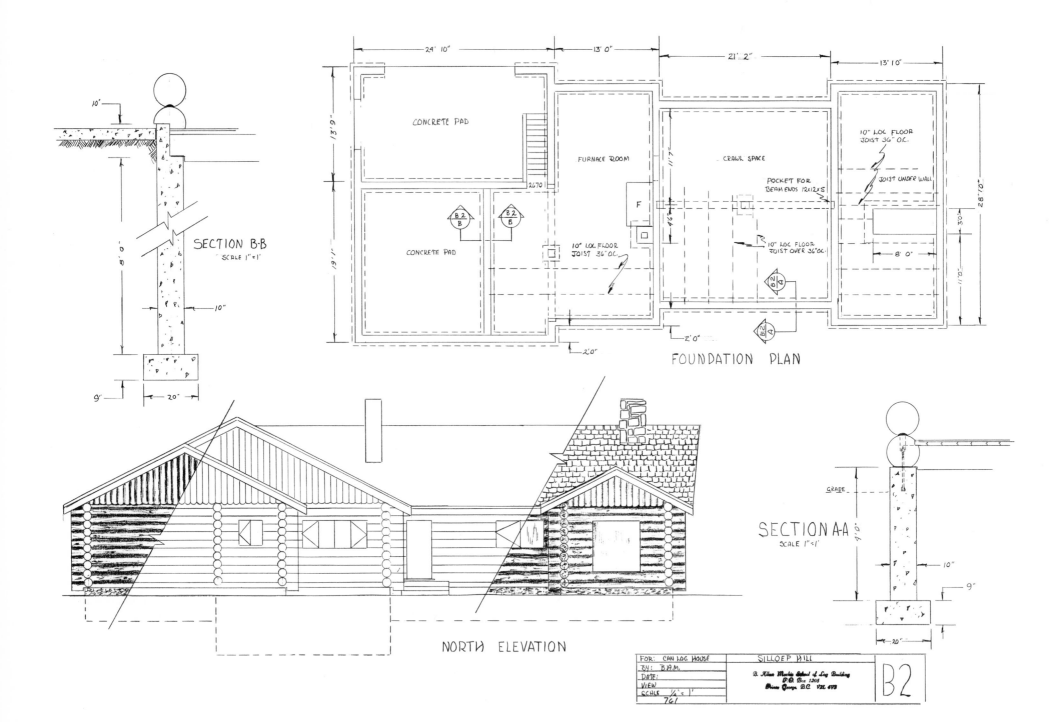

SECTION B-B
SCALE 1"=1'

10"

10"

5'0"

9"   20"

FOUNDATION PLAN

29'10"   13'0"   21'2"   13'10"

13'9"

CONCRETE PAD

FURNACE ROOM

CRAWL SPACE

10" LOG FLOOR
JOIST 36" O.C.

JOIST UNDER WALL

POCKET FOR
BEAM ENDS 12x12x5

11'7"

19'1"

CONCRETE PAD

2670

B2/B   B2/B

10" LOG FLOOR
JOIST 36" O.C.

10" LOG FLOOR
JOIST OVER 36" O.C.

F

28'0"

3'0"

8'0"

1'0"

B2/A

2'0"

2'0"

B2/A

NORTH ELEVATION

SECTION A-A
SCALE 1"=1'

GRADE

9'0"

10"

9"

20"

FOR: CAN LOG HOUSE   SILLOEP HILL
BY: B.A.M.
DATE:
VIEW:
SCALE: 1/2"=1'
    761

B. Allan Mackie School of Log Building
P.O. Box 1205
Prince George B.C. V2L 4V3

B2

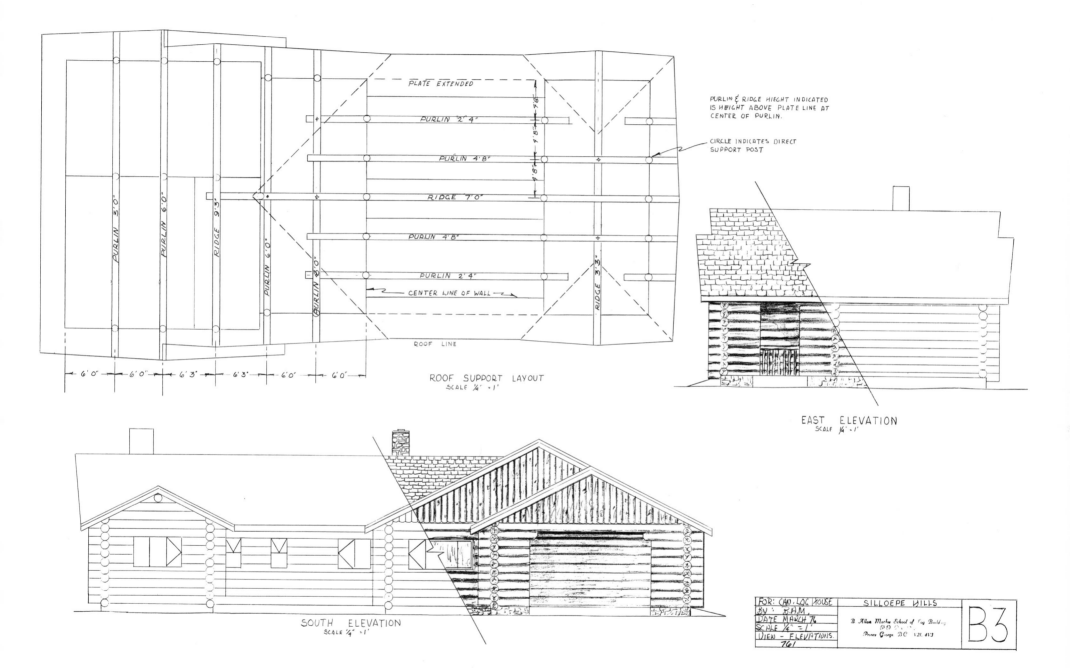

PLATE EXTENDED

PURLIN 2'4"

PURLIN 4'8"

RIDGE 7'0"

PURLIN 4'8"

PURLIN 2'4"

CENTER LINE OF WALL

ROOF LINE

PURLIN 3'0"
PURLIN 6'0"
RIDGE 9'3"
PURLIN 6'0"
PURLIN 3'0"
RIDGE 3'3"

6'0"   6'0"   6'3"   6'3"   6'0"   6'0"

ROOF SUPPORT LAYOUT
SCALE 1/4" = 1'

PURLIN & RIDGE HIEGHT INDICATED
IS HEIGHT ABOVE PLATE LINE AT
CENTER OF PURLIN.

CIRCLE INDICATES DIRECT
SUPPORT POST

EAST ELEVATION
SCALE 1/4" = 1'

SOUTH ELEVATION
SCALE 1/4" = 1'

FOR: CAN. LOG HOUSE   SILLOEPE HILLS
BY: B.A.M.
DATE MARCH 76   B. Allan Mackie School of Log Building
SCALE 1/4" = 1'   P.O.
VIEW - ELEVATIONS   Prince George, B.C. V2L 4V3
761

B3

#762 Square feet: 2,100

This design picks up the theme of self-sufficiency but it can be suited to the urban life as well as rural living.

This plan was drawn for a particular family whose lifestyle was informal yet busy. Thus the kitchen expanded to serve the many guests who tend to drop in unannounced, while the conventional dining and "living" rooms were virtually abolished in favour of the small conversation corner and its companion study room. The result is that each of the four members of the family may pursue their hobbies independently or may gather in entirely private reception rooms or flock together in the kitchen for food and drink.

In my opinion, this house reflects a good and serious attempt to think through personal lifestyles and to bend the house design to fit. All too often, houses are stereotyped, and we, the occupants, must bend to fit its restrictions. I often wonder how ballerinas get their start if they are raised in modern space-saving bungalows where even a cat can't take a hearty leap without crashing into a wall. In particular, the term "living" room troubles me, for it is the room in which the least living and the highest degree of decorum is observed. The "family" room is also a ponderous thing and much as I love my own brood, I'm daunted by the term and feel a distinct reluctance to have anything to do with the "family" room. Perhaps it is the stereotyping or labeling that is so awesome, as if it had been decreed what I could, or could not, do if I entered a certain room. Why not just a big, sunny pleasant room, "a room", placed lovingly in a house just in case one of the kids needed room . . . to dance. Just room. The "bed" room, the "bath" room seem more acceptable, since they refer to the objects in the rooms. It's when I myself am included in the stereotype that it troubles me and I begin wondering if those designations, such as "family" room, aren't meant to tell me what should not happen in there, rather than to explore the fullness of living in a home.

This design #762 may not be suited to a wide number of people since it was so individually designed . . . and yet, here again I often find myself wondering if the creative and unusual person is, in fact, so unusual. Surely if there is room to play, most of us play. Perhaps not the same game, but we play. For this reason, I've always urged people to build the house that bends to their lifestyle, and devil take those who plead for stereotyping as "resale" value. I firmly believe that a well-executed house which did meet a definite lifestyle is going to be recognized and snatched up very much more quickly than a stereotyped house.

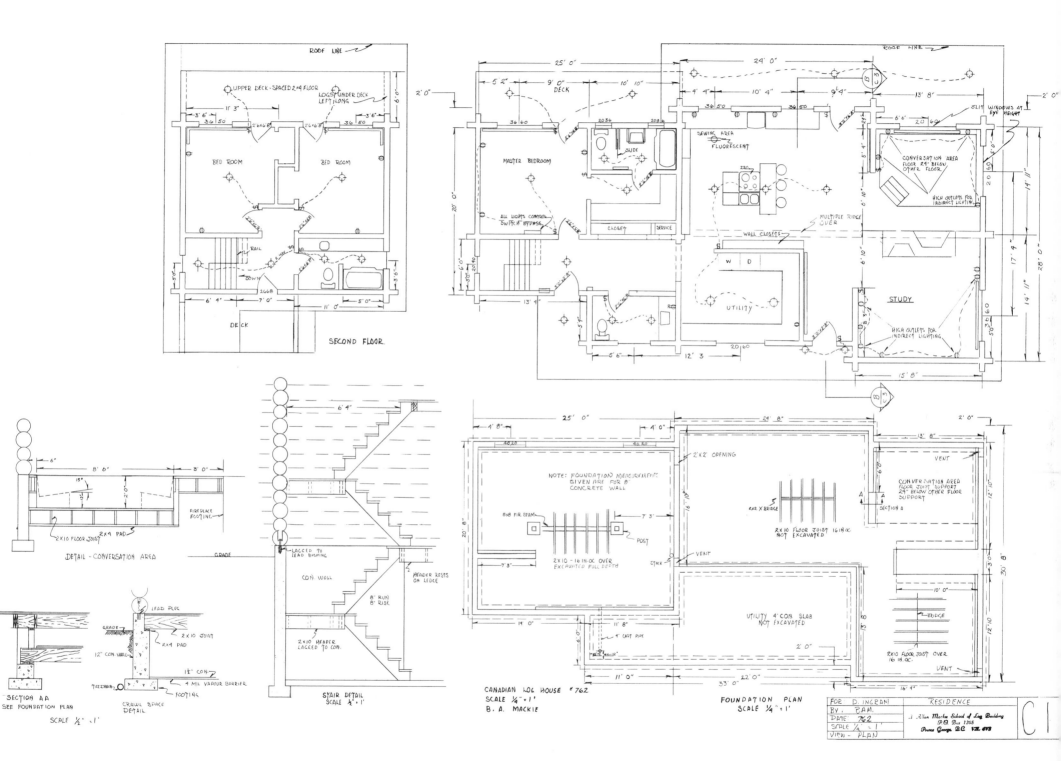

SECOND FLOOR

DETAIL - CONVERSATION AREA

SECTION AA
SEE FOUNDATION PLAN
SCALE ½" = 1'

CRAWL SPACE
DETAIL

STAIR DETAIL
SCALE ½" = 1'

CANADIAN LOG HOUSE #762
SCALE ¼" = 1'
B. A. MACKIE

FOUNDATION PLAN
SCALE ¼" = 1'

FOR D. INGRAM	RESIDENCE	
BY: B.A.M.		
DATE: 762	J. Allan Mackie School of Log Building	
SCALE ¼" = 1'	P.O. Box 1205	C1
VIEW: PLAN	Prince George B.C. V2L 4V3	

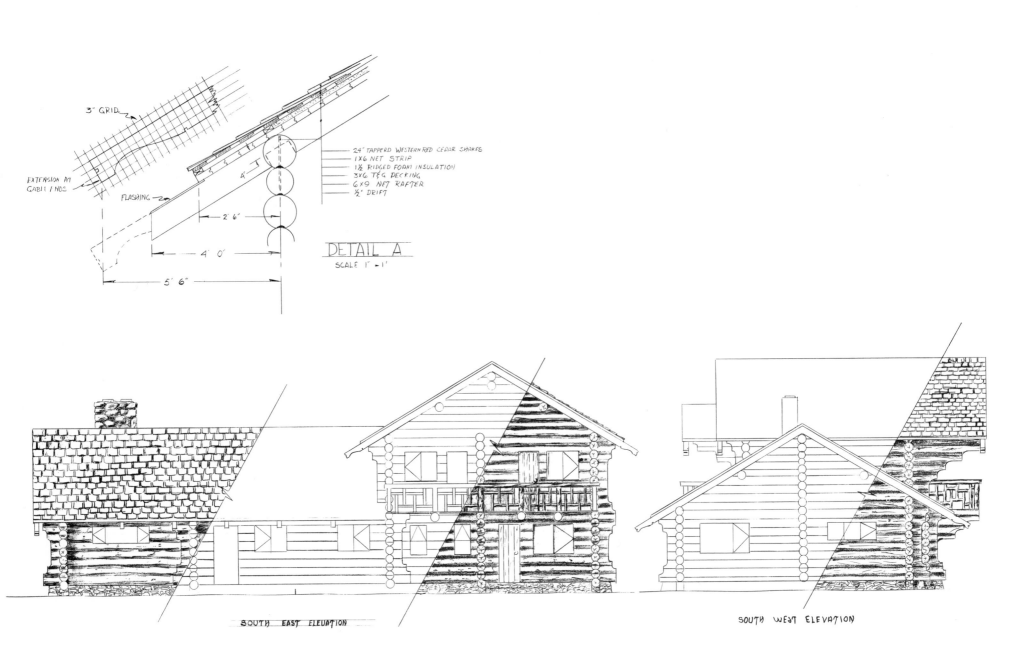

3" GRID

EXTENSION ON
GABLE / ENDS

FLASHING

24" TAPPERD WESTERN RED CEDAR SHAKES
1X6 NET STRIP
1½ RIDGED FOAM INSULATION
3X6 T&G DECKING
6X9 NET RAFTER
½" DRIFT

4'

2' 6"

4' 0"

5' 6"

DETAIL A
SCALE 1" = 1'

SOUTH EAST ELEVATION

SOUTH WEST ELEVATION

FOR: D. INGRAM	RESIDENCE	
BY: B.A.M		C2
DATE: 762		
SCALE ¼" = 1'		
VIEW ELEVATIONS		

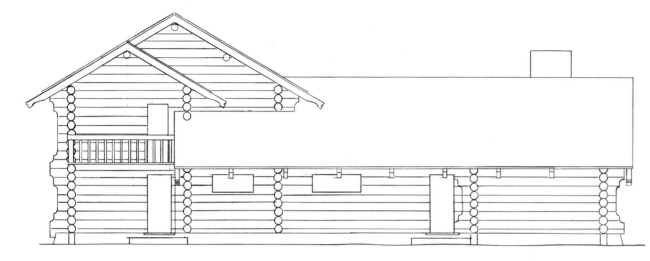

NORTHWEST ELEVATION

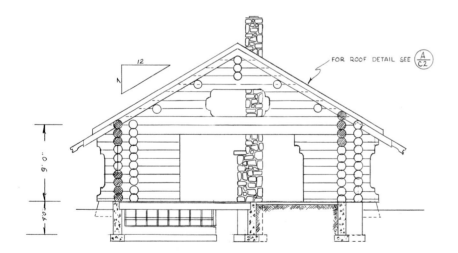

FOR ROOF DETAIL SEE $\frac{A}{C2}$

12

9'-0"

STRUCTURAL SECTION B-B

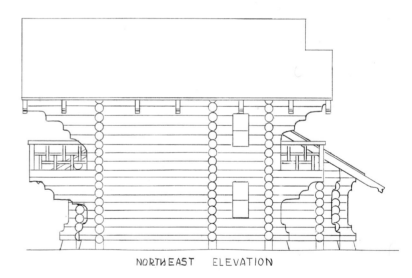

NORTHEAST ELEVATION

FOR D. INGRAM	RESIDENCE	C3
BY BAM.		
DATE 762		
SCALE 1/4" = 1'		
VIEW		

#763   *Square feet: 2,200*

This house has a symmetry which I find satisfying. Both the interior — in its pleasant yet formal separation of the rooms — and the exterior — in its balance and interplay of eaves, roof-pitch, and dormer.

Upstairs is designed to have either two large bedrooms or, with partitions, 4 smaller sized bedrooms.

There is a little extra work in its added corners but, in almost all cases of extra work, it yields a reward in interesting recesses, nooks and crannies.

With its full basement, this is a substantial home well suited to the family that enjoys formal dinner parties and entertaining.

Someone who bought this plan wrote to ask what the name "Nahanni" means. I'm not sure of the actual meaning of this Indian word but I adopted it from the northern British Columbia river by that name. To me, this house, on that river, would be paradise. Yet it's a house which would make a handsome addition to any urban or suburban neighbourhood.

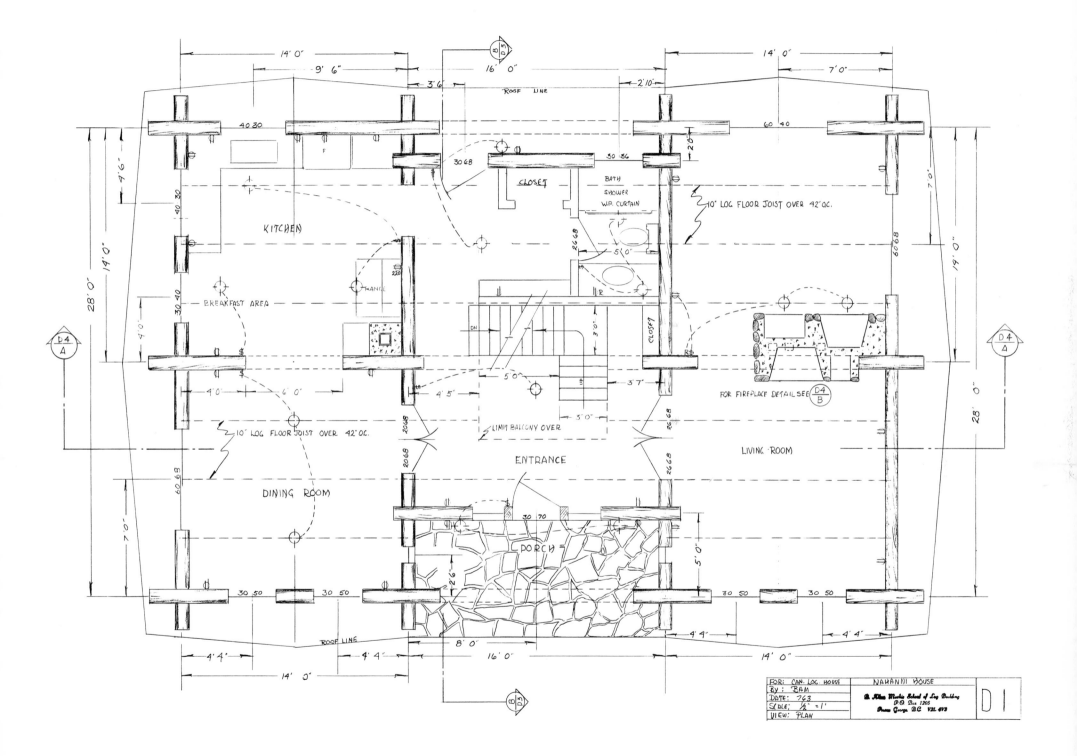

KITCHEN

BREAKFAST AREA

DINING ROOM

ENTRANCE

PORCH

CLOSET

BATH
SHOWER
W.P. CURTAIN

10" LOG FLOOR JOIST OVER 42" O.C.

CLOSET

FOR FIREPLACE DETAIL SEE $\frac{D4}{B}$

LIVING ROOM

10" LOG FLOOR JOIST OVER 42" O.C.

11mm BALCONY OVER

ROOF LINE

ROOF LINE

FOR:	CAN. LOG. HOUSE	NAHANNI HOUSE	D1
BY:	B.A.M.	B. Allan Mackie School of Log Building	
DATE:	7-63	P.O. Box 1205	
SCALE:	½" = 1'	Prince George BC V2L 4V3	
VIEW:	PLAN		

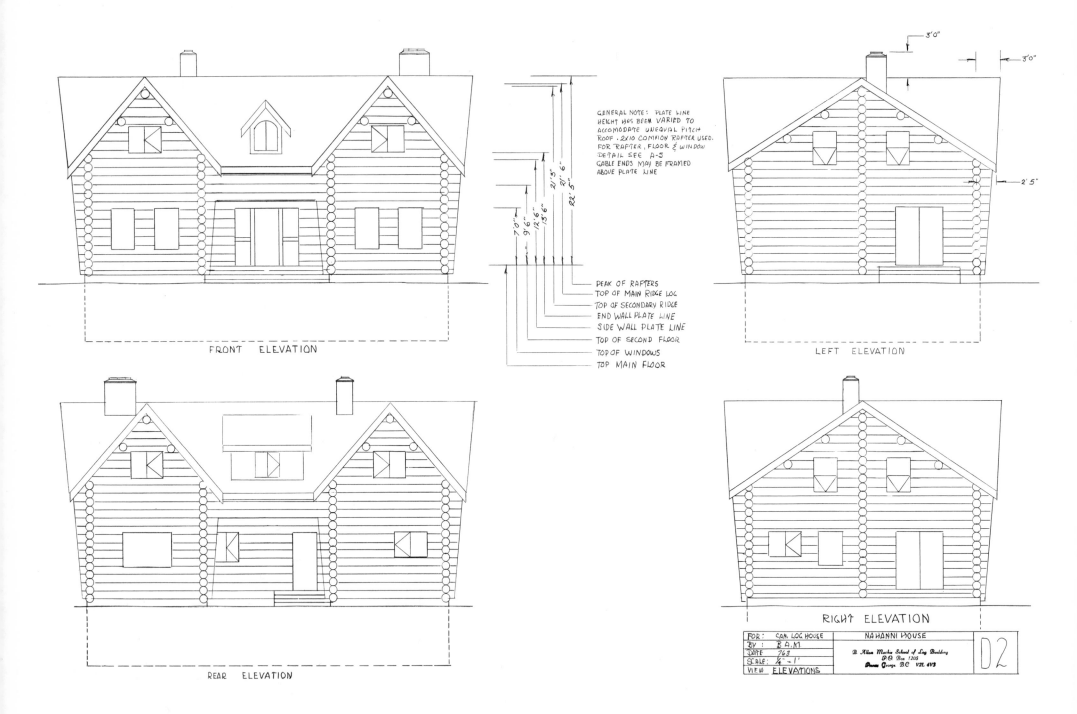

FRONT ELEVATION

GENERAL NOTE: PLATE LINE
HEIGHT HAS BEEN VARIED TO
ACCOMODATE UNEQUAL PITCH
ROOF. 2×10 COMMON RAFTER USED.
FOR RAFTER, FLOOR & WINDOW
DETAIL SEE A-5
GABLE ENDS MAY BE FRAMED
ABOVE PLATE LINE

PEAK OF RAFTERS
TOP OF MAIN RIDGE LOG
TOP OF SECONDARY RIDGE
END WALL PLATE LINE
SIDE WALL PLATE LINE
TOP OF SECOND FLOOR
TOP OF WINDOWS
TOP MAIN FLOOR

LEFT ELEVATION

REAR ELEVATION

RIGHT ELEVATION

FOR:	CAN. LOG HOUSE	NAHANNI HOUSE	
BY:	B. A. M		D2
DATE	763	B. Allan Mackie School of Log Building	
SCALE:	¼"~1'	P.O. Box 1205	
VIEW	ELEVATIONS	Prince George, B.C. V2L 4V3	

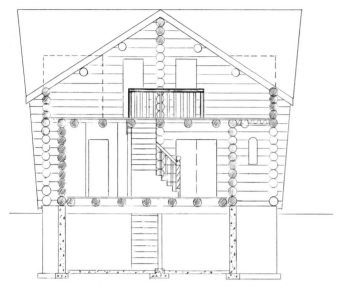

SECTION AT B-B

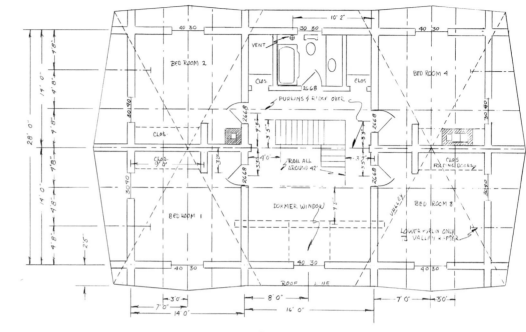

SECOND FLOOR PLAN

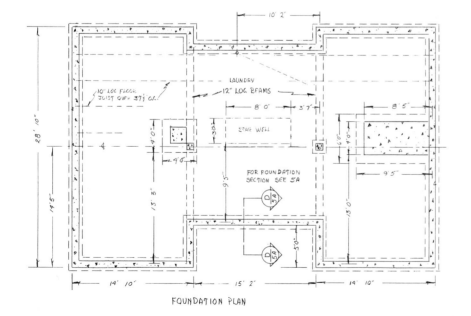

FOUNDATION PLAN

FOR: CAN LOG HOUSE	NAHANNI HOUSE	D3
BY: BAM	B. Allan Mackie School of Log Building	
DATE: 763	P.O. Box	
SCALE 1/4" = 1'	Prince George BC V2L 4V3	
VIEW		

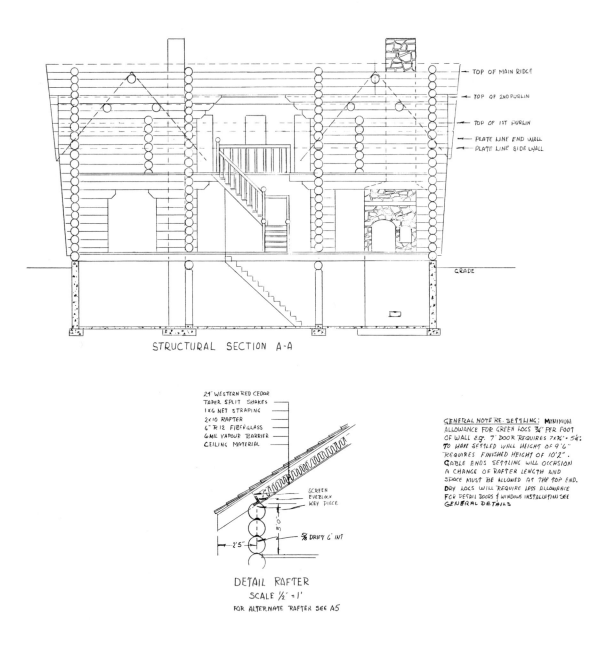

STRUCTURAL SECTION A-A

- TOP OF MAIN RIDGE
- TOP OF 2ND PURLIN
- TOP OF 1ST PURLIN
- PLATE LINE END WALL
- PLATE LINE SIDE WALL

GRADE

24" WESTERN RED CEDAR
TAPER SPLIT SHAKES
1x6 NET STRAPING
2x10 RAFTER
6" R 12 FIBERGLASS
6 MIL VAPOUR BARRIER
CEILING MATERIAL

SCREEN
EAVEBLOCK
KEY PIECE

5/8 DRIFT 6" INT

2'5"

DETAIL RAFTER
SCALE 1/2" = 1'
FOR ALTERNATE RAFTER SEE A5

GENERAL NOTE RE: SETTLING: MINIMUM
ALLOWANCE FOR GREEN LOGS 3/4" PER FOOT
OF WALL E.G. 7' DOOR REQUIRES 7x3/4" = 5 1/4":
TO HAVE SETTLED WALL HEIGHT OF 9'6"
REQUIRES FINISHED HEIGHT OF 10'2".
GABLE ENDS SETTLING WILL OCCASION
A CHANGE OF RAFTER LENGTH AND
SPACE MUST BE ALLOWED AT THE TOP END.
DRY LOGS WILL REQUIRE LESS ALLOWANCE
FOR DETAIL DOORS & WINDOWS INSTALLATION SEE
GENERAL DETAILS

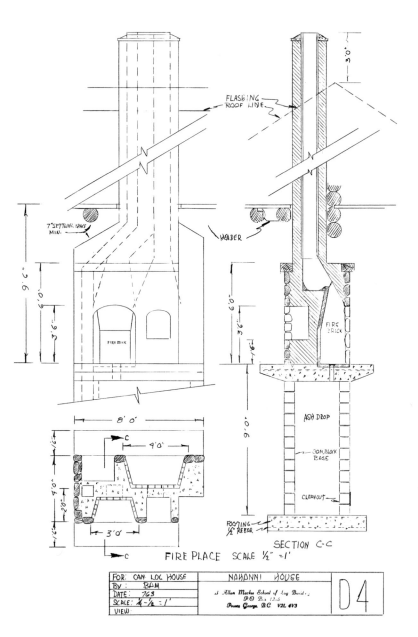

FLASHING
ROOF LINE

7" SETTLING SPACE
MIN.

HEADER

FIRE BOX

FIRE PLACE   SCALE 1/2" = 1'

SECTION C-C

FIRE BRICK

ASH DROP

CON. BLOCK BASE

CLEANOUT

FOOTING
1/2" REBAR

FOR:	CAN LOG HOUSE	NAHANNI HOUSE	
BY:	BAM		D4
DATE:	7/63	J. Allan Mackie School of Log Build.,	
SCALE:	1/4-1/2 = 1'	P.O. Box 1205	
VIEW:		Prince George B.C. V2L 4V3	

#764   *The Kerry Street House*   Square feet: 2,000

This house was originally designed and built for the lot at 598 Kerry Street, Prince George, bordering a well-treed city park. It was my own design, the logwork done by my own students, with the dual purpose of teaching men these skills as a career, and of establishing once and for all that the log home is just as suited to the modern urban environment as it is to the Nahanni River. It was a back-breaking job, one which would have been a thousand times easier if I had been entirely alone, building it myself. But I was the lone instructor with 20 novices, I was the sole purchasing agent, and at the end of March with only the ridgelog in place, I was the one who did all the completion plus answered 500 questions a day. Tour buses were re-routed to include the Kerry Street project, visitors came from all over Canada and beyond as far as Scotland, as well as delegations from various government departments. The doors were locked for the last few days when the rugs were laid and furniture was installed by several downtown department stores. The last smudge was wiped from the kitchen linoleum only minutes before the doors re-opened and the people surged in . . . they had been lined up in the rain for 2 blocks. It took me almost a year to recover from the demands of that pilot project and if anyone reading this was a visitor to the Kerry Street house during construction and did not get as long a conversation with me as they wished, I hope they understand. I often wondered if it had been worth that kind of punishment, but now I am sure it was. It provided a watershed in several areas. It helped to eliminate the word "cabin" from architectural references to timber con-

struction. It completely destroyed a most aggravating myth which held that building permits weren't issued for log construction. It established the fact that Central Mortgage & Housing Corporation was only too happy to advance the mortgage funds for a log house. It placed modern log construction alongside standard frame construction in a fairly high density urban subdivision, something which it was often said could not be done. And it established the fact that not only did the urban log house look good but, as one guest said, "It made the other houses look flimsy." Those were all big pluses for log construction which, before that, had been rarely acknowledged. So I look back on the construction of that pilot project with mixed feelings. But I've never doubted that collectively we owed this effort, this demonstration, to the craft. From Kerry Street onward (1974), both log homes and log builders, as well as the courses of instruction, were taken seriously. Because so many issues and developments arose from this project, it is hard for me to go back in my memory and recall the design of the house, simply as a design. But it does incorporate several fundamentals which make The Kerry Street design a good choice for many builders.

First, it maximizes the materials while it economizes to a high degree the effort involved in achieving a large house. It is a basic rectangle, with two partition walls not simply for aesthetics but also for the serious work of sway-bracing or cross supports. Thus, while fairly large and fairly simple, it is solid.

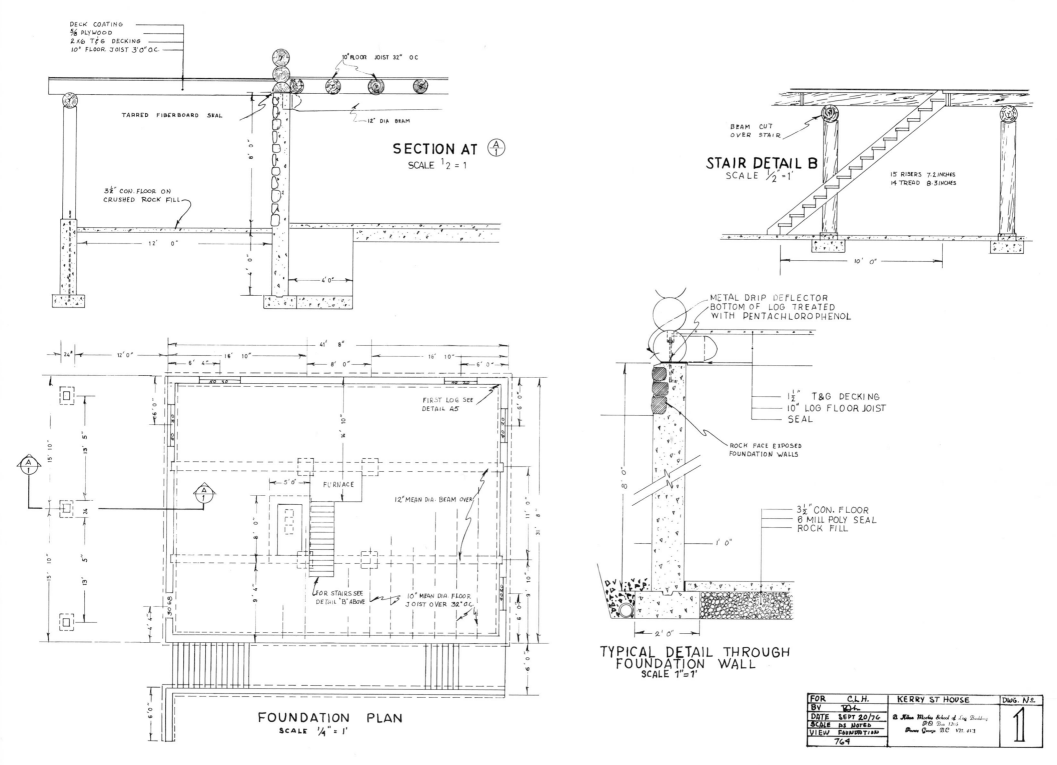

DECK COATING
⅝ PLYWOOD
2×6 T&G DECKING
10" FLOOR JOIST 3'0" O.C.

10" FLOOR JOIST 32" O.C.

TARRED FIBERBOARD SEAL

12" DIA BEAM

SECTION AT Ⓐ₁
SCALE ½ = 1

3½" CON. FLOOR ON
CRUSHED ROCK FILL

12' 0"

1' 0"

4' 0"

8' 0"

BEAM CUT
OVER STAIR

STAIR DETAIL B
SCALE ½ = 1'

15 RISERS 7.2 INCHES
14 TREAD 8.3 INCHES

10' 0"

METAL DRIP DEFLECTOR
BOTTOM OF LOG TREATED
WITH PENTACHLOROPHENOL

1½" T&G DECKING
10" LOG FLOOR JOIST
SEAL

ROCK FACE EXPOSED
FOUNDATION WALLS

3½" CON. FLOOR
6 MILL POLY SEAL
ROCK FILL

8' 0"

1' 0"

2' 0"

**TYPICAL DETAIL THROUGH
FOUNDATION WALL**
SCALE 1"=1'

24" 12' 0"

41' 8"

6' 4" 16' 10" 8' 0" 16' 10" 6' 0"

6' 6"

15' 10"

13' 5"

24

15' 10"

5"

13' 5"

4' 4"

FIRST LOG SEE
DETAIL A5

14' 10"

Ⓐ₁

Ⓐ₁

5' 0"

FURNACE

12" MEAN DIA. BEAM OVER

FOR STAIRS SEE
DETAIL "B" ABOVE

10" MEAN DIA. FLOOR
JOIST OVER 32" O.C.

8' 0"

9' 4"

11' 8"

31' 8"

9' 10"

6' 10"

6' 0"

6' 0"

FOUNDATION PLAN
SCALE ¼"= 1'

FOR	C.L.H.	KERRY ST HOUSE	DWG. No.
BY	TDL		
DATE	SEPT 20/76	B. Allan Mackie School of Log Building	**1**
SCALE	AS NOTED	PO Box 1205	
VIEW	FOUNDATION	Prince George B.C. V2L 4V3	
764			

116

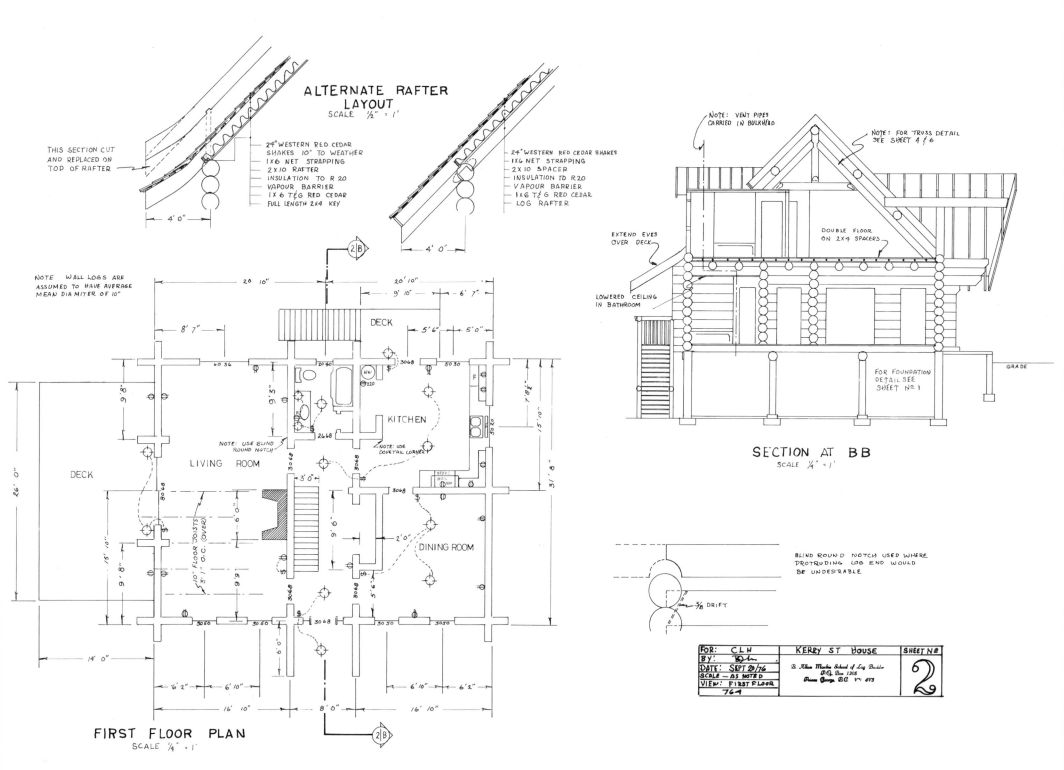

ALTERNATE RAFTER
LAYOUT
SCALE ½" = 1'

THIS SECTION CUT
AND REPLACED ON
TOP OF RAFTER

24" WESTERN RED CEDAR
SHAKES 10" TO WEATHER
1X6 NET STRAPPING
2X10 RAFTER
INSULATION TO R 20
VAPOUR BARRIER
1X 6 T&G RED CEDAR
FULL LENGTH 2X4 KEY

24" WESTERN RED CEDAR SHAKES
1X6 NET STRAPPING
2X10 SPACER
INSULATION TO R20
VAPOUR BARRIER
1X6 T&G RED CEDAR
LOG RAFTER

4' 0"

4' 0"

NOTE: VENT PIPES
CARRIED IN BULKHEAD

NOTE: FOR TRUSS DETAIL
SEE SHEET 4 & 6

EXTEND EVES
OVER DECK

DOUBLE FLOOR
ON 2X4 SPACERS

LOWERED CEILING
IN BATHROOM

FOR FOUNDATION
DETAIL SEE
SHEET N° 1

GRADE

SECTION AT BB
SCALE ¼" = 1'

NOTE   WALL LOGS ARE
ASSUMED TO HAVE AVERAGE
MEAN DIAMETER OF 10"

20' 10"

20' 10"

9' 10"

6' 7"

8' 7"

DECK

5' 6"

5' 0"

3068

5030

9' 8"

6036

2040

3068

HW
220

9' 3"

F

DECK

2668

KITCHEN

NOTE: USE
DOVETAIL CORNER

50 26

26' 0"

NOTE: USE BLIND
ROUND NOTCH

LIVING ROOM

3068

3068

3068

STOVE
HOT
220

15' 10"

7' 8½"

31' 8"

3' 0"

15' 10"

9' 8"

8068

3'-0" FLOOR JOISTS
3'-1" O.C. (OVER)

6' 0"

9' 6"

DINING ROOM

2' 0"

9' 8"

9' 9"

3068

3068

5' 6"

BLIND ROUND NOTCH USED WHERE
PROTRUDING LOG END WOULD
BE UNDESIRABLE

14' 0"

6' 0"

3050

30 50

3068

3050

3050

⅜ DRIFT

6' 2"

6' 10"

6' 10"

6' 2"

16' 10"

8' 0"

16' 10"

FIRST FLOOR PLAN
SCALE ¼" = 1'

FOR:	CLH	KERRY ST HOUSE	SHEET N°
BY:		B. Allan Mackie School of Log Buildg	
DATE:	SEPT 20/76	P.O. Box 1205	2
SCALE — AS NOTED		Prince George B.C. V²ⁿ 4V3	
VIEW: FIRST FLOOR			
761			

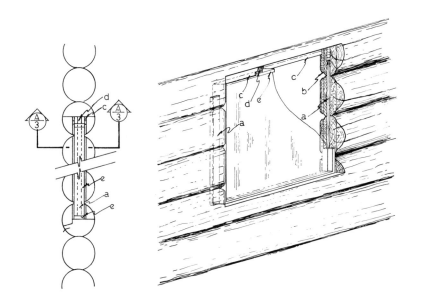

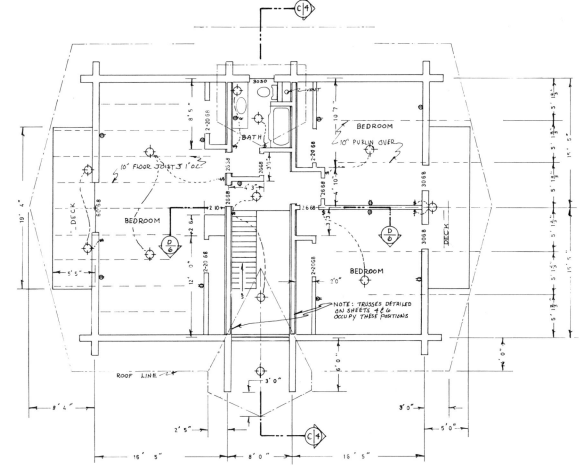

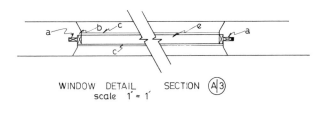

WINDOW DETAIL   SECTION (A|3)
scale 1' = 1'

a   KEY PIECE (2×4)
b   JAMB FOR WINDOW FRAME
c   SKIRTING FOR SETTLING SPACE
d   INSULATION
e   WINDOW FRAME

SECOND FLOOR PLAN
SCALE ¼ 1

BEDROOM

BATH

BEDROOM

BEDROOM

DECK

DECK

ROOF LINE

NOTE: TRUSSES DETAILED
ON SHEETS 4 & 6
OCCUPY THESE POSITIONS

10" FLOOR JOIST 3' 1" O.C.

10" PURLIN OVER

FOR:	C.L.H.	KERRY ST HOUSE	DWG Nº
BY:	BAM.		**3**
DATE:	OCT 18/76		
SCALE:	¼" = 1'		
VIEW:	SECOND FLOOR		
764			

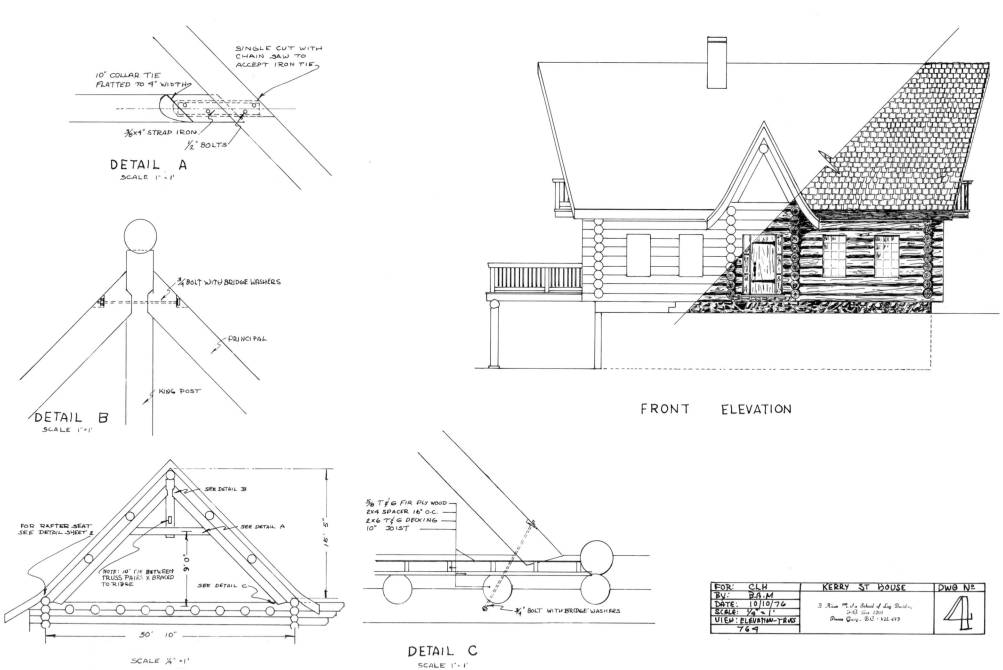

SINGLE CUT WITH
CHAIN SAW TO
ACCEPT IRON TIE

10" COLLAR TIE
FLATTED TO 4" WIDTH

3/8 x 4" STRAP IRON
1/2" BOLTS

DETAIL A
SCALE 1" = 1'

3/4 BOLT WITH BRIDGE WASHERS

PRINCIPAL

KING POST

DETAIL B
SCALE 1" = 1'

SEE DETAIL B

FOR RAFTER SEAT
SEE DETAIL SHEET 2

SEE DETAIL A

(NOTE: 10" TIE BETWEEN
TRUSS PAIRS X BRACED
TO RIDGE

SEE DETAIL C

16' 5"

9' 0"

50' 10"

SCALE 1/4" = 1'

SECTION C-C

5/8 T&G FIR PLY WOOD
2x4 SPACER 16" O.C.
2x6 T&G DECKING
10" JOIST

3/4" BOLT WITH BRIDGE WASHERS

DETAIL C
SCALE 1" = 1'

FRONT ELEVATION

FOR:	CLH	KERRY ST HOUSE	DWG Nº
BY:	B.A.M		
DATE:	10/10/76	B. Allan M. et a School of Log Building	4
SCALE:	1/4" = 1'	S.O. Box 1205	
VIEW:	ELEVATION-TRUSS	Prince George, B.C. V2L 4V3	
	769		

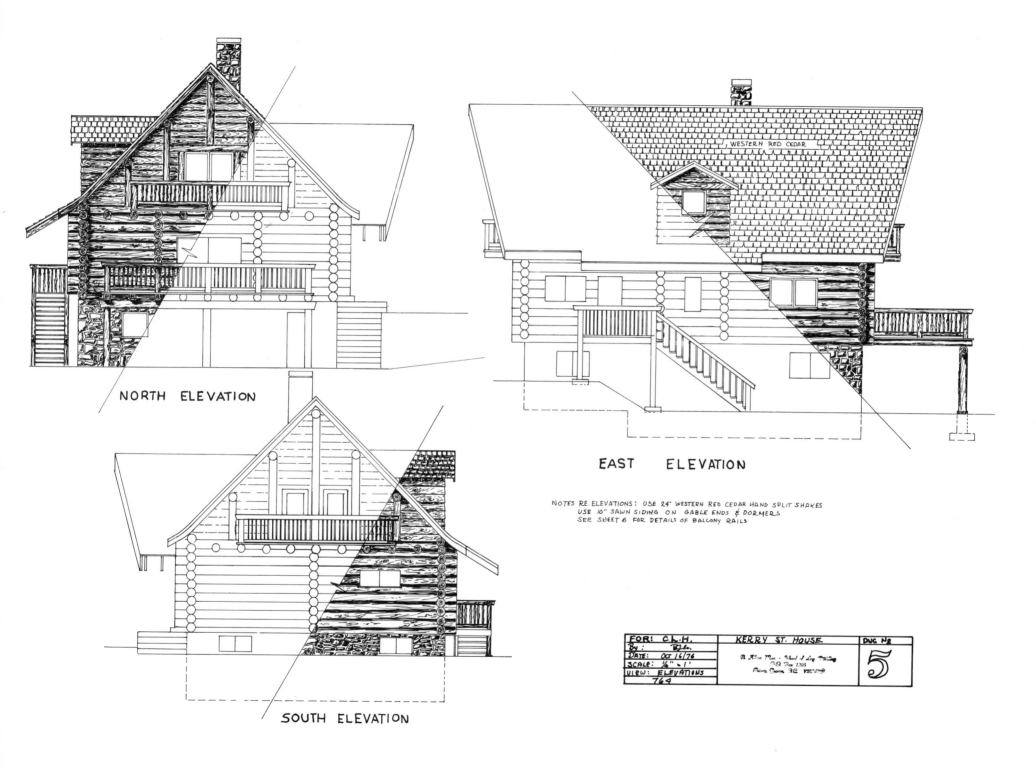

NORTH ELEVATION

EAST ELEVATION

SOUTH ELEVATION

, WESTERN RED CEDAR

NOTES RE. ELEVATIONS: USE 24" WESTERN RED CEDAR HAND SPLIT SHAKES
USE 10" SAWN SIDING ON GABLE ENDS & DORMERS
SEE SHEET 6 FOR DETAILS OF BALCONY RAILS

FOR: CL.H.	KERRY ST. HOUSE	DWG N<u>o</u>
BY: BJ.m.		
DATE: OCT 16/76	B. Allan Mac. School of Log Building	5
SCALE: ¼" = 1'	P.O. Box 1305	
VIEW: ELEVATIONS	Prince George, B.C. V2L 4V3	
764		

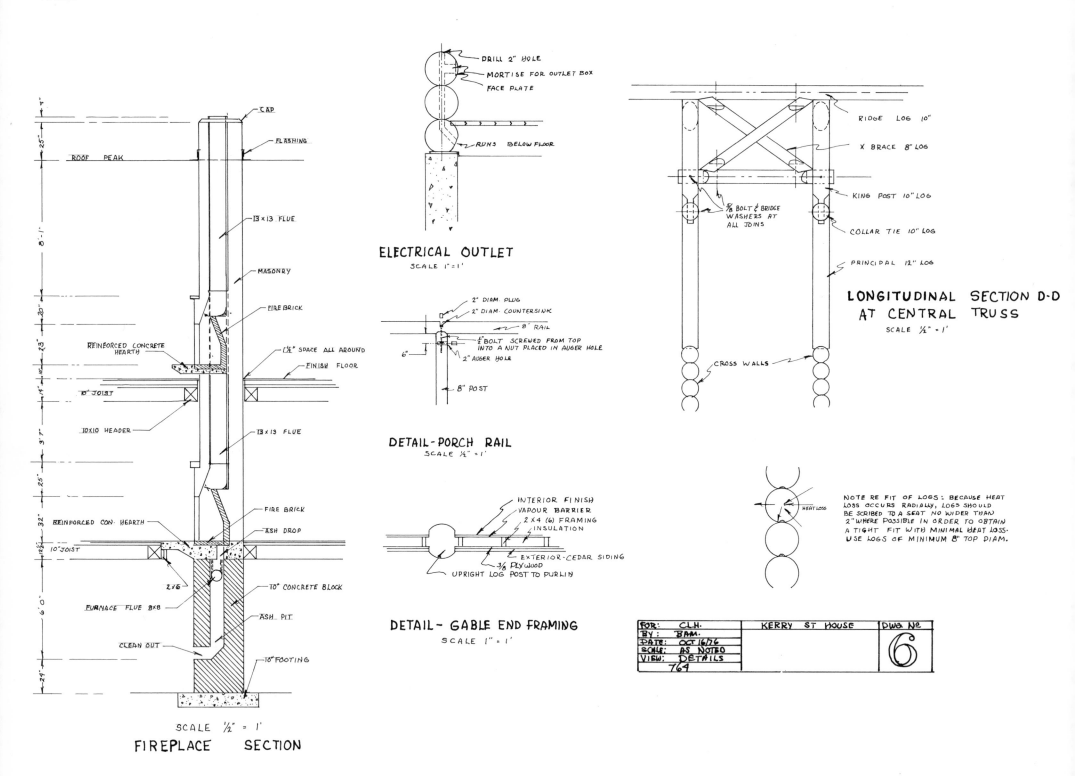

FIREPLACE SECTION
SCALE ½" = 1'

CAP
FLASHING
ROOF PEAK
13 × 13 FLUE
MASONRY
FIRE BRICK
1½" SPACE ALL AROUND
REINFORCED CONCRETE HEARTH
FINISH FLOOR
10" JOIST
10×10 HEADER
13 × 13 FLUE
FIRE BRICK
REINFORCED CON. HEARTH
ASH DROP
10" JOIST
2 × 6
10" CONCRETE BLOCK
FURNACE FLUE 8×8
ASH PIT
CLEAN OUT
10" FOOTING

ELECTRICAL OUTLET
SCALE 1" = 1'

DRILL 2" HOLE
MORTISE FOR OUTLET BOX
FACE PLATE
2" RUNS BELOW FLOOR

DETAIL - PORCH RAIL
SCALE ½" = 1'

2" DIAM. PLUG
2" DIAM. COUNTERSINK
8" RAIL
½" BOLT SCREWED FROM TOP INTO A NUT PLACED IN AUGER HOLE
6"
2" AUGER HOLE
8" POST

DETAIL - GABLE END FRAMING
SCALE 1" = 1'

INTERIOR FINISH
VAPOUR BARRIER
2 × 4 (6) FRAMING INSULATION
EXTERIOR CEDAR SIDING
3/8 PLYWOOD
UPRIGHT LOG POST TO PURLIN

LONGITUDINAL SECTION D-D AT CENTRAL TRUSS
SCALE ½" = 1'

RIDGE LOG 10"
X BRACE 8" LOG
KING POST 10" LOG
COLLAR TIE 10" LOG
PRINCIPAL 12" LOG
5/8 BOLT & BRIDGE WASHERS AT ALL JOINS
CROSS WALLS

HEAT LOSS

NOTE RE FIT OF LOGS: BECAUSE HEAT LOSS OCCURS RADIALLY, LOGS SHOULD BE SCRIBED TO A SEAT NO WIDER THAN 2" WHERE POSSIBLE IN ORDER TO OBTAIN A TIGHT FIT WITH MINIMAL HEAT LOSS. USE LOGS OF MINIMUM 8" TOP DIAM.

FOR:	CLH.	KERRY ST HOUSE	DWG №
BY:	BAM.		
DATE:	OCT 16/76		**6**
SCALE:	AS NOTED		
VIEW:	DETAILS		
	764		

Many, many people who visited the home said how beautiful, how grand it was . . . and yet, if you examine it in the blueprint, it is in actuality only a basic house. It is simple, uncluttered, and I think, quite realistic. If it becomes grandly beautiful, then, it is only because the builder cares enough to execute the work well, and the owners care enough to furnish the home well. And I like that aspect of the house responding to people's efforts.

The upstairs provides one very large bedroom and two normal sized bedrooms plus a full bathroom. These are achieved within the high-pitched roof, and is also an economy in both time and materials.

In drawing the original design, I included far more detail than is usually done in order to show building practices which otherwise may be unfamiliar. This was primarily for my own students' understanding. But many others have used these blueprints simply for study. They are unusual in this respect.

I believe that the Kerry Street, then, is the basic log house which anybody could build with a reasonable prospect of achieving a fine home. It is straightforward, very strong, economical of time and materials, handsome, and is, I've been told, a most pleasant home to live in.

For those interested in dollars and cents, it cost $68,300.00 to build the house and to buy the lot, in 1974 and was sold at cost by the College where I, at that time, taught. When the young owners were transferred to Greenland in 1978, the house went on the market for just over $100,000.00.

There's a remarkable thing about the Kerry Street house and its blueprint. This is the most popular of all the blueprints offered in the past 6 years by way of The Canadian Log House magazine. I've seen the Kerry Street houseplan built many times by many different builders. It is never the same house twice; each time it is built, despite its straightforward simplicity, it is the reflection of a new builder, a new owner, or a new location.

I once requested permission from a log home owner to show their house and plan. It was politely refused on the basis that the owners didn't want to see "rows and rows of houses just like theirs". This puzzled me, but I certainly accepted their right to any opinion that pleased them. They welcomed me into their home, incidentally, and I was completely astonished to discover that its interior was an absolute stereotype of any "3-br bung" in any city suburb. There would have been nothing to show off. Only the exterior was handsome, for it was natural log in very pleasing proportions. So I developed a strong hunch, then and there, even though it was very early in the log construction "boom", that no two log houses would ever be recognizably alike. The Kerry Street house proved it. I've only seen echoes of it, and a delightful harmonious song it does make, all across this nation, now.

#751

This house provides solid design with a high degree of style and efficiency. It makes maximum use of the logs and it also makes maximum use of floor area.

Square feet: 1,200

Originally designed as a project which my young son built, the design has been picked up by others who have built it in several regions of Canada.

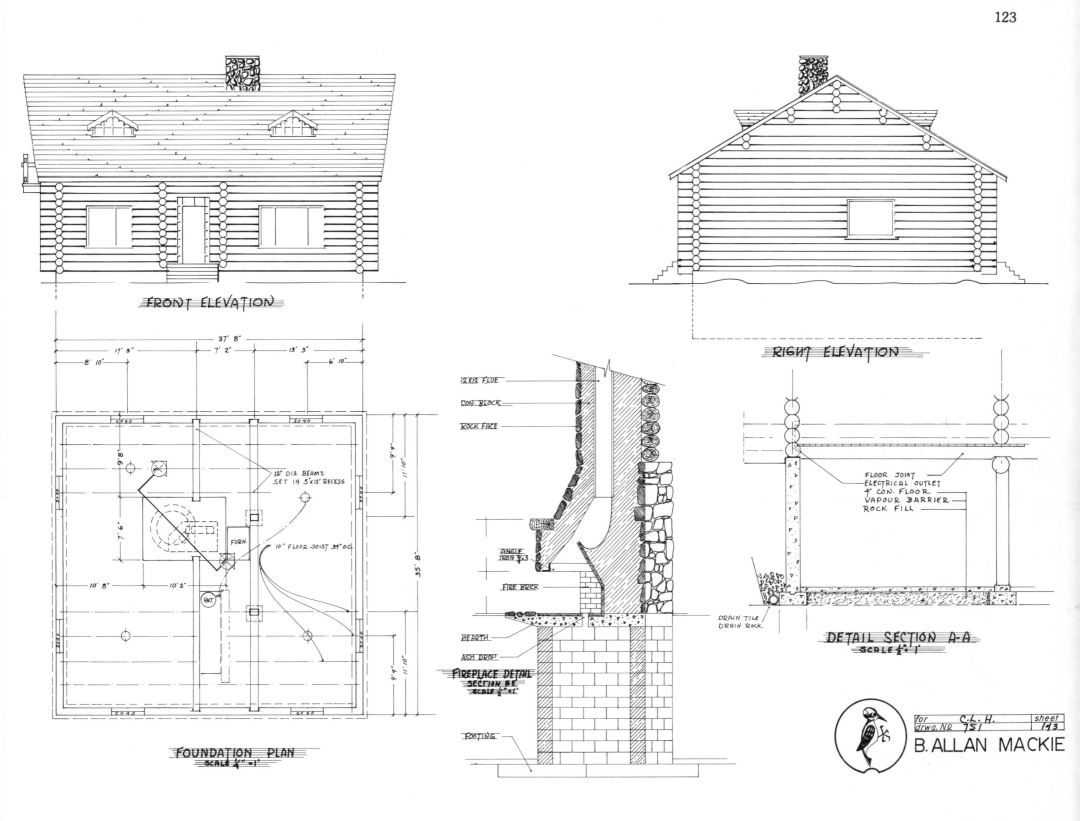

FRONT ELEVATION

RIGHT ELEVATION

FOUNDATION PLAN
SCALE ¼"=1'

FIREPLACE DETAIL
SECTION B-E
SCALE ¼"=1'

DETAIL SECTION A-A
SCALE ¼"=1'

37' 8"
17' 3"
7' 2"
13' 3"
8' 10"
6' 10"
9' 8"
9' 3"
11' 10"
35' 8"
7' 6"
10' 8"
10' 2"
9' 3"
11' 10"

12" DIA. BEAMS
SET IN 5"×12" RECESS

10" FLOOR JOIST 34" O.C.

FURN.

HWT.

12×12 FLUE
CON. BLOCK
ROCK FACE
ANGLE IRON ⅜×3
FIRE BRICK
HEARTH
ASH DROP
FOOTING

FLOOR JOIST
ELECTRICAL OUTLET
4" CON. FLOOR
VAPOUR BARRIER
ROCK FILL

DRAIN TILE
DRAIN ROCK.

for C.L.H.
drwg. No 951
sheet 143

B. ALLAN MACKIE

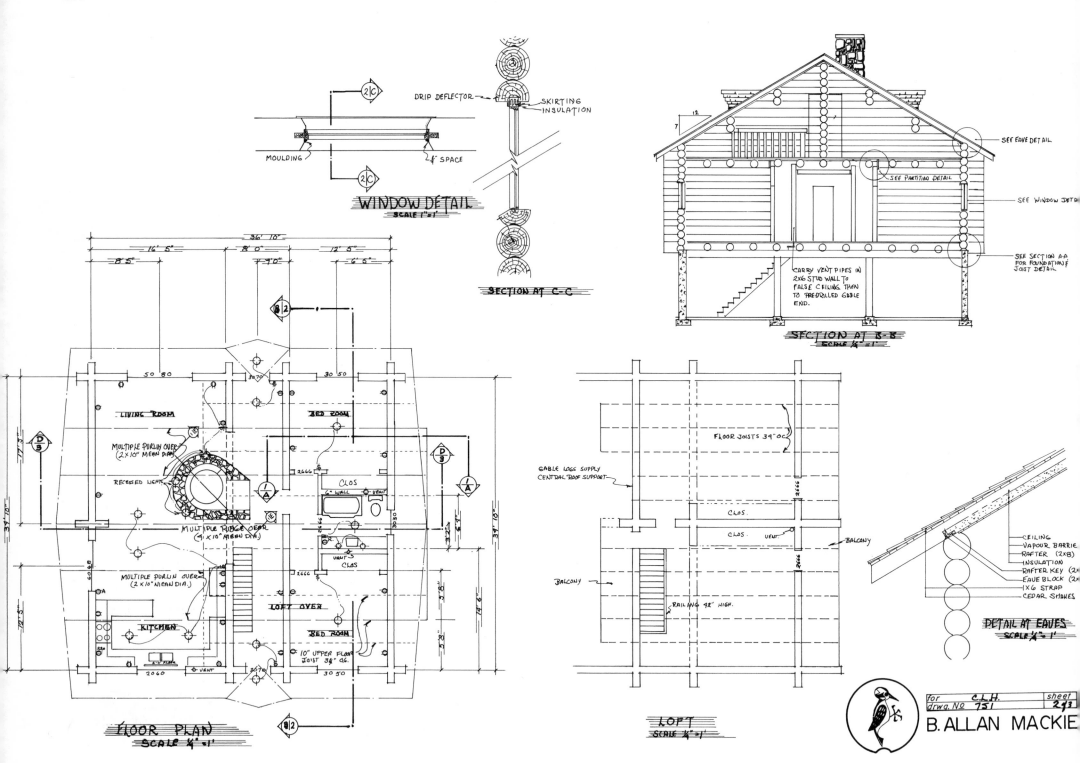

DRIP DEFLECTOR
SKIRTING
INSULATION
MOULDING
4" SPACE

WINDOW DETAIL
SCALE 1"=1'

SECTION AT C-C

SEE EAVE DETAIL

SEE PARTITION DETAIL

SEE WINDOW DETAIL

SEE SECTION A-A
FOR FOUNDATION &
JOIST DETAIL

CARRY VENT PIPES IN
2x6 STUD WALL TO
FALSE CEILING THEN
TO PREDRILLED GABLE
END.

SECTION AT B-B
SCALE ¼"=1'

36' 10"
16' 5"   8' 0"   12' 5"
8' 5"   7' 0"   6' 5"

LIVING ROOM
BED ROOM

50 80   30 50

MULTIPLE PURLIN OVER
(2x10" MEAN DIAM.)

RECESSED LIGHTS

CLOS
6" WALL   VENT

MULTIPLE RIDGE OVER
(4x10" MEAN DIA.)

CLOS

MULTIPLE PURLIN OVER
(2x10" MEAN DIA.)

2666

LOFT OVER

KITCHEN

BED ROOM

10" UPPER FLOOR
JOIST 34" OC.

2060   VENT   30 50

FLOOR PLAN
SCALE ¼"=1'

FLOOR JOISTS 39"OC

GABLE LOGS SUPPLY
CENTRAL ROOF SUPPORT

CLOS.
CLOS.   VENT

BALCONY

BALCONY

RAILING 42" HIGH.

LOFT
SCALE ¼"=1'

CEILING
VAPOUR BARRIER
RAFTER (2x8)
INSULATION
RAFTER KEY (2x
EAVE BLOCK (2x
1x6 STRAP
CEDAR SHAKES

DETAIL AT EAVES
SCALE ¼"=1'

for   C.L.H.   sheet
drwg. No. 751   2 of 3

B. ALLAN MACKIE

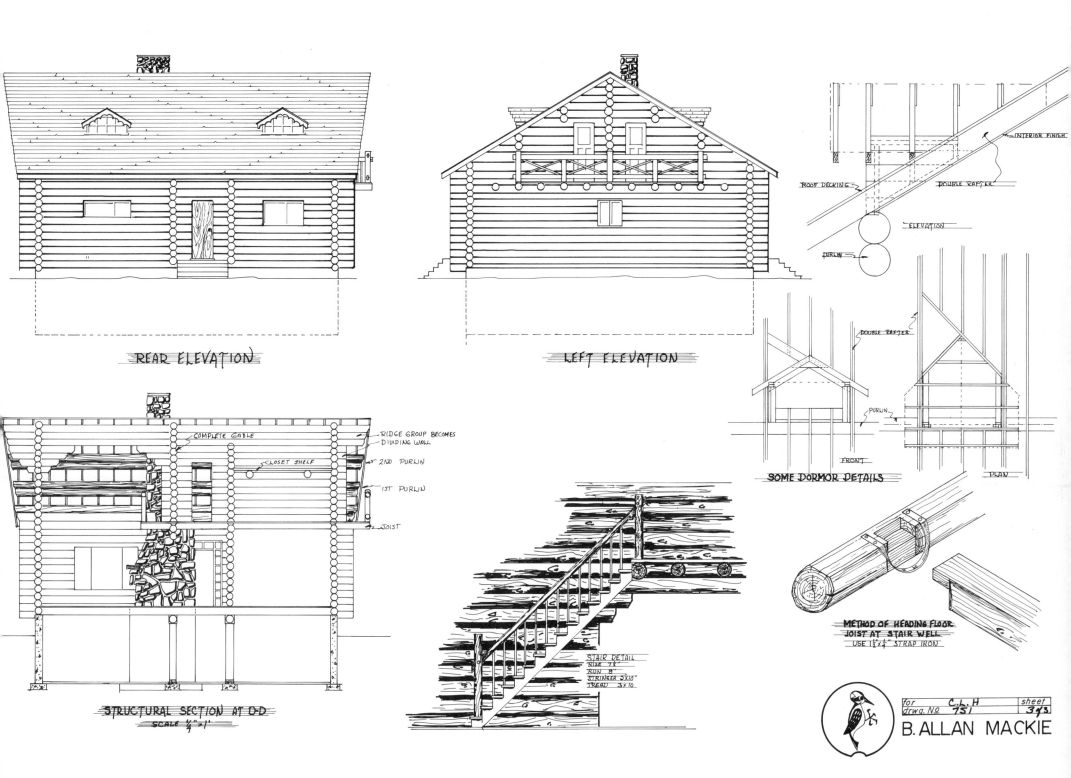

REAR ELEVATION

LEFT ELEVATION

INTERIOR FINISH

ROOF DECKING

DOUBLE RAFTER

ELEVATION

PURLIN

DOUBLE RAFTER

PURLIN

FRONT

PLAN

SOME DORMOR DETAILS

COMPLETE GABLE

RIDGE GROUP BECOMES
DIVIDING WALL

CLOSET SHELF

2ND PURLIN

1ST PURLIN

JOIST

STRUCTURAL SECTION AT D-D
SCALE ¼" = 1'

STAIR DETAIL
RISE 7⅜"
RUN 8"
STRINGER 3x10"
TREAD 3x10

METHOD OF HEADING FLOOR
JOIST AT STAIR WELL
USE 1½"x¼" STRAP IRON

for C.L.H   sheet
drwg. No. 751   3/3

B. ALLAN MACKIE

#752 **Square feet: 1,000**

I have lived in this house and can vouch for the fact that it provides free, casual, yet efficient living space. It is a good, unassuming little house suited to almost any environment.

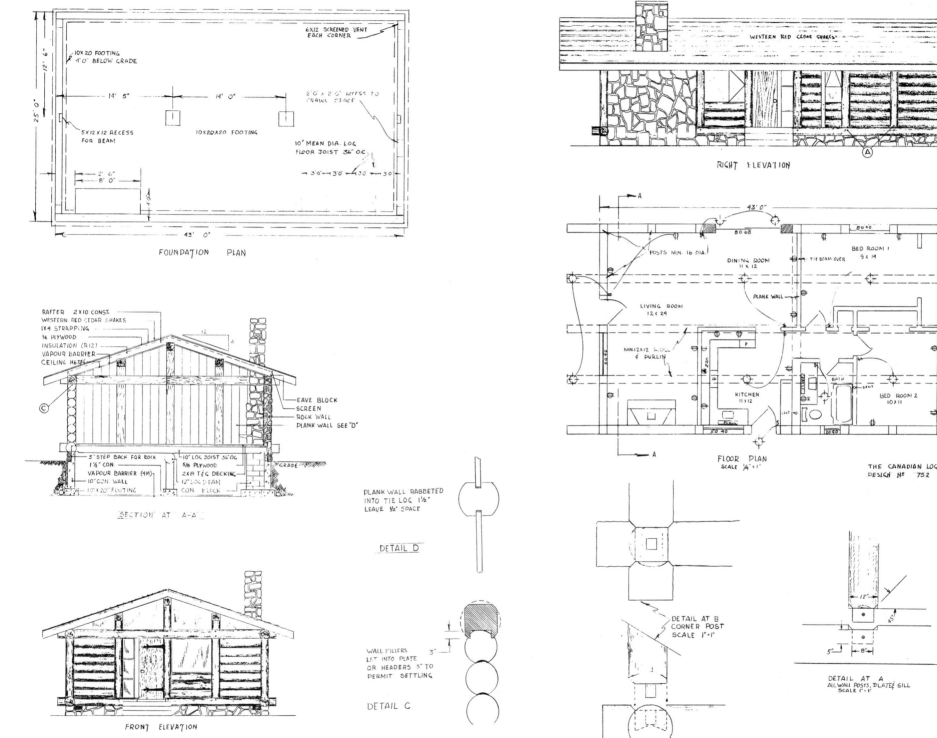

FOUNDATION PLAN

10X20 FOOTING 4'0" BELOW GRADE

6X12 SCREENED VENT EACH CORNER

5X12X12 RECESS FOR BEAM

10X20X20 FOOTING

2'0" X 2'0" ACCESS TO CRAWL SPACE

10" MEAN DIA. LOG FLOOR JOIST 36" OC

WESTERN RED CEDAR SHAKES

RIGHT ELEVATION

RAFTER 2X10 CONST.
WESTERN RED CEDAR SHAKES
1X4 STRAPPING
⅜ PLYWOOD
INSULATION (R12)
VAPOUR BARRIER
CEILING 1467G

EAVE BLOCK
SCREEN
ROCK WALL
PLANK WALL SEE "D"

5" STEP BACK FOR ROCK
1½" CON.
VAPOUR BARRIER (4M)
10" CON. WALL
10" X 20" FOOTING

10" LOG JOIST 36"OC
5/8 PLYWOOD
2X8 T&G DECKING
12" LOG BEAM
CON. BLOCK

GRADE

SECTION AT A-A

PLANK WALL RABBETED INTO TIE LOG 1½" LEAVE ½" SPACE

DETAIL D

WALL FILLERS LET INTO PLATE OR HEADERS 3" TO PERMIT SETTLING

DETAIL C

FLOOR PLAN
SCALE ¼"=1'

POSTS MIN. 16 DIA.

DINING ROOM 11 X 12

TIE BEAM OVER

BED ROOM 1 9 X 14

LIVING ROOM 12 X 29

PLANK WALL

MIN 12X12 RIDGE & PURLIN

KITCHEN 11 X 12

BATH

BED ROOM 2 10 X 11

THE CANADIAN LOG HOUSE
DESIGN Nº 752 B.A. MACKIE

FRONT ELEVATION

DETAIL AT B
CORNER POST
SCALE 1"=1'

DETAIL AT A
ALL WALL POSTS, PLATE& SILL
SCALE 1"=1'

#753 Square feet: 1,500

This is a very solid two-bedroom house which I designed for two purposes. First, it maximizes the flexibility and beauty of timber and stone. Second, it provided enough corners, or notches, to keep a highly enthusiastic, very energetic group of students busy. There are 23 corners in a complete round, including a dovetailed bow window, which put an absolute stop to all complaints by students of having to wait while others completed their notch. The building provided a challenge to this group and caught their imagination by its growth. We were all very pleasantly surprised by its beauty which, in large part, was due to the efforts of that special group.

Designed to be fussy, pretty, and a compliment to the skill of the builder as well as to the materials, this house will tax the energy of the builder as well as his expertise. It might be especially appropriate for the home of a builder who wishes to use it as a display home. There's much truth in the saying that a man's buildings are his diploma.

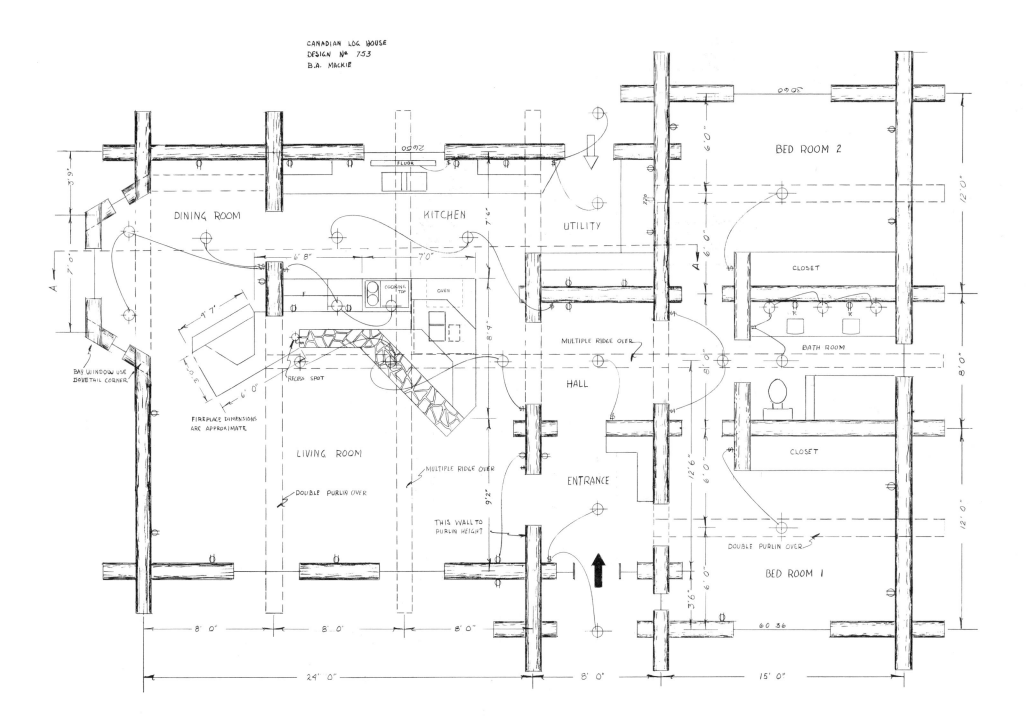

CANADIAN LOG HOUSE
DESIGN Nº 753
B.A. MACKIE

BED ROOM 2

DINING ROOM

KITCHEN

UTILITY

CLOSET

BATH ROOM

COOKING TOP

OVEN

FLUOR

BAY WINDOW USE
DOVETAIL CORNER

RECESS SPOT

FIREPLACE DIMENSIONS
ARE APPROXIMATE

MULTIPLE RIDGE OVER

HALL

LIVING ROOM

MULTIPLE RIDGE OVER

ENTRANCE

CLOSET

DOUBLE PURLIN OVER

THIS WALL TO
PURLIN HEIGHT

DOUBLE PURLIN OVER

BED ROOM 1

2650

3060

6' 8"   7' 0"

4' 7"

3' 0"

6' 0"

3' 9"

7' 0"

7' 6"

8' 9"

9' 2"

8' 0"

12' 6"

6' 0"

6' 0"

6' 0"

6' 0"

8' 0"

12' 0"

12' 0"

3' 6"

60 36

8' 0"   8' 0"   8' 0"

24' 0"

8' 0"

15' 0"

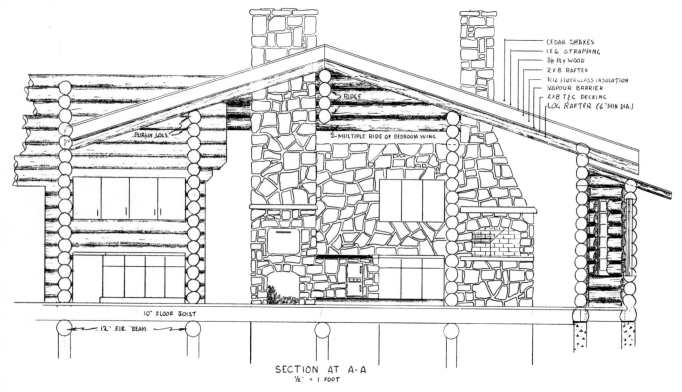

CEDAR SHAKES
1 X 6 STRAPPING
3/8 PLY WOOD
2 X 8 RAFTER
R12 FIBERGLASS INSULATION
VAPOUR BARRIER
2 X 8 T&G DECKING
LOG RAFTER (6" MIN DIA.)

RIDGE

PURLIN LOGS

2-MULTIPLE RIDE OF BEDROOM WING

10" FLOOR JOIST

12" FIR. BEAM

SECTION AT A-A
1/2" = 1 FOOT

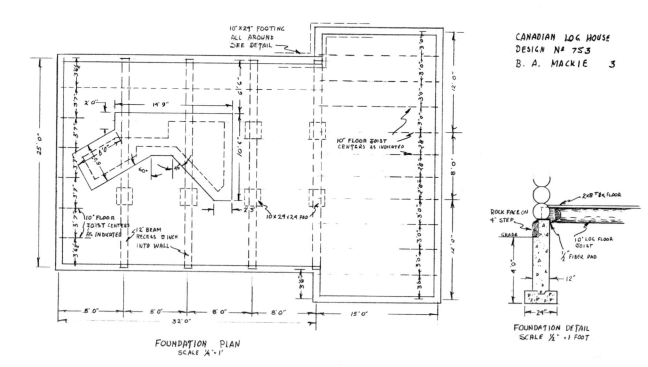

10"X24" FOOTING
ALL AROUND
SEE DETAIL

CANADIAN LOG HOUSE
DESIGN Nº 753
B. A. MACKIE   3

19'9"

2'0"

25'0"

6'0"

60°   45°

10" FLOOR JOIST
CENTERS AS INDICATED

10" FLOOR
JOIST CENTERS
AS INDICATED

12" BEAM
RECESS 3 INCH
INTO WALL

10 X 24 X 24 PAD

8'0"   8'0"   8'0"   8'0"   15'0"

32'0"

12'0"

8'0"

12'0"

FOUNDATION PLAN
SCALE 1/8" = 1'

2 X 8 T&G FLOOR

ROCK FACE ON
4" STEP

GRADE

10" LOG FLOOR
JOIST

1/2 FIBER PAD

4'0"

12"

24"

FOUNDATION DETAIL
SCALE 1/2" = 1 FOOT

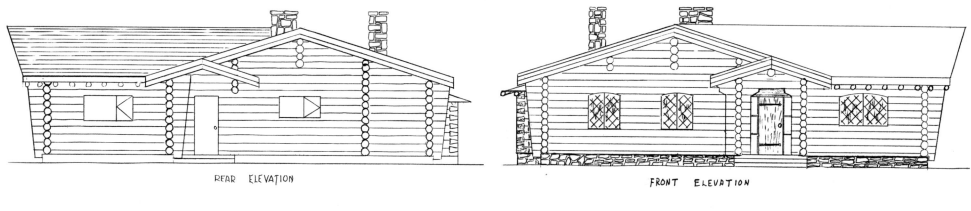

REAR ELEVATION

FRONT ELEVATION

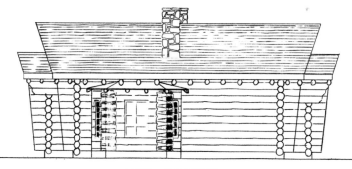

LEFT ELEVATION
SCALE ¼" = 1'

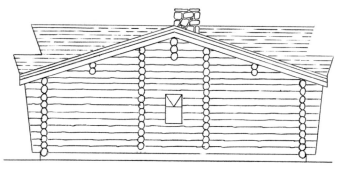

RIGHT ELEVATION
SCALE ¼" = 1'

CANADIAN LOG HOUSE
DESIGN Nº 753
B. A. MACKIE

#741   **Square feet: 3,300**

This large house contains a swimming pool and sauna as well as three additional bedrooms over the living room end of the house.

The design is sprawling, and yet not too complicated, but it will require the expert builder. It is capable of supplying gratifying accommodation for those who like this style.

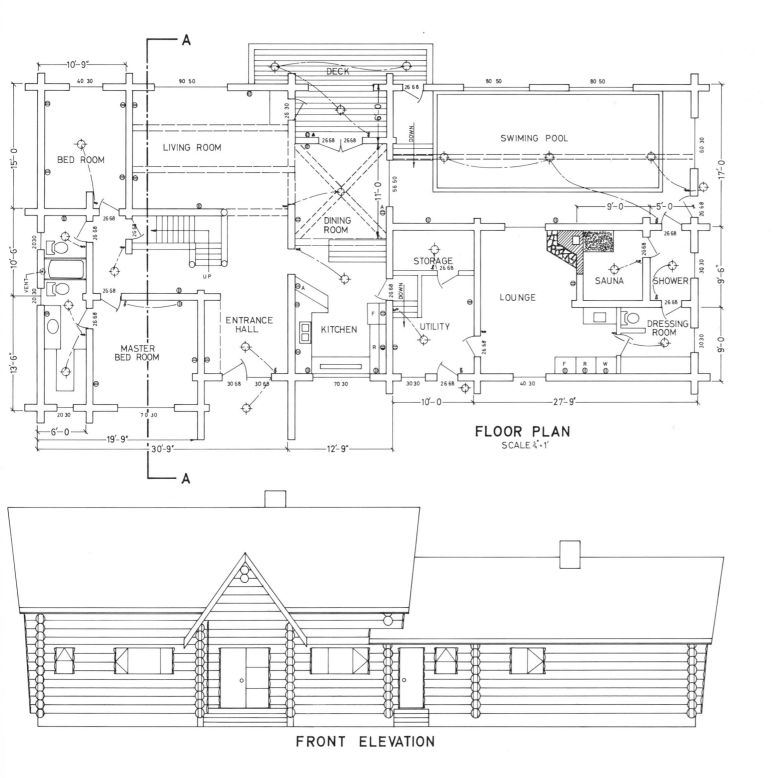

FLOOR PLAN
SCALE ¼"·1'

Rooms labeled: BED ROOM, LIVING ROOM, DECK, SWIMING POOL, DINING ROOM, STORAGE, SAUNA, SHOWER, LOUNGE, DRESSING ROOM, MASTER BED ROOM, ENTRANCE HALL, KITCHEN, UTILITY

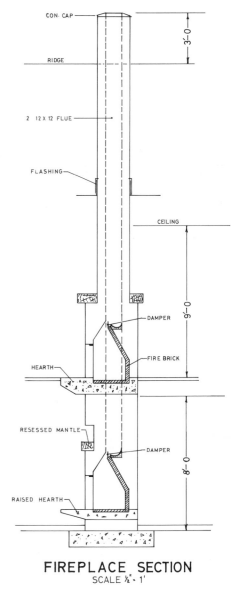

FIREPLACE SECTION
SCALE ¼"·1'

Labels: CON·CAP, RIDGE, 2 12 X 12 FLUE, FLASHING, CEILING, DAMPER, FIRE BRICK, HEARTH, RESESSED MANTLE, RAISED HEARTH

FRONT ELEVATION

for drwg. No 741   sheet 1-3

B. ALLAN MACKIE

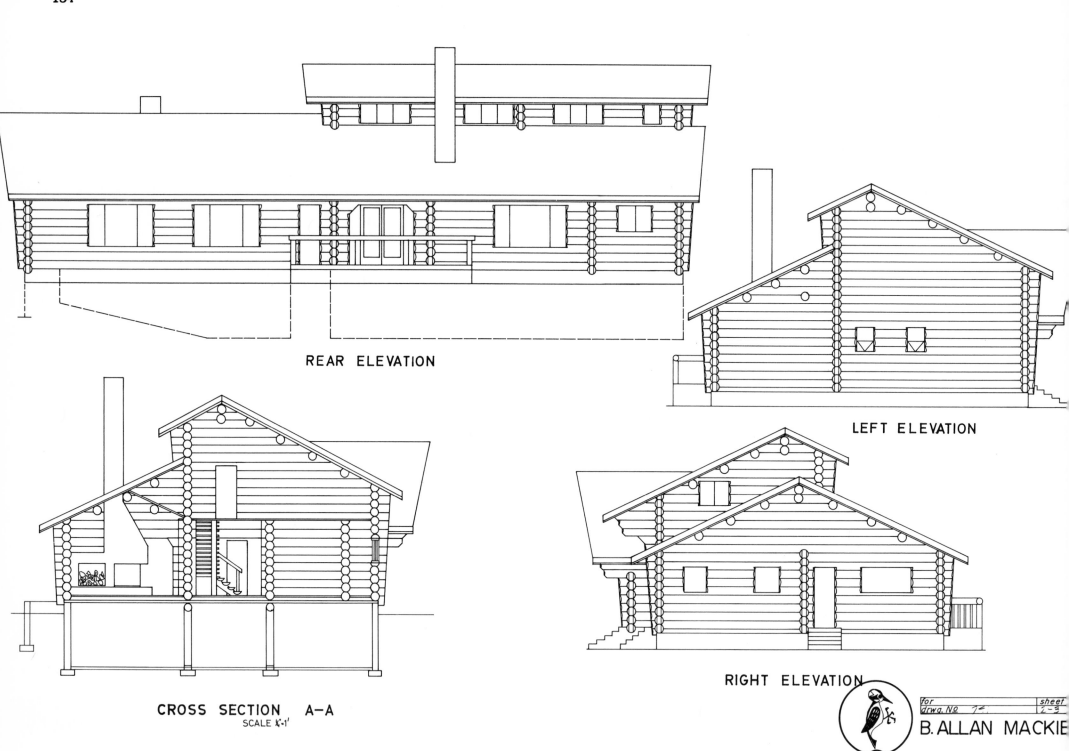

REAR ELEVATION

LEFT ELEVATION

CROSS SECTION A—A

SCALE ¼"-1'

RIGHT ELEVATION

for drwg. No 12

sheet 2-3

B. ALLAN MACKIE

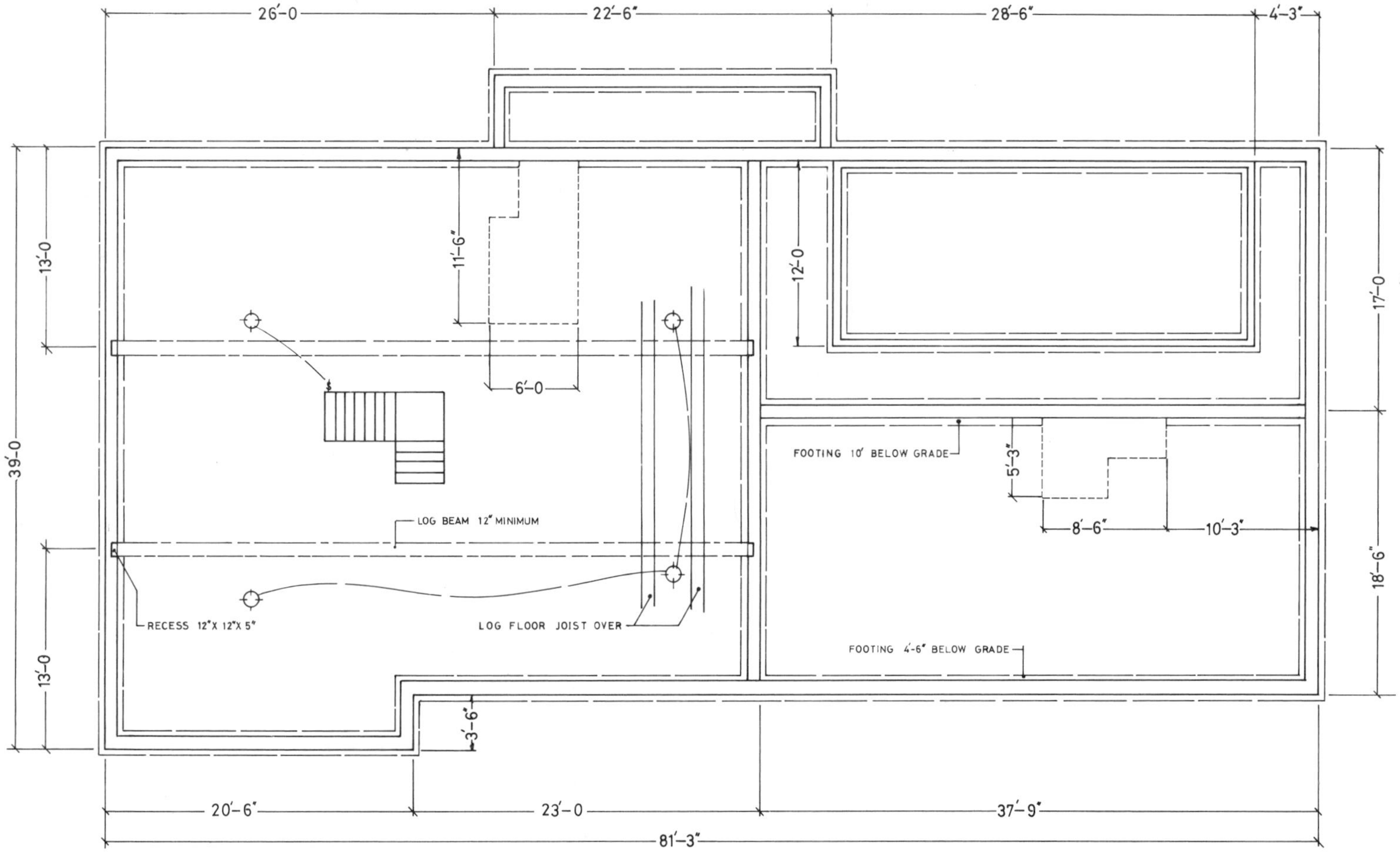

CUT OUT FOR BOX

2" HOLE

ELEVATION   SECTION

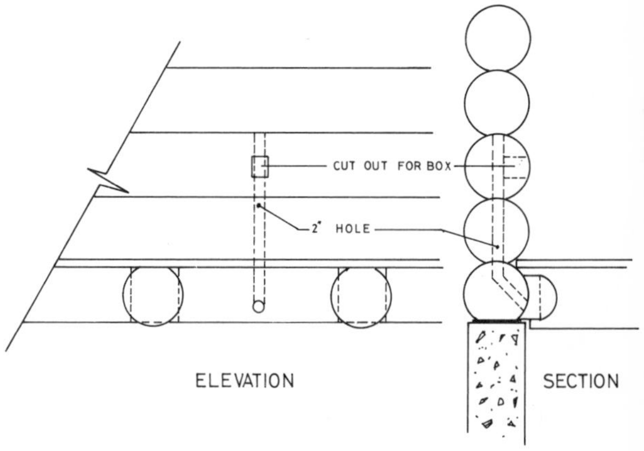

ELECTRICAL OUTLETS
SCALE 1"=1'

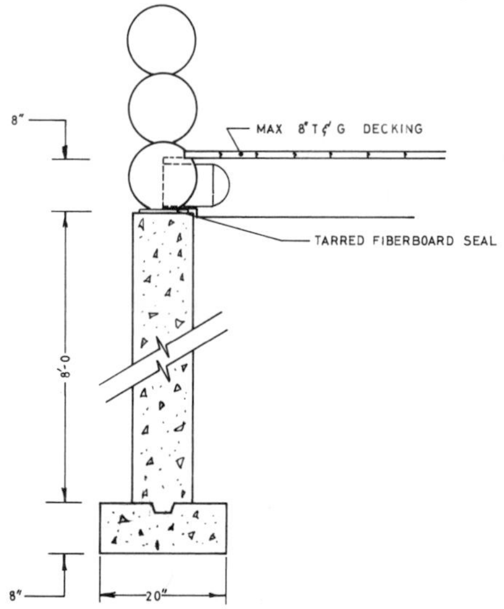

26'-0"   22'-6"   28'-6"   4'-3"

13'-0"

11'-6"

12'-0"

17'-0"

39'-0"

6'-0"

LOG BEAM 12" MINIMUM

FOOTING 10' BELOW GRADE

5'-3"

8'-6"   10'-3"

18'-6"

RECESS 12"X 12"X 5"

LOG FLOOR JOIST OVER

FOOTING 4'-6" BELOW GRADE

13'-0"

3'-6"

20'-6"   23'-0"   37'-9"

81'-3"

FOUNDATION PLAN
SCALE ¼"=1'

MAX 8" T & G DECKING

8"

TARRED FIBERBOARD SEAL

8'-0"

8"   20"

FOUNDATION DETAILS
SCALE 1"=1'

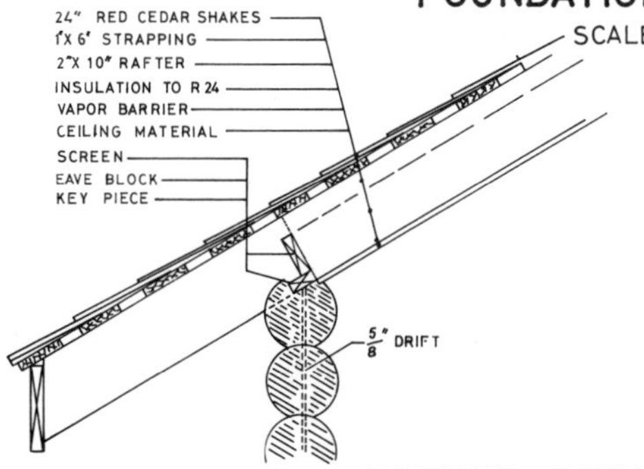

24" RED CEDAR SHAKES
1"X 6" STRAPPING
2"X 10" RAFTER
INSULATION TO R 24
VAPOR BARRIER
CEILING MATERIAL
SCREEN
EAVE BLOCK
KEY PIECE

5/8" DRIFT

RAFTER DETAILS
SCALE 1"=1'

for
drwg. No 72

sheet
8-9

B. ALLAN MACKIE

#742   *Square feet: 1,630*

This is another large house and fairly straightforward. Every corner of the basement is expected to perform some useful service.

In considering this plan, or the previous one, I would urge the home-owner to consider whether or not all these facilities could be consolidated into a more energy-efficient, two-storey house, before making the final choice.

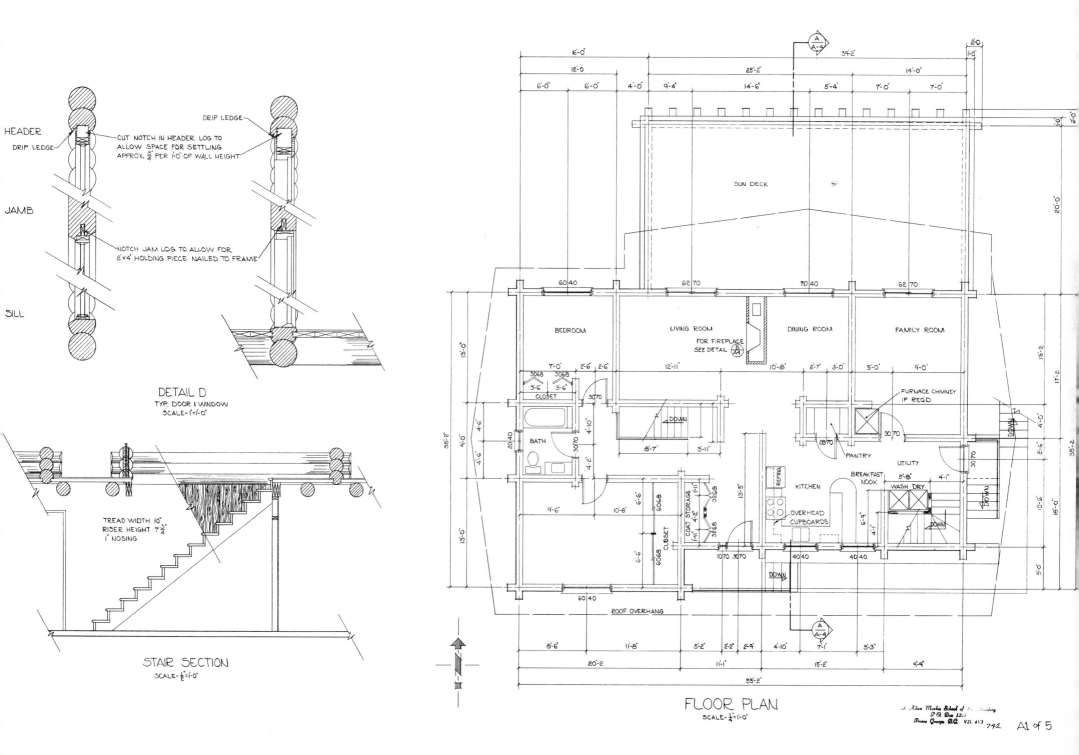

HEADER
DRIP LEDGE

DRIP LEDGE
CUT NOTCH IN HEADER LOG TO ALLOW SPACE FOR SETTLING APPROX. ⅜" PER 1'-0" OF WALL HEIGHT

JAMB

NOTCH JAM LOG TO ALLOW FOR 2"×4" HOLDING PIECE NAILED TO FRAME

SILL

DETAIL D
TYP. DOOR & WINDOW
SCALE- 1"=1'-0"

TREAD WIDTH 10"
RISER HEIGHT 7¼"
1" NOSING

STAIR SECTION
SCALE- ½"=1'-0"

FLOOR PLAN
SCALE- ¼"=1'-0"

A1 of 5

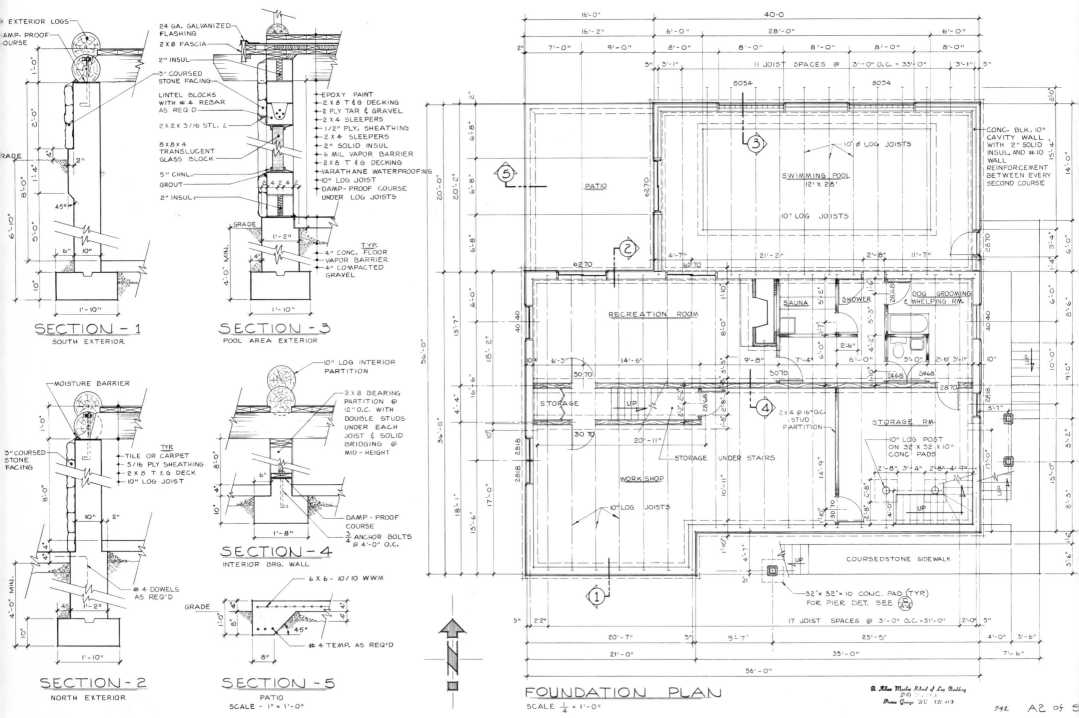

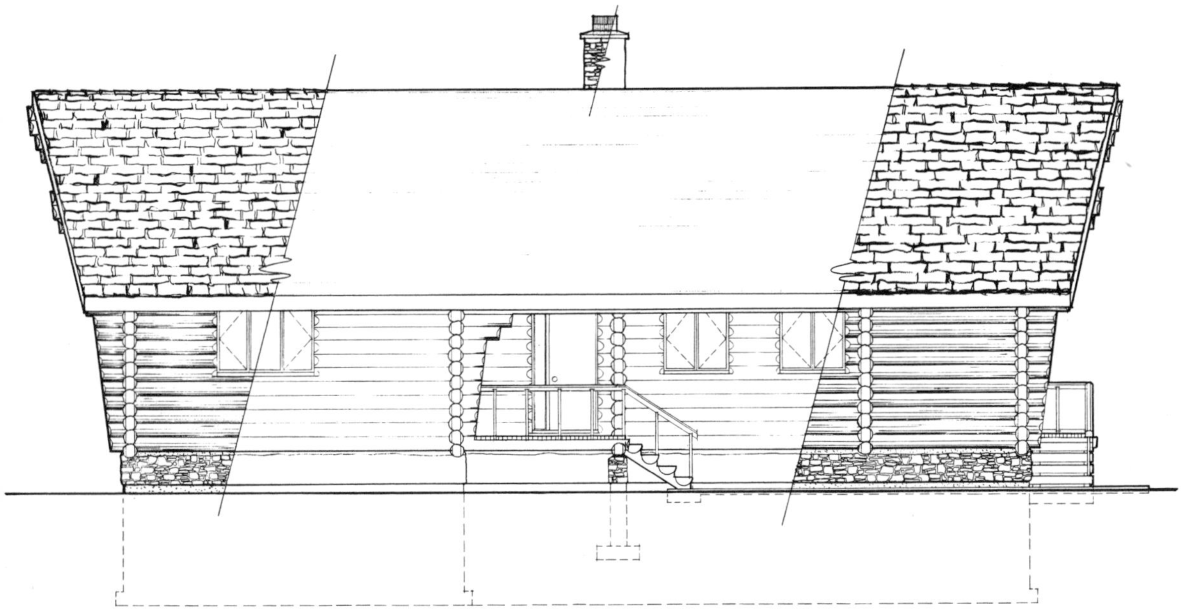

SOUTH ELEVATION

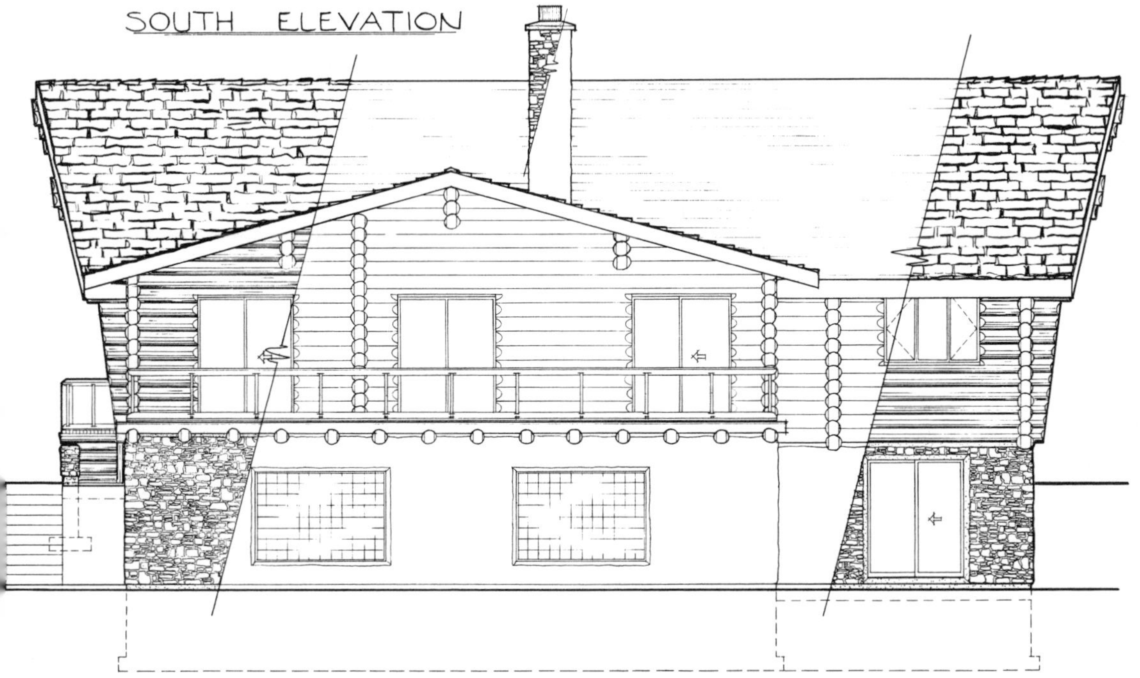

NORTH ELEVATION

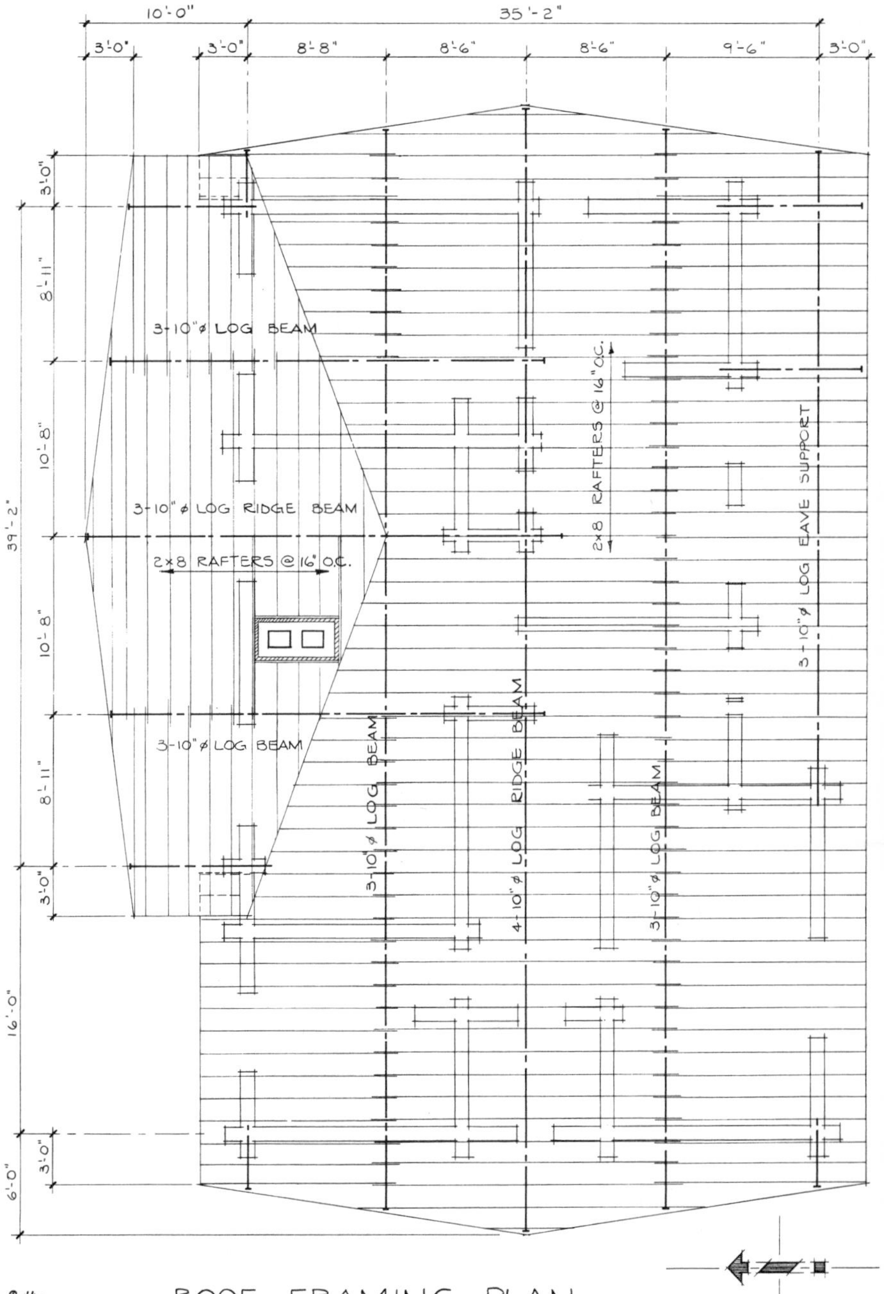

ROOF FRAMING PLAN

SCALE - ¼" = 1'-0"

3'-10"ø LOG BEAM

3'-10"ø LOG RIDGE BEAM

2×8 RAFTERS @ 16" O.C.

3'-10"ø LOG BEAM

2×8 RAFTERS @ 16" O.C.

3'-10"ø LOG EAVE SUPPORT

3'-10"ø LOG BEAM

4'-10"ø LOG RIDGE BEAM

3'-10"ø LOG BEAM

B. Allan Mackie School of Log Building
P.O. Box 1205
Prince George B.C. V2L 4V3

10'-0"   35'-2"

3'-0" 3'-0" 8'-8" 8'-6" 8'-6" 9'-6" 3'-0"

3'-0" 8'-11" 10'-8" 10'-8" 8'-11" 3'-0"

39'-2"

16'-0" 6'-0"

792   A3 of 5

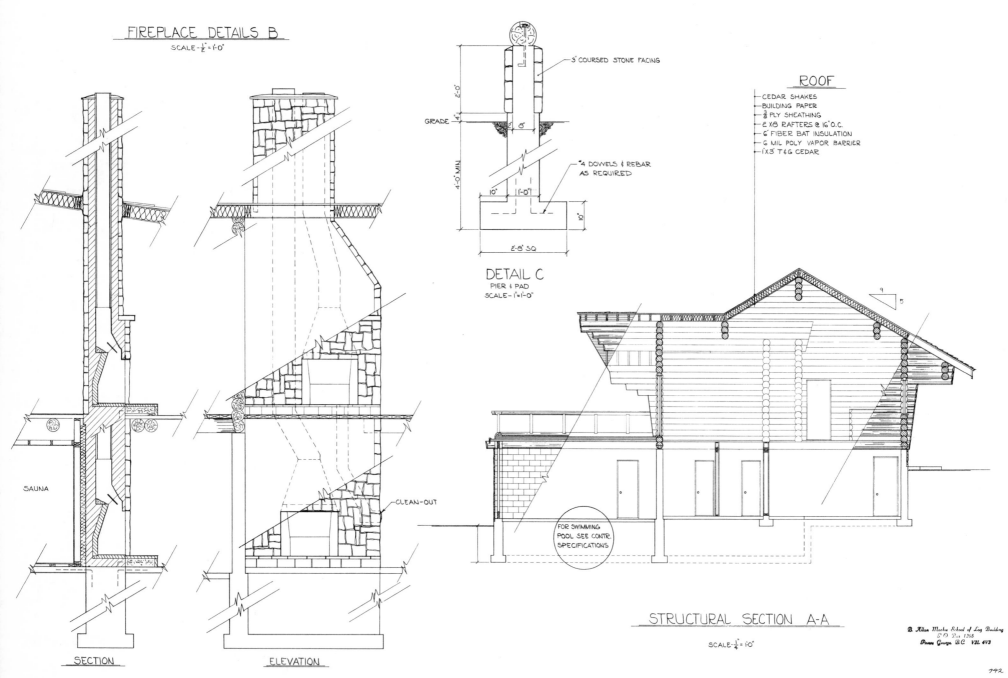

FIREPLACE DETAILS B
SCALE- $\frac{1}{2}$"=1'-0"

SECTION

ELEVATION

SAUNA

CLEAN-OUT

3" COURSED STONE FACING

GRADE

2'-0"

4"

4'-0" MIN

10"

1'-0"

10"

2'-8" SQ

#4 DOWELS & REBAR
AS REQUIRED

DETAIL C
PIER & PAD
SCALE-1"=1'-0"

ROOF

- CEDAR SHAKES
- BUILDING PAPER
- $\frac{3}{8}$ PLY SHEATHING
- 2 X 8 RAFTERS @ 16" O.C.
- 6" FIBER BAT INSULATION
- 6 MIL POLY VAPOR BARRIER
- 1"X 3" T & G CEDAR

9
5

FOR SWIMMING
POOL SEE CONTR.
SPECIFICATIONS

STRUCTURAL SECTION A-A

SCALE- $\frac{1}{4}$"=1'-0"

B. Allan Mackie School of Log Building
P.O. Box 1205
Prince George BC V2L 4V3

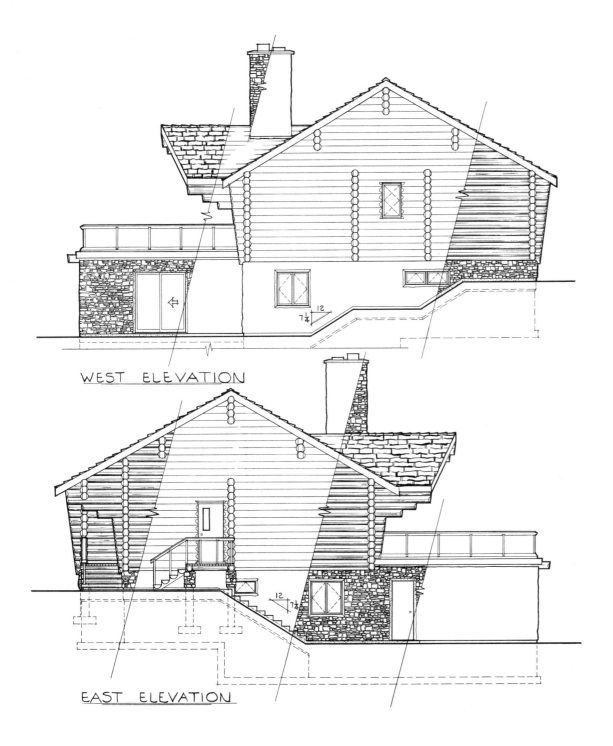

WEST ELEVATION

EAST ELEVATION

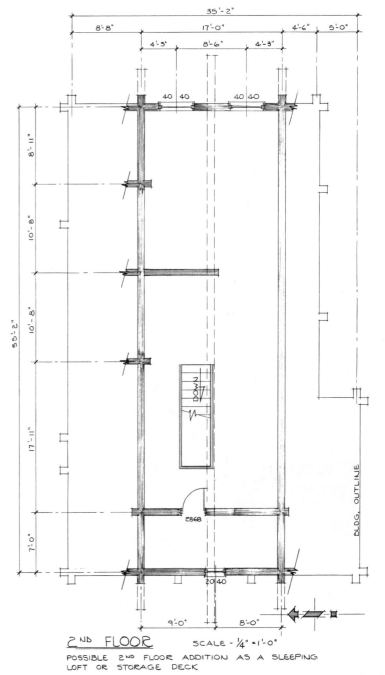

2ND FLOOR   SCALE - ¼" = 1'-0"

POSSIBLE 2ND FLOOR ADDITION AS A SLEEPING
LOFT OR STORAGE DECK

792   A5 of 5

#743

Square feet: 1,250

The design here permits casual living yet with all the facilities. I believe it is a compromise, in the real sense, falling midway between an energy-efficient log house and the suburban frame house which tends to sprawl.

Some people contend that logs themselves being an energy-efficient building material, those who care enough to handcraft them into homes ought to go all the way, trying by every means to eliminate the wasteful aspects of "conspicuous consumption" which have entered into house design between the Depression Years and the Oil Crisis. I tend to agree with that evaluation. But I offer these designs because, for various and valid reasons, people need to have a good look at the full spectrum, before making that final choice.

Well-constructed, this design can supply the backdrop for gracious living.

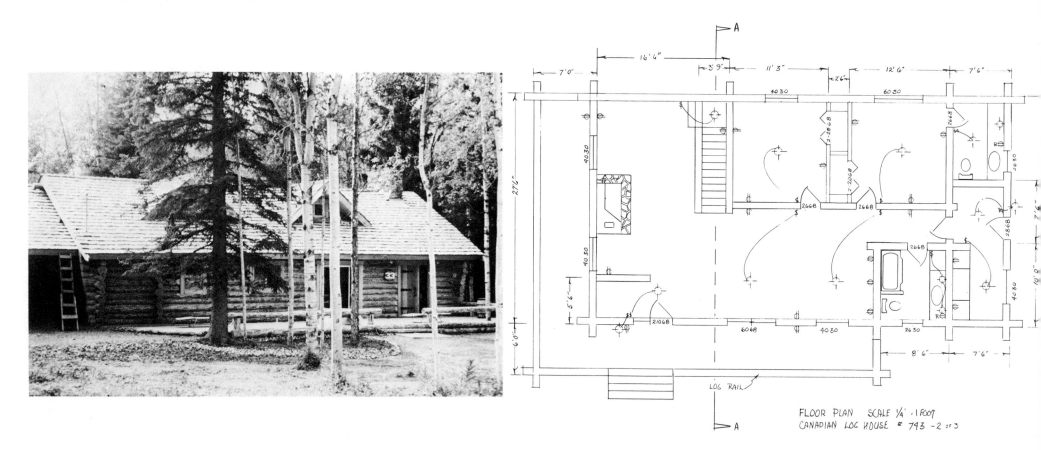

FLOOR PLAN   SCALE ¼" = 1 FOOT
CANADIAN LOG HOUSE # 743 - 2 OF 3

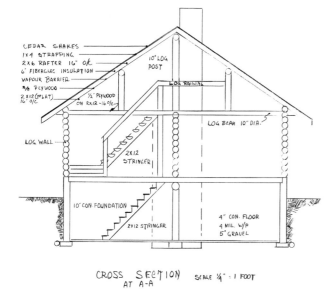

CEDAR SHAKES
1x4 STRAPPING
2x6 RAFTER 16" O/C
6" FIBERGLAS INSULATION
VAPOUR BARRIER
3/8 PLYWOOD
2x12 (FLAT)
16" O/C

10" LOG POST

LOG RAILING

1/2 PLYWOOD
ON 2x12 - 16 O/C

LOG BEAM 10" DIA.

LOG WALL

2x12 STRINGER

10" CON. FOUNDATION

2x12 STRINGER

4" CON. FLOOR
4 MIL W/P
5" GRAVEL

CROSS SECTION AT A-A   SCALE 1/4" = 1 FOOT

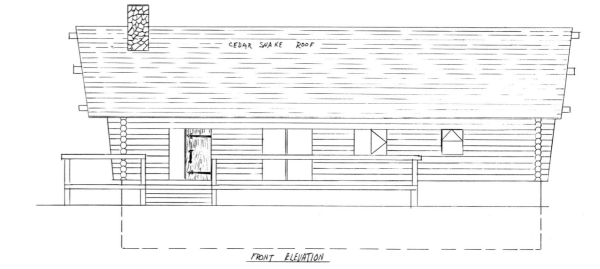

CEDAR SHAKE ROOF

FRONT ELEVATION

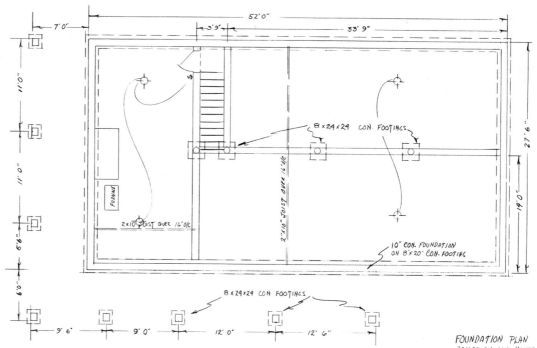

7'0"
52'0"
3'9"
33'9"

11'0"
11'0"
6'6"
6'0"

27'6"

19'0"

8x24x24 CON. FOOTINGS

2x10 JOIST OVER 16" O/C

2x10 JOIST OVER 16" O/C

10" CON. FOUNDATION
ON 8"x20" CON. FOOTING

FURNACE

8x24x24 CON FOOTINGS

9'6"   9'0"   12'0"   12'6"

FOUNDATION PLAN   SCALE 1/4" = 1'
CANADIAN LOG HOUSE # 743 - 1 OF 3
P.O. BOX 1205
PRINCE GEORGE B.C.
DESIGN N.J. ITKONEN

#744

Square feet: 2,000

Although this is a large house, the space is obtained with a minimum of material and will require a minimum of heating for a standard house.

It was designed originally for a Yukon site but it has since been built in a great many locations from there to Nova Scotia.

This design is worth considering if the owner feels that someday the house will require expansion. It would be possible to leave the upstairs unfinished until that time.

I'd like to mention here the comments of a Central Mortgage & Housing Corporation's district manager, who said he felt that the 1½ storey house was an excellent choice for people who thought they'd like to build in two stages. "Finish the main floor," he said, "and the CM&HC mortgage requirements are fulfilled. Then, when circumstances permit, finish the upstairs."

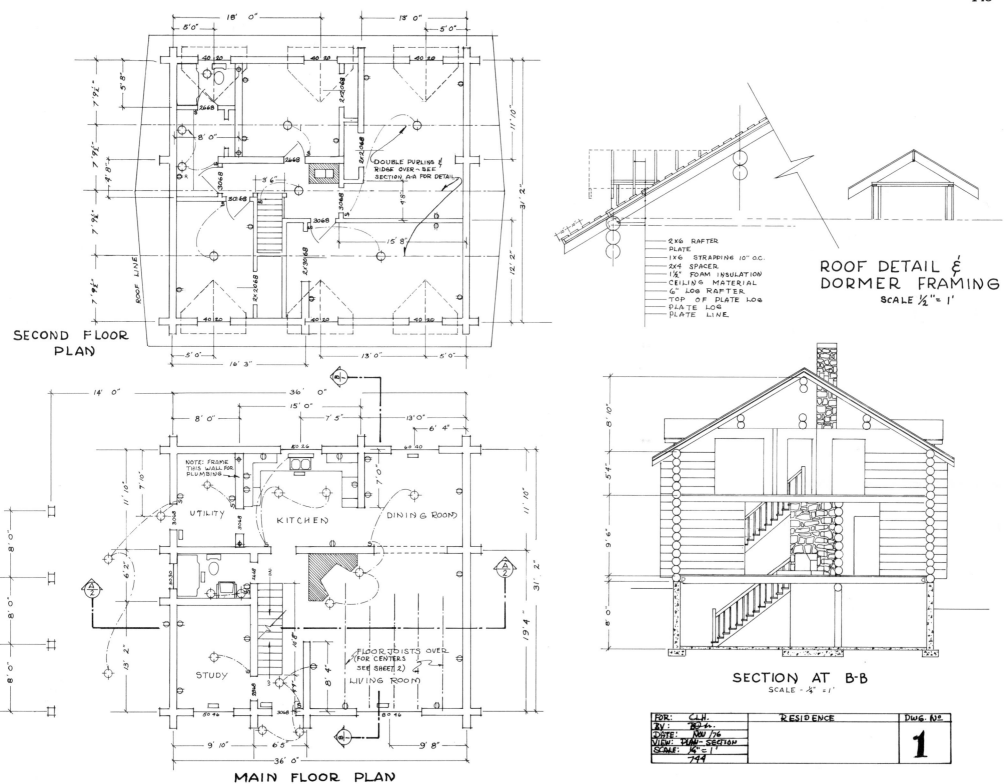

SECOND FLOOR
PLAN

DOUBLE PURLINS &
RIDGE OVER ~ SEE
SECTION A-A FOR DETAIL

ROOF LINE

2X6 RAFTER
PLATE
1X6 STRAPPING 10" O.C.
2X4 SPACER
1½" FOAM INSULATION
CEILING MATERIAL
6" LOG RAFTER
TOP OF PLATE LOG
PLATE LOG
PLATE LINE

ROOF DETAIL &
DORMER FRAMING
SCALE ½" = 1'

NOTE: FRAME
THIS WALL FOR
PLUMBING

UTILITY

KITCHEN

DINING ROOM

STUDY

LIVING ROOM

FLOOR JOISTS OVER
(FOR CENTERS
SEE SHEET 2)

MAIN FLOOR PLAN

SECTION AT B-B
SCALE - ¼" = 1'

FOR: C.H.	RESIDENCE	DWG. No.
BY: B.J.h.		
DATE: NOV /76		**1**
VIEW: PLAN-SECTION		
SCALE: ¼" = 1'		
744		

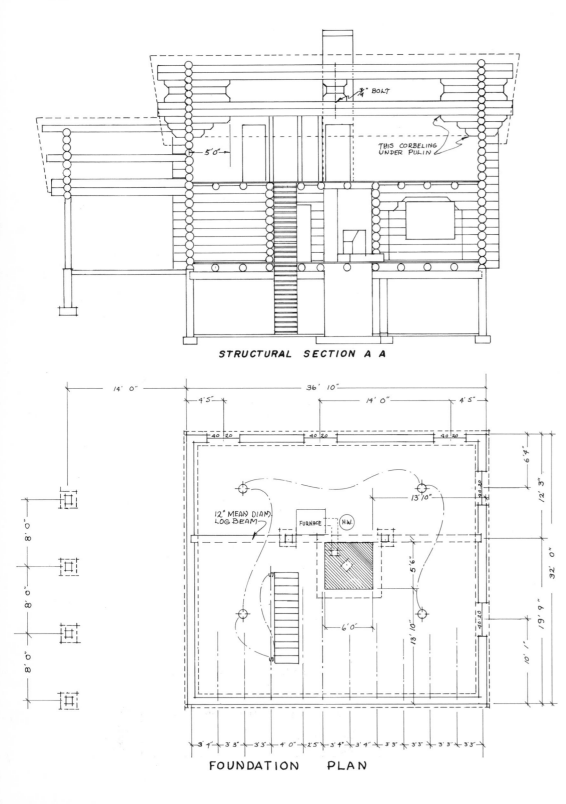

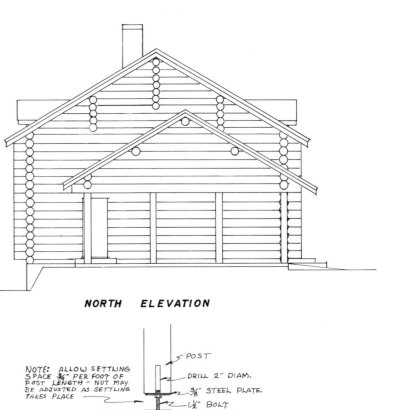

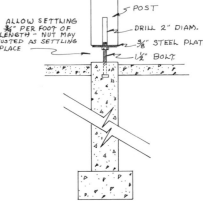

¾" BOLT

THIS CORBELING
UNDER PULIN

5'0"

STRUCTURAL SECTION A A

NORTH ELEVATION

NOTE: ALLOW SETTLING
SPACE ¾" PER FOOT OF
POST LENGTH - NUT MAY
BE ADJUSTED AS SETTLING
TAKES PLACE

POST

DRILL 2" DIAM.

⅜" STEEL PLATE

1½" BOLT

DETAIL— CARPORT POST

SCALE — 1"= 1'

14' 0"   36' 10"
4'5"   14' 0"   4'5"

40 20   40 20   40 20

6' 4"
12' 3"
32' 0"
19' 9"
10' 1"

13' 10"

12" MEAN DIAM)
LOG BEAM

FURNACE   H.W.

5' 6"

13' 10"

6' 0"

8' 0"   8' 0"   8' 0"

3' 1" 3' 3" 3' 3" 4' 0" 2'5" 3' 4" 3' 4" 3' 3" 3'3" 3' 3" 3'3"

FOUNDATION   PLAN

FOR:	CLH.	RESIDENCE	DWG. N°
BY			
DATE:	DEC 76		**2**
VIEW:			
SCALE:			
	7-11		

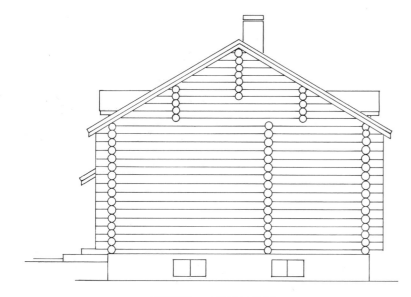

SOUTH   ELEVATION

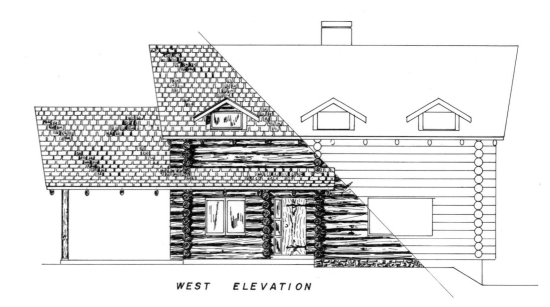

WEST   ELEVATION

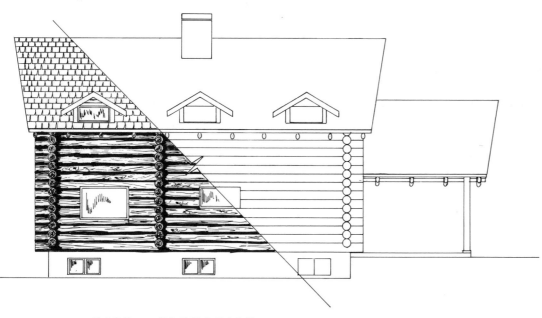

EAST   ELEVATION

FOR: C.L.H.	RESIDENCE	DWG. N⁰
BY:		**3**
DATE: Dec 19/76		
VIEW: ELEV.		
SCALE 1/4" = 1'		
744		

#745

Square feet: 2,000

This has been a popular design, judging from the number of blueprints ordered in the past.

There is considerable work to the building, and it is possible to achieve the same amount of space in a 2-storey house with half the roof area. But if, after considering these factors, you decide to go with this design, I might add that many novice builders have taken on this project with real success.

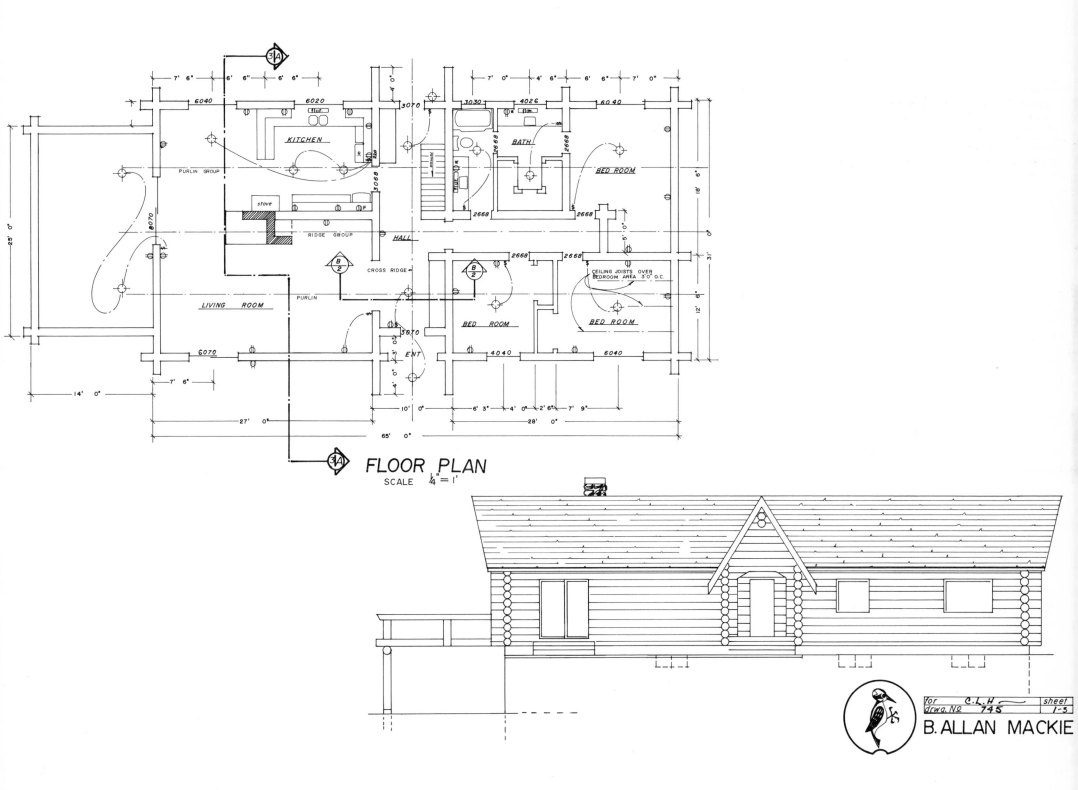

FLOOR PLAN
SCALE ¼" = 1'

for C.L.H.
drwg. Nº 745
sheet 1-3
B. ALLAN MACKIE

CROSS RIDGE · RIDGE

PURLIN

SECTION B-B
SCALE ½"=1'

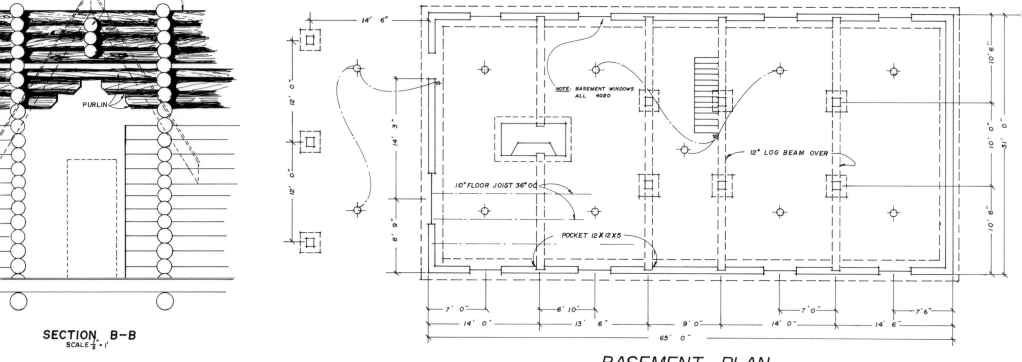

14' 6"

12' 0"

12' 0"

14' 3"

8' 9"

10½" 0"

10' 0"

31' 0"

10' 6"

NOTE: BASEMENT WINDOWS ALL 4020

12" LOG BEAM OVER

10" FLOOR JOIST 36" OC

POCKET 12X12X5

7' 0"   6' 10"   7' 0"   7' 6"

14' 0"   13' 6"   9' 0"   14' 0"   14' 6"

65' 0"

BASEMENT PLAN
SCALE ¼"=1'

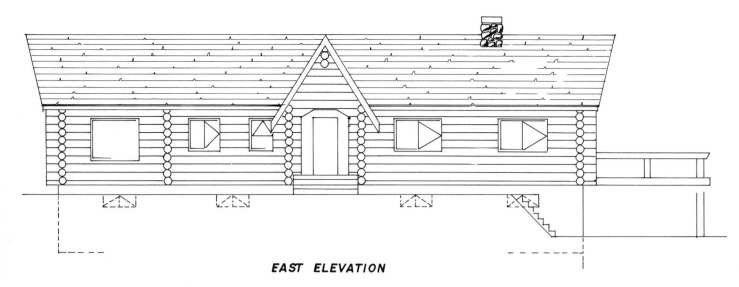

EAST ELEVATION

for C.L.H.   sheet
drwg. No. 745   L-3

B. ALLAN MACKIE

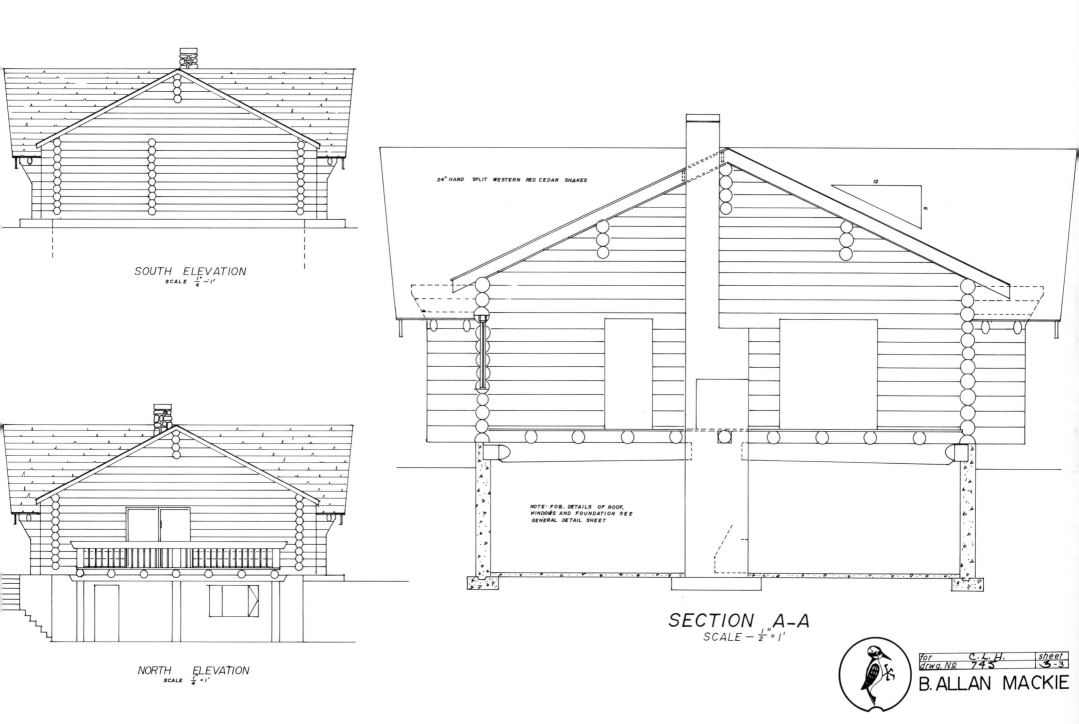

SOUTH ELEVATION
SCALE ¼"=1'

NORTH ELEVATION
SCALE ¼"=1'

24" HAND SPLIT WESTERN RED CEDAR SHAKES

12

NOTE: FOR DETAILS OF ROOF,
WINDOWS AND FOUNDATION SEE
GENERAL DETAIL SHEET

SECTION A-A
SCALE — ½"=1'

for C.L.H.
drwg. No 745
sheet 3-3

B. ALLAN MACKIE

APPENDIX I

Log House Construction

There are now a great many books on the market describing in varying detail just how one should go about the construction of a log house. This gives the would-be builder a wider choice in his approach to any given task. To the novice who is seeking an ever-easier way of doing a job, which must seem large and ominous to his inexperienced eyes, I'd say that no matter how much the subject of log construction is discussed, it seems there is always more to be said or a new idea to offer. The great challenge is to be able to discern between a sound construction technique and a slipshod one. It's one of the great disappointments, to complete a project and only then, in the light of newly acquired wisdom, to be able to see that one could have used a better method to have achieved a better project . . . usually with the same quantity of effort and materials.

Discussion and variety and new ideas being all to the good, I now add an abbreviated chapter to the body of information because it just seems that it should be there. It's offered for those who may be very new to the trade of the log builder or for those who may be collecting various ideas. Most of the following information is basic practice, while some of it is a result of refinements on the trade, which have developed at the Mackie School of Log Building or amongst other builders. This, then, is one of the benefits of continuing discussion and varied input. The enthusiasm with which the debates continue is a sure sign of the good health of the industry. When the builders become uncaring and all procedures are cut and dried and uninteresting, then we may properly consider that we have problems.

Footings

Footings should be, in most cases, double the foundation width and consequently 20 inches wide, since a 10-inch thick foundation wall has become generally accepted as a good standard (Fig. I).

If the soil is very wet or soft, and if the area has shifting soil, it will be advisable to reinforce both footings and foundations or perhaps to increase the size.

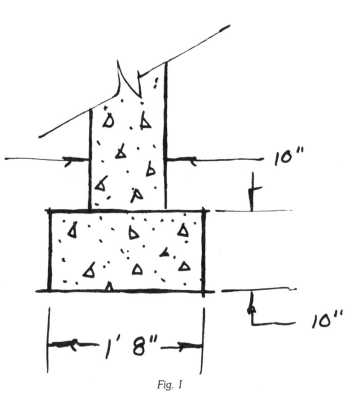

Fig. I

Footings usually are poured level with concrete, between either 2x-8" or 2x10" forms. The forms are spaced with 1x2 nailed across what will become the bottom . . . turned over, and spaced at the top (Fig. II).

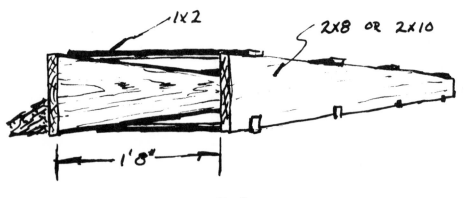

Fig. II

A sufficient number of cross-spacers should be nailed in place to prevent distortion of the form when the wet concrete is poured.

The form should then be carefully located and squared up, levelled, then staked into position. Banking up the sides with soil will also help keep the form in place.

Masonry or concrete block walls may require more substantial footings. Check with other builders in your area.

Foundation Walls

These can be solid concrete, concrete block, masonry, wood, or a combination of these.

Solid concrete is customarily poured between 8-foot sheets of plywood with a variety of metal spacer straps available for rapid construction. Eight feet is a very minimal height, in my opinion, and 9 feet is better, to ensure good head-room in a full basement.

Concrete blocks can be recommended as a do-it-yourself material. The skill required to put up a good, clean block wall is not great, and additional height may be built on easily. Blocks used in a combination with a rock facing can give very pleasing results (Fig. III). Walls that are totally masonry require more skill, but they're not beyond the ability of most people after they've had a bit of practice. I often drive past a place where the owners built a dog house as a practice project. It's a real beauty done square and true with fieldstone, which is a little more difficult to work. I admire the owner's skill, every time I go past there, and I respect his determination. But I pity the poor mutt who must live there in below zero temperatures unless there's an electrically-heated floor in the rock doghouse that I don't know about. In honour of that canine, I'd like to suggest a compost box as being a much more suitable object for masonry practice.

There are good books on this subject of do-it-yourself masonry. The one I recommend is "Stone Masonry for the Owner Builder" — Kemp Owner Builders Series.

Wood foundations are a different subject and for information on these, I think you would have to go to the dealers. While I do not like treated plywood framed basements, I do think there is a place for piling to be used in non-basement houses (Fig. IV). A New Zealand publisher

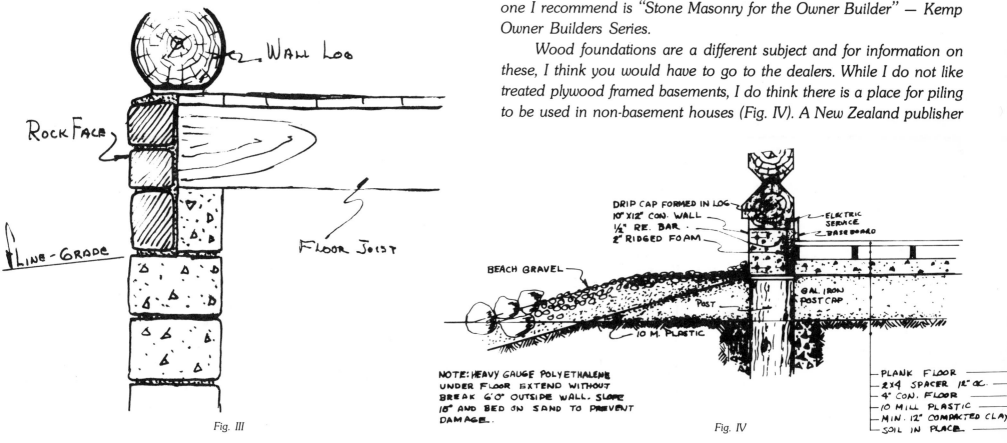

Fig. III

Fig. IV

has an interesting book of pole houses called "Poles Apart" in which pilings are taken as quite a commonplace thing. This is interesting in a country where earthquake is common. I think that pilings are vastly underrated as a foundation and, while I am becoming more and more suspicious of chemicals used to preserve wood, in particular P.C.P., posts treated with creosote or with copper sulphate solution should, under certain conditions, provide extended service without environmental hazard.

Main Floor

Main floor joists can be notched into the first (sill) log or set flush with the foundation, or, in fact, placed into the wall at a height of several feet above the concrete, depending upon the elevations desired.

I prefer log floor joists as I like to avoid as much millwork material as possible. I have been putting these log joists in as level as possible,

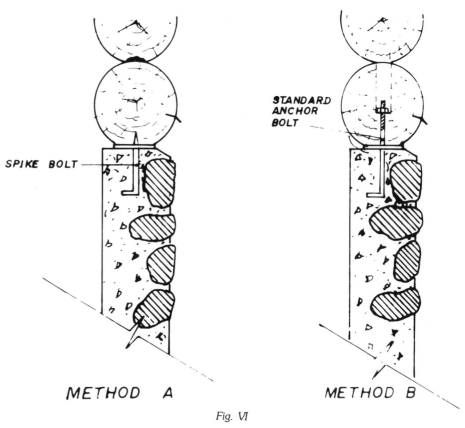

SPIKE BOLT

STANDARD ANCHOR BOLT

METHOD A

METHOD B

Fig. VI

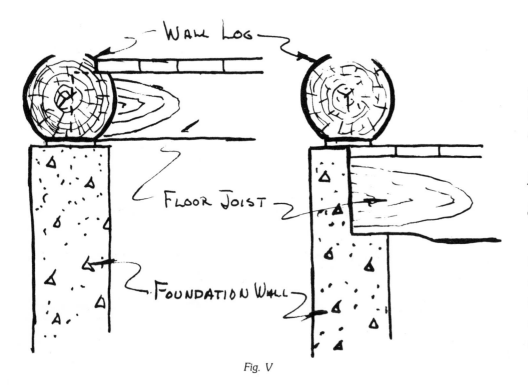

WALL LOG

FLOOR JOIST

FOUNDATION WALL

Fig. V

then adzing them off to a chalk line when they are all in place. Be careful to get the top of the sub-floor even with the top of the foundation wall in order to avoid difficult fitting along the length of the sill logs.

Log floor joists should be spaced according to size. Spacing up to 4 ft. 0 inches is possible, if 2x6" tongue and groove sub-flooring is used.

Sill Logs

Sill logs are usually good-sized, straight logs. Avoid excessive bow in these logs and swing part of the bow out in order to obtain a straighter line on the upper and lower surfaces of the sill log. The butts should be the same direction for parallel logs in the same course. The bottoms should be flattened for a width of 3 or 4 inches and secured to the foundation in accordance with local regulations (Fig. VI).

If sill logs are of sufficient size, they may be shaped to provide a drip shield. Otherwise, a metal flashing may be used. Fig. VII

Fig. VII

In round log construction, the sill logs on the other two (usually shorter) walls are most often half-logs. These may be either blind-notched into the other two sill logs, or they may extend as round logs beyond the foundation.

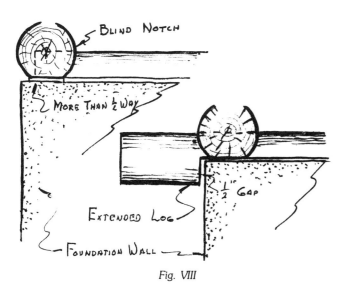

Fig. VIII

Wall Logs

Wall logs are a continuation of the first or sill logs in whatever style of notching is being used. Careful attention should be paid to maintaining a uniform wall extension so that a well-controlled profile may be trimmed, later.

For the techniques of notching and for cutting the essential lateral groove, see my previous books, BUILDING WITH LOGS and NOTCHES OF ALL KINDS, A Book of Timber Joinery.

In the above photo, log partitions were constructed with the walls.

Partitions

Partitions, for the most part, should be built of logs at the same time as the exterior walls are built. This is not only for aesthetic reasons. It also builds in strength and sway-bracing. I would never recommend that anyone eliminate a log partition in favour of a lumber framed partition on the basis of it being quicker. Ask any log builder. It definitely is not quicker to build a frame partition because any interior framed wall must have ample provision for the inevitable settling which will take place in the log walls. This is far less of a problem if the interior walls are also log, and all the logs settle at the same time and in the approximately the same amounts.

Door and Window Openings

When the lintel log is reached — the log which will house the tops of the doors and windows — levels should be located on the lintel log when it has been fully fitted and in its final place. Then, one more time, turn the log up. The window and door header cuts should be made at this time. This makes the job very much easier, safer and the quality of the cuts a great deal better.

The top of the windows and doors should eventually be at about 7 ft. 0 inches above the floor, consequently the expected settling distance should be added to the height of the opening. In the case of a door, this would be 5 inches; for a window of 3 ft. 6 in. height, add at least 2-¾ inches to allow for settling.

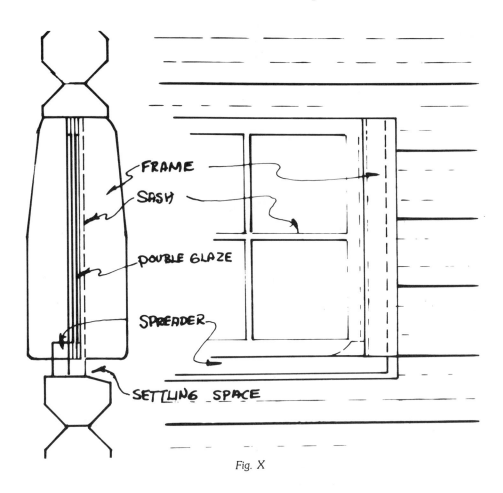

Fig. X

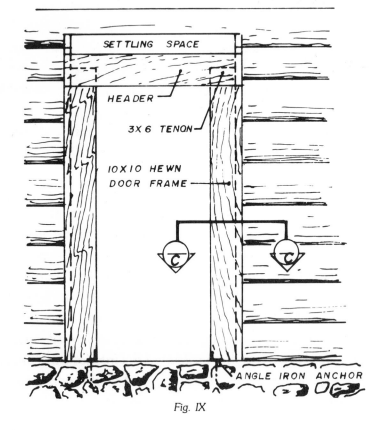

SETTLING SPACE

HEADER

3 X 6 TENON

10 X 10 HEWN
DOOR FRAME

ANGLE IRON ANCHOR

Fig. IX

If the window sizes have been fully decided, there is much to recommend that the final cuts be made at this time, as well, both from the point of view of safety as of efficiency.

At the Mackie School of Log Building, we have done a number of experiments with the use of timber framing around the doors and windows. I feel the results have been most satisfactory.

These openings have been built in two types: the first (Fig. IX) using 10 to 12 inch squared timbers with a header and rabbeted to receive a tenon on the log ends, the second (Fig. X) using thinner jambs that have the key-piece rabbeted into it and a keyway, in turn, in the log ends. This jamb is pinned at the top and knee braces are used at the bottom to keep the jamb in place.

Second Floor Joists

These are placed when the height is reached. It is important to the house that this height be correct. First, be aware that the eye will pick up the bottom of the floor joists as being the visual ceiling height. Therefore, the top surface of the joists should be at least 9 ft. 0 inches high and should have the anticipated settling added onto this (9 feet + approx. 7 inches). Walls nearing 10 feet in height may seem vastly high indeed. But persevere. It will be right in the end. But real problems occur when insufficient height has been allowed and the settling brings the ceiling down around one's ears ... or so it feels, when the ceiling is constructed of a massive material.

Cut the way for the second floor decking at the time the cap log is put on top of the floor joists, in order to save time later on.

Photo shows unique hewn floor joists that are double notched into wall and capped with two logs.

Gable Ends

Gable ends may be framed or built of logs. It is unquestionably more trouble to build them with logs. But there is also more satisfaction in it. The purlins can be mathematically located on log gable ends in accordance with the house design. But leave the gable end logs plenty long so that they don't prove to be a little too short when it comes to trimming down the slope.

Gable logs should extend right to the shingles and, in order to have the various levels come out right, a good deal of sketching is required of the builder (see Fig. XI).

Roof, Roof Support System, and Roofing Material

This is an extensive subject, worthy of an entire book to itself.

The tendency has been toward double-framed roofs with insulation following the roof line. This permits the use of the area under the roof either as a second storey or as loft space. To date, the practice has been to use principal rafters in the form of a truss, or of trusses supporting purlins and common rafters and, of course, the roofing material. Some of these undertakings have been most successful. In future, well-designed and tastefully executed roof support systems will, I hope, become more common. And we may then be able to avoid the collections of bolts, strap iron, and rough-sawn materials often being recommended in recent times by inspection "authorities".

In the question of design and construction, the considerations are these:

To design a roof system that permits an economic use of space and material. This means that as much of the roofed area as possible should be accessible. But, too, large and high vaulted areas may have great visual impact which may make their lack of utility entirely acceptable. Costs will, in this latter instance, be high.

The roof will be the most expensive single item in the building and, for this reason, designs which tend toward square and two-storey buildings contain a far greater area under a given amount of roof with a consequently much higher E.R. or efficiency ratio.

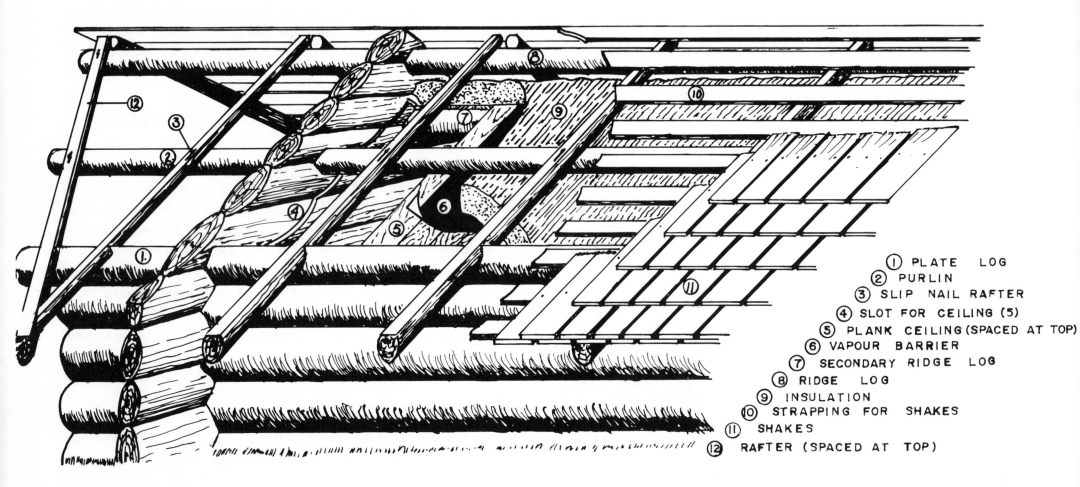

1. PLATE LOG
2. PURLIN
3. SLIP NAIL RAFTER
4. SLOT FOR CEILING (5)
5. PLANK CEILING (SPACED AT TOP)
6. VAPOUR BARRIER
7. SECONDARY RIDGE LOG
8. RIDGE LOG
9. INSULATION
10. STRAPPING FOR SHAKES
11. SHAKES
12. RAFTER (SPACED AT TOP)

Fig. XI

Above illustration shows cut away view of a log framed roof with the ceiling dropped for additional insulation space.

The problem, then, is to design a roof support system which will embody the required strength for the spans involved. Log span tables are published separately by Log House Publishing Company Ltd., and are contained in my book, NOTCHES OF ALL KINDS as well.

It has become more and more apparent that the greatest possibility for heat loss in a building will be through the roof. As a result, design for improved insulation has been increasing steadily. (Figs. XII and XIII.)

Heat loss will occur, no matter how much insulation is used, and a point is reached where the savings do not warrant further additional costs. Thus the present R-40 has become an accepted figure to aim for in ceiling or roof insulation and should prove to be an entirely satisfactory goal in future.

The roof design must, therefore, provide for this heavy insulation as well as for ventilation space in a visually pleasing way.

24" SHAKES
IX6 STRAPPING
2 X 8 RAFTER
12" FIBERGLASS
VAPOUR BARRIER
DECKING
10" JOIST
BLOCK
SCREEN

RAFTER DETAIL SECTION B-B
SCALE I"= I'
Fig. XIII

24" SHAKES
IX6 STRAPPING
2 X 8 RAFTER
4" FOAM INSULATION
VAPOUR BARRIER
DECKING
LOG RAFTER

EAVE BLOCK
SCREEN

RAFTER DETAIL SECTION A-A
SCALE I" = I'

Fig. XII

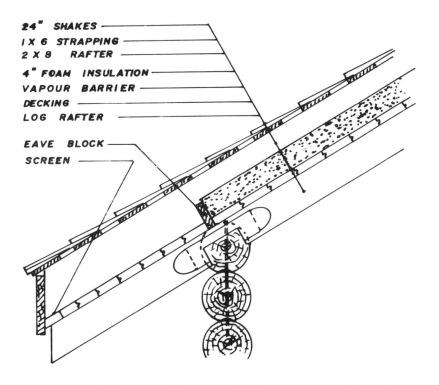

Piece-Sur-Piece Construction

Piece-sur-piece design has blossomed considerably in popularity once again, over the last few years, and some good buildings have resulted.

The system offers a great flexibility and, at the same time, can utilize much shorter logs than is possible in horizontal round log construction.

Most of the building principles discussed so far will apply, in large part, to piece-sur-piece buildings. The area of special concern with this style of building is: what to do with the wall panels as they settle.

In century-old piece-sur-piece buildings such as the Hudson's Bay Company store at Fort St. James on Stuart Lake in north-central British Columbia, the upper storey could be expected to serve as fur storage that would not be heated. When the wall panel logs shrank and settled, a gap would develop at the top but to them this was of no great consequence. This same tendency does, however, pose a problem today in a modern house.

Several solutions have been tried with varying success.

1) To build the wall filler logs up between a double plate which is, in turn, bolted to the upright post (Fig. XIV).

This approach appears to work. It is structurally sound. But it is not historically correct and while I do not advocate a strict adherence to all historical methods, I do have a great admiration for many of the fine buildings that were constructed in this style by the early French and I am a bit sad to see their techniques subjected to any modification.

2) Another system which succeeds in permitting the settling of the wall fillers without producing a void at the top is illustrated in Figure XV. This approach consists of a 4 to 6 inch wide apron between the posts which can be removed for servicing occasionally. If well-dried logs are used, and a solid fit between the filler logs (Fig. XVI) is made, very little settling should then occur.

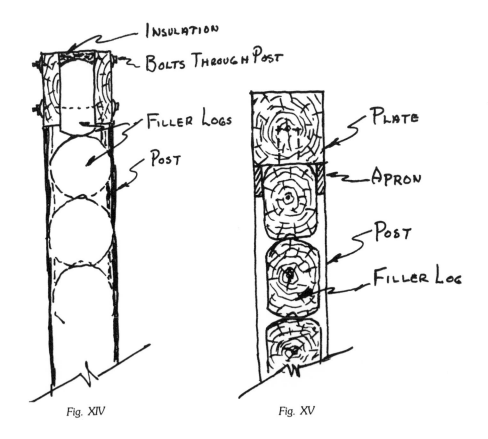

Fig. XIV

Fig. XV

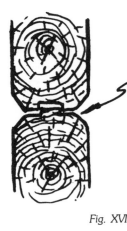

Fig. XVI

OAKUM

Fig. XVII

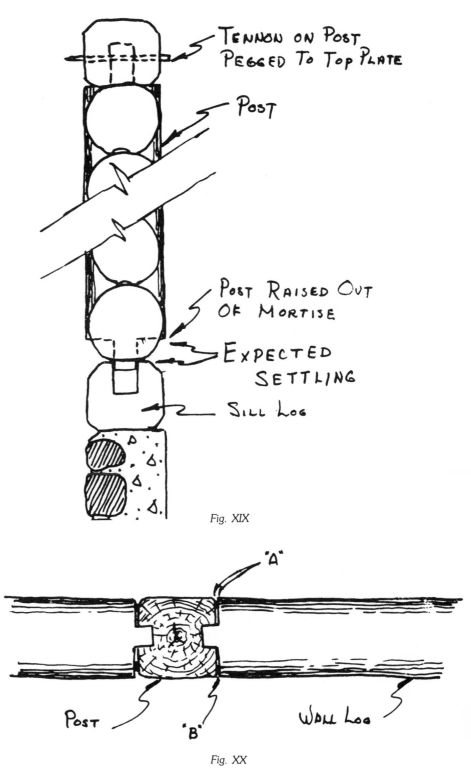

TENNON ON POST PEGGED TO TOP PLATE

POST

POST RAISED OUT OF MORTISE

EXPECTED SETTLING

SILL LOG

Fig. XIX

3) Yet another method is to have the filler logs flatted on top and bottom and to drive oakum between (Fig. XVII). When the logs shrink, more oakum can be driven, to lift the logs back to their original position. This, too, would require dry logs.

4) If the wall panels are fairly long, so that doors and windows may be framed in the manner previously described, the best solution to the settling problem is to raise the post out of mortise in the bottom plate, and to allow the entire weight of the building to rest on the wall fillers (Fig. XIX). In this configuration there is no problem with the walls being hung up for lack of weight and as long as sufficient settling space is allowed, there need be no anxiety about annual maintenance because no service would be required.

Questions have been raised about possible air leakage between the posts and the filler logs. While this is strictly a matter of the quality of workmanship, a leakage for whatever reason is of real concern, as it can cause the formation of frost indoors during winter when the cold outer air contacts the warm, moist, interior air of the household. Many proposals for the sealing of these joints have been put forward. The main thing is to keep the interior warm and the internal space dry: that is, seal both interior and exterior walls and provide for a vapour barrier on the interior. One suggestion is made in Fig. XX. Do not make the join at "A" too tight. Allow about ¼" of space into which oakum may be firmly placed. This, in turn, may be filled on the inside with a caulking compound "B" to provide the necessary vapour seal.

"A"

POST

"B"

WALL LOG

Fig. XX

The rabbeted groove in the posts may vary in size depending upon the size of the logs, but it should always be cut with the greatest degree of accuracy. At the School, we have been rabbeting a matching groove in the log ends in order to facilitate fitting, then using a key instead of a tenon on the log end (Fig. XXI). Whichever system is used, a greater accuracy may be obtained by placing the wall panel in a jig and making the complete cut at one time.

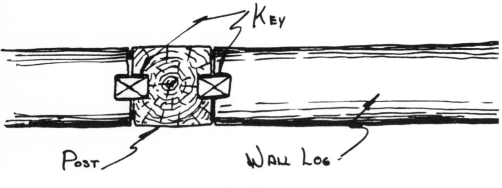

Fig. XXI

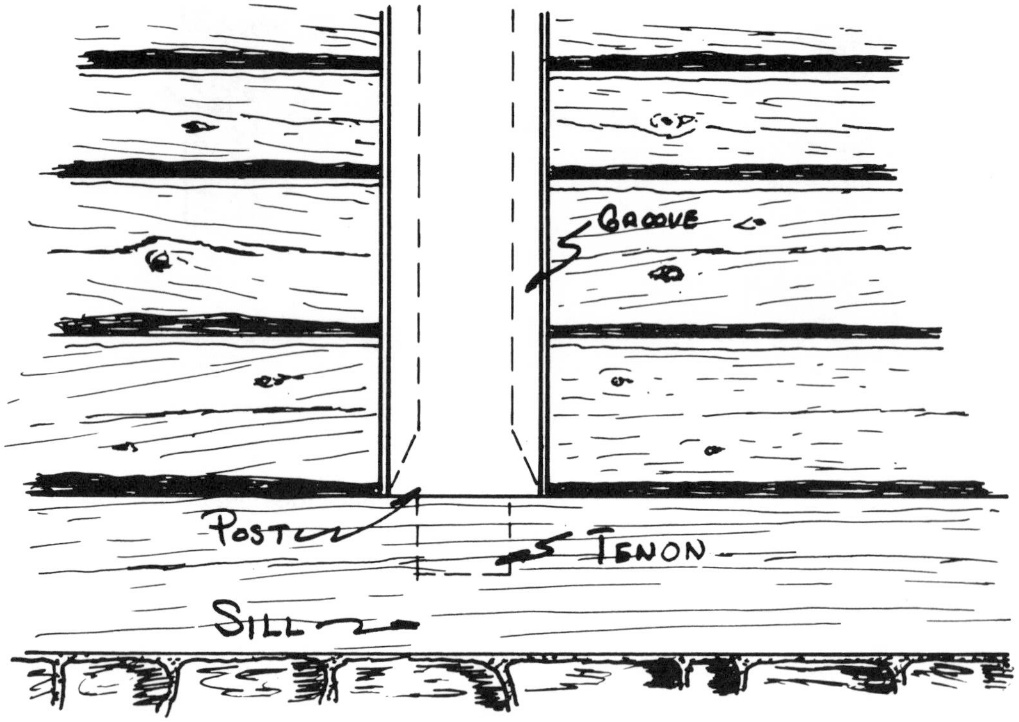

The groove at the bottom of the post should run out at the bottom to provide protection for the bottom mortise (Fig. XXII).

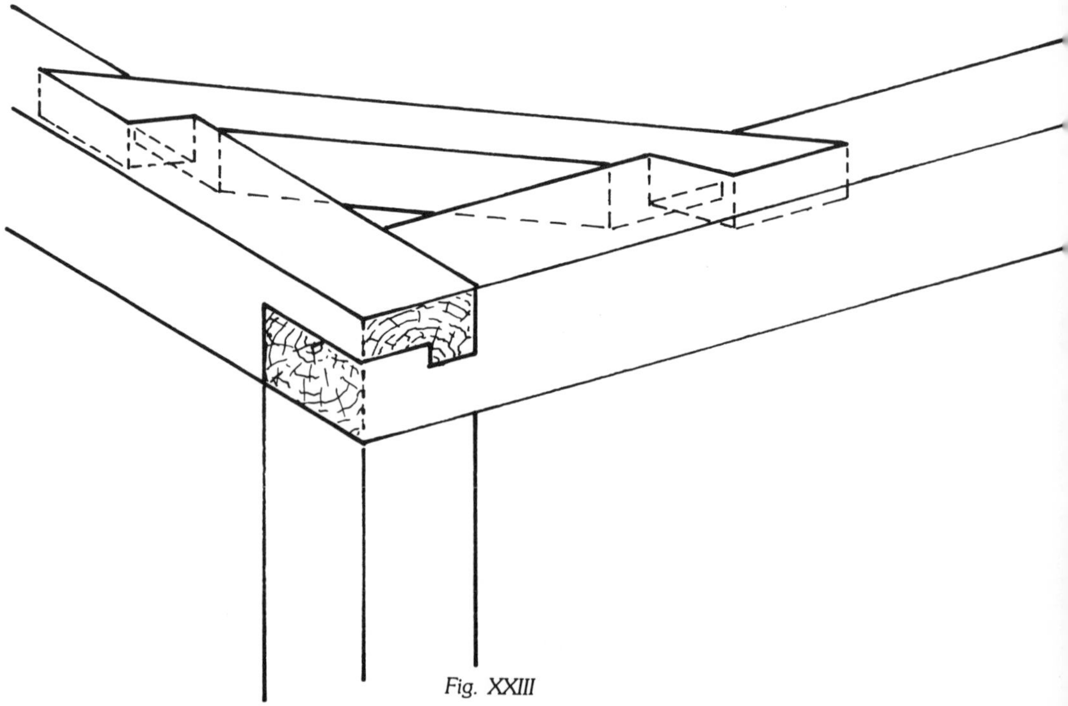

Angle braces of a substantial nature, that are dovetailed across the corner of the top plates (Fig. XXIII) will provide torque bracing. The best possible pegs to use in these instances are made of white oak. But for most of us a lesser, straight-grained hardwood will have to suffice. Pegs are traditionally 1 inch in diameter and while many buildings have countersunk bolts with a peg-like plug in many locations, a good peg will surely look better and be plenty durable.

Now, with the addition of a good, substantial roof of proportions worthy of the rest of the building, the piece-sur-piece project is complete.

Fig. XXII

Fig. XXIII

APPENDIX II

Finishing and Preserving

These two topics are very closely related subjects. May I begin with a note of caution. The tendency has become widespread to use chemicals instead of knowledge and skill, in the preservation of timber buildings. In some parts of the world, undoubtedly, where there is fungus, bacteria, and insects posing a real threat, the preservation of a wood building is a challenge. But for areas where this is not the case, I caution that chemicals should be avoided as much as possible.

Only recently have we begun to assess the problem to health and to the general environment caused by the use of Pentachlorophenol. It indicates that PCPs should be avoided. I am sure that if a building has been designed, planned, and constructed with the purpose (among all its other considerations) of avoiding the attacks of fungus, bacteria, insects, bleaching, and so forth, then the building will easily last as long as it would take to grow new building logs . . . and then some.

Since we cannot . . . and indeed, should not, expect our work to last forever, a reasonable life expectancy should be an entirely acceptable goal. By reasonable, in the case of logs, I should think that a century is quite within reason for most timber species that we use in Canada.

Deterioration in a wood building is caused by the following elements:

1) Moisture, in the form of rain, condensation, or humidity. The only real solution to this problem is to protect the building from moisture. Use a good overhang at the eaves. Locate the building out of moisture-laden winds. Provide porches or trees as wind-break on the exposed walls.

Condensation is largely controlled by proper provision of vapour barrier and ventilation. To avoid the condensation of humid air in such places as crawl spaces, attics, soffits, or other dead air areas, ventilation must be supplied.

2) Sun. Ask any Albertan. Sunshine is responsible for the breakdown of fibre. Cracks and checks can occur, then, which may further aggravate the problem by holding water, at other times. The warmth of the sun, plus the moisture, provide a most favourable environment for bacterial action. Solar collectors and greenhouses may channel this energy to better purposes. Otherwise, provide protection from the sun by means of roof design, siting, or plantings.

3) Wind. In seacoast areas, particularly, there is wind-driven moisture even on days when it isn't raining. This wreaks havoc upon masonry buildings whenever a hard frost follows on one of these drenching winds. The well-built log house is much better able to fend off the problem but help can be provided in the form of wind-breaks and good site selection.

4) Mechanical damage. A great variety of hazards, from insects to urban renewal, can occur. Most of these can be avoided in the original design, in construction, and in good maintenance.

Bear in mind, always, that insects require moisture if they are to survive and work their mischief. Therefore good design, good ventilation, and some weather protection constitutes the best lines of defence.

Wear, abrasion, and overload failure are all design faults and to these there are practical solutions. But no solution has yet been formed for the mechanical damage often caused by the attacks of over-zealous civic employees.

Logs As Building Material

Logs are an organic material designed by nature to break down and decay under the warm moist conditions which encourage the activities of organisms.

The builder must presume that such organisms are always present and that the life-support needs of these organisms are not unlike our own except that they seem to have a far wider tolerance range.

Preservation of logs, then, is a matter of limiting the availability of these life-support substances of warmth and moisture, while keeping the wood.

Chemicals, on the other hand, attempt to remove the organisms. I believe this is unnecessary. We, too, are organisms and for my part I am reluctant to be removed. And make no mistake, we risk that possibility whenever we take up any kind of partnership with a deadly chemical solution, such as PCP.

Log builders can accomplish excellent results in wood preservations, with very few exceptions, by controlling the moisture and humidity levels necessary for infestation.

GLOSSARY

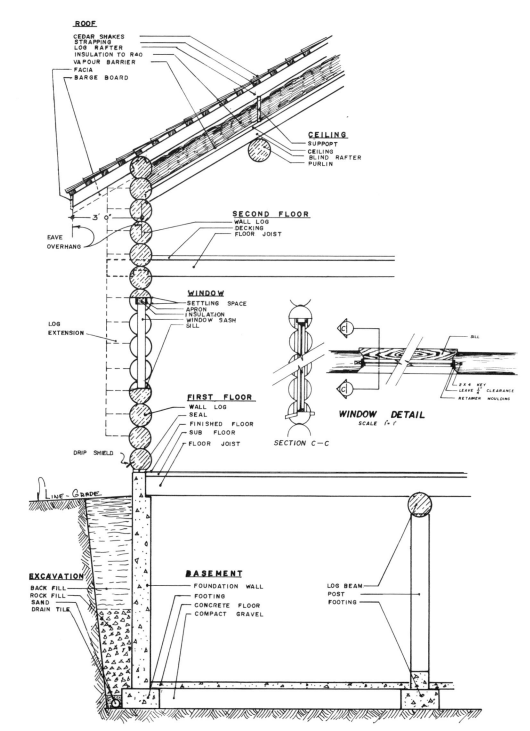

ROOF
CEDAR SHAKES
STRAPPING
LOG RAFTER
INSULATION TO R40
VAPOUR BARRIER
FACIA
BARGE BOARD

CEILING
SUPPOPT
CEILING
BLIND RAFTER
PURLIN

SECOND FLOOR
WALL LOG
DECKING
FLOOR JOIST

EAVE OVERHANG

3'0"

WINDOW
SETTLING SPACE
APRON
INSULATION
WINDOW SASH
SILL

LOG EXTENSION

FIRST FLOOR
WALL LOG
SEAL
FINISHED FLOOR
SUB FLOOR
FLOOR JOIST

DRIP SHIELD

LINE-GRADE

EXCAVATION
BACK FILL
ROCK FILL
SAND
DRAIN TILE

BASEMENT
FOUNDATION WALL
FOOTING
CONCRETE FLOOR
COMPACT GRAVEL

LOG BEAM
POST
FOOTING

SILL
2 X 4 KEY
LEAVE ¼ CLEARANCE
RETAINER MOULDING

WINDOW DETAIL
SCALE 1"·1'

SECTION C—C

ARCH — An assembly of two or more members, all of which are under compression, used to span a distance.

BARGE BOARD — Ornamental or protective board on a gable end, under roof.

BATTEN — Narrow wooden strip used to cover joins or as a decorative strip.

CANTILEVER — Structural member supported at one end but extending beyond its support at the other end.

CHECKING — Longitudinal splits in timber caused by rapid drying.

CONDUCTION — Transfer of heat through a material.

CONVECTION — Heat transfer resulting from the motion of the air.

CORBEL — Building out of one layer of material beyond another.

DOG — An iron bar having a right angle bend at each end capable of being driven into logs to secure them in place.

DORMER — Smaller roofed structure protruding from a roof.

DOUBLE FRAME (Roof) — Common rafters supported by principal rafters and purlins.

EAVE BLOCK — Piece of timber used to block space between rafters at the top of the plate.

EFFICIENCY RATIO (E.R.) — The useable floor area of a house divided by the exposed area and expressed as a decimal equivalent: Floor area = E.R.

EXTENSION — Portion of a log protruding beyond the notch on the outside of a corner.

FASCIA — The trim board at end of rafters or overhang.

FOOTING — Initial construction, usually concrete, to form a level base and to support a foundation wall. It is generally twice the width of the wall it supports.

FURRING — Strips of wood applied to a surface to even the plane of the material.

GLASS (types) — INSULATING GLASS: Factory-sealed, double or triple paned glass with air space between.

PLATE AND FLOAT GLASS: Glass which is manufactured in the flat and can be made thicker and stronger than sheet glass.

SHEET GLASS DOUBLE STRENGTH (⅛") is the most useful.

SINGLE STRENGTH (3/32") breaks easily. Also made in 3/16" and 7/32".

TEMPERED GLASS: Glass which is heat-treated to produce tension at the outer surfaces. Stronger and safer than other glass.

GRADE — The slope of the land.

GRAIN — Direction of cellular arrangement in wood.

HEADER — Structural member supporting other members such as joists or rafters where they are cut around a horizontal opening.

JAMB — Side and head lining of a door or window.

KEYING — Similar to notching but without extended log ends.

KEYWAY — Rabbet cut in log ends to receive a scantling so that lateral support may be obtained.

LATERAL GROOVE — Longitudinal groove cut on the underside of a log so that it will fit the log below.

LINTEL — Horizontal support member spanning an opening in the wall.

MASONRY — Stone, brick, or concrete bonded to form a mass of any kind.

MORTISE — Square or rectangular recess cut into a timber which a tenon will fit.

NOTCH — Recess cut in a log to accept another log at an angle to it.

OVERHANG — Part of roof extending beyond the exterior of the wall.

PIER — Column of masonry used to support another structure.

PITCH — Slope of roof expressed in terms of the total span of the roof. E.g., a half-pitch roof is one in which the rise is half the span or 12 feet high on a building 24 feet wide.

PERMEABILITY — Ability to accept water.

PLANE — A flat surface which has width and length but no thickness.

PLATE LOG — Log at the top of wall on which rafters are resting.

PLUMB — Vertical position.

POST — Column of wood used to support other structure.

PRINCIPAL — Main structural member supporting other members.

PURLIN — Horizontal roof beams, usually supporting common rafters.

RABBET — Three-sided groove.

RESISTANCE — The ability of material to impede transfer of heat. Opposite to conductivity. Generally referred to as R value.

ROOF TYPES — GAMBREL
GABLE
HIP
MANSARD

SASH — Light frame containing one or more panes of glass.

SCANTLING — Piece sawn from a timber parallel to grain.

SCARFED — Cut at a long angle in the direction of the timber.

SCORE — Preliminary cutting into, or along, a line.

SCRIBER — Device used to mark parallel lines between two logs or other members.

SILL — Bottom member of wall, door, or window.

SLAB — One unit floor and foundation installed directly on grade.

SLOPE — Angle expressed in degrees from horizontal or in terms of run and rise, e.g., a "6 in 12 slope" meaning 6" rise for each 12" of run.

SOLAR TEMPERING — Modifying of temperature in a given area by the inclusion of sunlight.

SPLINE — Narrow strip of wood placed in matching rabbets cut in two adjacent pieces of wood.

STAIR TYPES — STRAIGHT: As the name applies, it proceeds in a straight line from landing to landing.
PLATFORM: Stair rises to platform, then proceeds again at an angle from this platform.
SPIRAL: Stair that curves from landing to landing.

TEMPLATE — A pattern whose outline conforms to a desired shape. Used for repeated modules.

TENON — Square or rectangular extension to a timber to fit a mortise. (Or, as one of my students explained, it's one better than a nine-on.)

TRUSS — A beam made up of three or more lighter members, at least one of which will be under tension. Used to span a distance.

WINDOW TYPES — AWNING: Hinged to swing out at the bottom.
Casement. Hinged to swing to one side.
CLERESTORY: Window placed vertically in a wall above the line of vision, to provide natural light. Usually at the intersection of two offset roof planes.
DOUBLE HUNG: Upper sash and lower sash, each of which may slide.
FIXED SASH: Non-opening window.
SKYLIGHT: A clear or translucent pane set into a roof at or near a horizontal angle to provide natural light.

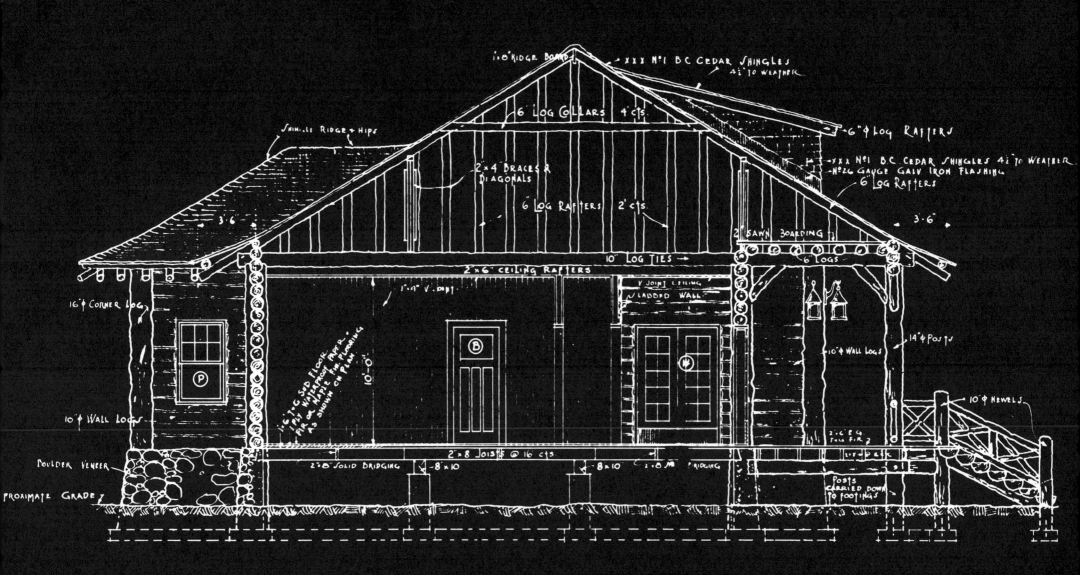

1·0" RIDGE BOARD

XXX N°1 B.C CEDAR SHINGLES 4½" TO WEATHER

SHINGLE RIDGE + HIPS

6 LOG COLLARS 4 cts.

6" Ø LOG RAFTERS

2"x4 BRACES & DIAGONALS

XXX N°1 B.C CEDAR SHINGLES 4½" TO WEATHER
N°26 GAUGE GALV IRON FLASHING
6" LOG RAFTERS

6 LOG RAFTERS 2' cts.

2" SAWN BOARDING

3·6"

3·6"

10" LOG TIES

6" LOGS

2"x6 CEILING RAFTERS

16" Ø CORNER LOG

1'·0" V. JOINT

V JOINT CEILING
LADDED WALL

10'·0"

14" Ø POSTS

10" Ø WALL LOGS

1½"T·G SUB FLOOR PAPER
FIR OR MAPLE FIR FLOORING
AS SHOWN ON PLAN

10" Ø NEWELS

10" Ø WALL LOGS

2'·6"&4"
T·G FIR?

BOULDER VENEER

2"x8 JOISTS @ 16 cts.

2"x8 SOLID BRIDGING

8"x10

8"x10

2"·8 M BRIDGING

POSTS
CARRIED DOWN
TO FOOTINGS

PROXIMATE GRADE

SECTION · ON · LINE · A·A

ORDER FORM

To: LOG HOUSE PUBLISHING COMPANY LTD.
P.O. Box 1205
Prince George, British Columbia, V2L 4V3

From: _____   Date: _____

_____

_____

Postal Code:_____ or Zip Code _____   _____

I enclose my Certified Cheque or Money Order in the amount of $_____ (from U.S. points, kindly remit in U.S. funds and add $3.00 postage) covering the cost of a set of blueprints,

Design No._____ , according to the prices shown below. Please allow 3 to 6 weeks for normal delivery. Absolutely no telephone orders will be accepted. At times, we may be able to expedite delivery by using Air Express, Loomis Courier, or Greyhound, but only if (a) you agree to accept the additional delivery charges (if so, please state here:_____), and (b) if you provide a telephone number so that you can be notified by the Carrier on arrival of the parcel in your town.

Design	Price	Design	Price
791	$45.00	784	$45.00
792	$45.00	771	$50.00
793	$50.00	772	$45.00
794	$50.00	773	$45.00
795	$50.00	774	$45.00
796	$50.00	775	$55.00
797	$60.00	776	$50.00
798	$45.00	761	$50.00
799	$45.00	762	$50.00
7910	$15.00	763	$50.00
7911	$15.00	764	$60.00
7912	$50.00	751	$50.00
7913	$50.00	752	$45.00
7914	$50.00	753	$50.00
7915	$45.00	741	$50.00
781	$45.00	742	$60.00
782	$45.00	743	$45.00
783	$50.00	744	$50.00
		745	$50.00

Note: All prices quoted are subject to change without notice.